THE 6 PRINCIPLES

FOR EXEMPLARY TEACHING OF ENGLISH LEARNERS®

ADULT EDUCATION AND WORKFORCE DEVELOPMENT

Andrea B. Hellman
Kathy Harris
Amea Wilbur

Deborah J. Short, *Series Editor*

FOREWORD **BY JOHAN E. UVIN**

This book has a
companion website. Go to
www.the6principles.org/adult-education
for additional resources.

www.tesol.org/bookstore

TESOL International Association
1925 Ballenger Avenue
Alexandria, VA 22314 USA
www.tesol.org

Director of Publishing and Product Development: Myrna Jacobs
Copy Editor: Tomiko Breland
Cover and Interior Design: Citrine Sky Design
Layout: Capitol Communications, LLC
Printing: Gasch Printing, LLC

The 6 Principles for Exemplary Teaching of English Learners® and The 6 Principles® is a registered trademark of TESOL International Association, Inc.

Every effort has been made to copyright holders for permission to reprint borrowed material. We regret any oversights that may have occurred and will rectify them in future printings of this work.

Recommended citation:
Hellman, A. B., Harris, K., & Wilbur, A. (2019). *The 6 principles for exemplary teaching of English learners: Adult education and workforce development*. Alexandria, VA: TESOL International Association.

ISBN 978-1-945351-66-2
eBook ISBN 978-1-945351-73-0
Library of Congress Control Number 2018964147

BULK PURCHASES
Quantity discounts are available for workshops and staff development.
Visit www.tesol.org/read-and-publish/bookstore/book-ordering-policies or call 1 888-891-0041.

First edition, 2019
1 2 3 4 5 6 7 8 9 10

CONTENTS

FOREWORD

There are many policies and services that facilitate the integration of adult immigrants and refugees, but without access to high-quality English language instruction, the returns on those policies and services will be limited for individuals, communities, economies, and governments.

English proficiency matters a lot today. It is a gateway to jobs, education and training, and better wages, if you have it. It is a gatekeeper of opportunity, if you don't. A fast-growing group of immigrants, resettled refugees, asylum claimants, and temporary workers in English-speaking countries understand very well the premium that comes with proficiency. They want to learn English to get access to a better job or career. In a growing number of other nations, adults want to improve their English skills so they can get to work in sectors where English has become the language of business. It goes without saying that high-quality instruction is essential, as adults have many responsibilities and have no time to waste. That instruction, if it is to be of high quality and grounded in research, needs to accommodate the significant diversity in the backgrounds, circumstances, goals, and aspirations of adult English learners.

Every day in tens of thousands of classrooms around the world, adult English to speakers of other languages (ESOL) teachers—often in isolation and frequently unappreciated or inadequately compensated—selflessly work hard to support the educational opportunities of adult immigrants, refugees, asylees, and everyone who sees opportunity in advancing their work and life outcomes through learning English. As a former adult English as a second language (ESL) teacher, I aspired to excellence in my teaching but did not always have access to examples of what that looked like or to supports that could help me get to exemplary teaching.

The 6 Principles for Exemplary Teaching of English Learners: Adult Education and Workforce Development, by Andrea Hellman, Kathy Harris, and Amea Wilbur (Deborah Short, Series Editor), shares with us TESOL's vision for exemplary teaching of adults who are learning English as a part of their preparation for the workforce. This book is written for the large and growing international audience of English teachers who instruct adult English learners in a variety of settings (adult learning centers, adult basic education programs, family literacy programs, workplace education, career training, settlement programs, and refugee serving agencies).

This book is an extraordinary resource for anyone who is part of the global community of English teachers, and by extension administrators, for many reasons. The book opens with solid data on the size and composition of the growing population of adult English learners, offers a comprehensive profile using learner vignettes, and presents a good overview of the institutional contexts in which learning English is facilitated, along with TESOL's statement of the characteristics of effective programs. It then provides a clear and comprehensive view of all the findings from language acquisition and literacy development research that teachers should know about and be mindful of when designing teaching and learning experiences and activities. The book then introduces and discusses in select chapters The 6 Principles for effective teaching. Illustrating each principle with practice tips and vignettes, the book helps the reader develop a mental picture of what research- and principle-based effective teaching looks like. The discussion in Chapter 4 of the various supports learners may need with issues of disability, mental health, and other challenges that can affect the learning of adult English learners is invaluable. The description of the principles in five different institutional contexts and geographies in Chapter 5 brings it all to life in a very real way. The clarity of the manuscript's language makes it easy to imagine how one could be applying these practices in one's own context. Always with an eye toward application, the practices—including numerous hands-on techniques, tips, and teaching advice—are informative, motivating, and actionable. It seldom happens that a book for teachers about teaching and learning provides the reader with confidence and enthusiasm about enhancing one's practice. This book does. In addition, the book adopts a view of adult English learners that acknowledges and leverages the many assets that learners bring and which often remain unlocked, unless teachers are intentional about using a holistic approach. The cultural sensitivity and commitment to creating culturally respectful and responsive learning experiences are two additional strengths the authors have brought forth throughout the manuscript.

One particular area where this book is so unlike many other books for teachers is related to the sixth principle, "Engage and collaborate within a community of practice." The view of teachers as advocates for learners and policies and as leaders in their respective communities, focused on working with others to ensure access to integrated support services, is refreshing, inspiring, and beyond symbolic.

The 6 Principles for Exemplary Teaching of English Learners: Adult Education and Workforce Development validates the experiences of seasoned practitioners and provides a well-researched set of practices that all teachers will find useful in their pursuit of excellence. Perhaps more importantly, implementing many of the practices presented in this book will markedly accelerate the integration of adult English learners at work and in our communities.

Johan E. Uvin
Institute for Educational Leadership, Washington, DC

3. Design high-quality lessons for language development.
4. Adapt lesson delivery as needed.
5. Monitor and assess student language development.
6. Engage and collaborate within a community of practice.

These statements are the armature around which we mold our field's best ideas to form a coherent model. The practices, which show how exemplary teachers achieve these principles, give the model its true shape. As with a sculpture, once the structure is in place, the details add to the main function. The 6 Principles framework allows us to convey the most important elements of expertise in our field to anyone with a desire to understand and to improve the education of English learners.

Audience

The intended audience for this book includes

- teachers in adult education programs in countries where adults have a reason to learn English as a new language,
- instructors who work with English learners in workplace education and career preparation,
- teachers in integrated English language and citizenship education programs,
- ESOL and literacy tutors who serve adults,
- volunteers in faith-based and community-based English language programs, and
- staff and volunteers at agencies that serve adults who need to learn English.

The secondary audience is

- teacher educators in TESOL and adult education programs,
- consultants who deliver professional development to teachers of adult English learners worldwide,
- trainers of ESOL and literacy tutors,
- creators of English language teaching materials for adults, and
- administrators of adult and workplace education programs.

Overview

We present the principles and practices of exemplary teaching of adult learners in five chapters:

Chapter 1: Teaching Adults English Language and Literacy with The 6 Principles offers the rationale for raising the bar for adult English learners' proficiency to meet the demands of the 21st-century workplace. We outline the characteristics of programs that effectively serve adult English learners and introduce The 6 Principles for teaching these learners.

Chapter 2: What Teachers Should Know about English Language and Literacy Development to Plan Instruction for Adult Learners summarizes the main factors of learning a new language in adulthood and the role of literacy development for boosting proficiency with English. We emphasize the need for adults to have functional practice with language skills as opposed to receiving knowledge about the English language as an academic subject. We reference the standards documents that are in place to guide the instruction of adult learners whose skills with listening, speaking, reading, and writing are at various proficiency levels. The fundamentals explained in this chapter provide the necessary working knowledge for The 6 Principles.

Chapter 3: Teaching with The 6 Principles, which is the core of this book, defines and illustrates each principle. We supply several high-leverage practices that are evidence based and that add depth and clarity to what each principle means. We elaborate Principle 3 the most—design high-quality lessons for language development—because we must plan lessons carefully before delivering instruction, and there are many nuanced ways to create an effective lesson.

Chapter 4: Addressing the Challenges with Adult English Learners describes the inevitable obstacles that educators of adult learners face daily with learners' participation and attendance, their struggles to adapt to new conditions in a new culture, and the burdens of low literacy, special needs, or trauma. We place our recommendations within The 6 Principles framework to encourage systematic, proactive practices, which we can thoughtfully plan.

Chapter 5: The 6 Principles in Different Program Contexts shows how we can recognize exemplary teaching in very different classrooms by applying The 6 Principles framework. We feature the classes of five English teachers, who instruct adult learners in five different programs in three countries. All of them deliver high-quality lessons consistently. We point out where and how The 6 Principles are in action in these contexts. Our purpose is to demonstrate what these principles look and sound like in a variety of classrooms to help you picture what it would mean for you to realize them in your own teaching.

Moving Forward

TESOL's mission is to advance the quality of English language teaching around the world. The 6 Principles framework is an important strategy for that mission. The framework is the result of a two-year process by a team of language experts and educators, who participated in collaborative inquiry and lengthy discussions. The writing team of this current volume accepted the charge to build on the existing framework and adapt it for teaching adult learners. We were able to achieve this by altering the practices slightly where necessary and adding several new teaching practices.

Our work in this volume is consistent with the first 6 Principles book. We use the same framework and terminology to feature teaching practices. Readers who are already familiar with The 6 Principles may recognize that we have continued to refine the practices by adding examples and explanations to those concepts that are not as well known to adult educators in the international context as they are to K–12 educators in the United States. We show, for example, how to plan language objectives based on standards documents and detail the techniques that can help teachers make different types of input—speech, text, content—comprehensible to learners whose English language skills vary. We hope to inspire by revealing the strategies and thoughtful teaching approaches of many exemplary adult educators in action in their classes.

We are excited to contribute a new strand to TESOL International Association's 6 Principles initiative, whose goal is to bring high-quality instruction to every English language classroom across the globe. We hope that you will become an active participant to make your mark, not only by implementing these principles with your own classes but also by joining TESOL International Association as a member and becoming a 6 Principles trainer for your own colleagues.

Andrea B. Hellman
Kathy Harris
Amea Wilbur

Acknowledgments

This volume reflects the abundant contributions of many amazing individuals who are passionate about the subject and care deeply about English learners. They were generous with their expertise and mentored us graciously with valuable remarks.

We are indebted to our editor, Deborah J. Short, who directed the writing with sharp focus, guiding us along any time we needed support and contributing her wealth of experience with publications. Myrna Jacobs, Director of Publications and Product Development, commissioned the work and led it expertly at every stage of development and production. We are grateful to Johan Uvin, President of the Institute for Educational Leadership, who served as Acting Assistant Secretary for the Office of Career, Technical, and Adult Education (OCTAE) at the U.S. Department of Education; he encouraged this work and wrote the Foreword.

We acknowledge the TESOL Writing Team who created the first volume in The 6 Principles series, which served as the foundation and main structure for this book: Deborah J. Short, Helene Becker, Nancy Cloud, Andrea B. Hellman, and Linda New Levine. Additional contributors to the original volume were Sherry Blok, Karen Woodson, Christel Broady, and Ximena Uribe-Zarain. We borrowed, preserved, and adjusted many parts of the text in the original volume in Chapters 1–3.

We deeply appreciate the contributions of the wonderful colleagues who supplied vignettes, examples, and/or information for the case studies: Ximena Uribe-Zarain, Morie Ford, Sara Yuen, Diana Jeffries, Sandra Slind, Erin Good, Pamela McPherson, Patricia Ruiz, and Ning Zhang. We thank those who guided us with resources: Debra Suarez and Pamela McPherson. Our copy editor, Tomiko Breland, sharpened the prose and added grace.

The reviewers provided invaluable assistance with their constructive feedback, which significantly shaped both the content and the presentation in this book. We thank them for their knowledge as well as for making it a priority to respond to the manuscript with helpful suggestions within a tight schedule. Their encouragement was astonishing. We applaud them for their dedication.

Emily Albertsen
Natalia Balyasnikova
Miriam Burt
MaryAnne Cunningham
　　Florez
Maria Dantas-Whitney
Andrea DeCapua

Diane Hardy
Christina Kitson
Christine Nicodemus
Betsy Parrish
Joy Kreeft Peyton
Laura Ramm
Sarah Rilling

Tanis Sawkins
Julie Ship
Cristine Smith
Thu H. Tran
Jen Vanek
Ke Xu

1
TEACHING ADULTS ENGLISH LANGUAGE AND LITERACY WITH THE 6 PRINCIPLES

Morgan points to the board to present today's content and language objectives for her level 3 English as a Second Language class at the adult learning center: "Our content objective is to compare standards for food safety. We all work with food. We work with different foods. We cook for different people. We must keep foods safe. Our language objective is to discuss and write rules for food safety." She also writes several key vocabulary items on the board and prompts her students to be on the lookout for these words and keep using them throughout the lesson. For key vocabulary, she chose words that have useful parts that can help produce other words: safer, safety, safely, and keep safe.

Morgan shows four photographs that depict people handling food safely in various situations: the kitchen of a childcare facility, a food stand at a festival, a restaurant kitchen, and a home cook: "Which picture is important to you?" She prompts learners to join one of four groups based on the image that depicts a situation relevant for them. Having four options helps Morgan differentiate her instruction for learners who have varied learning purposes and background knowledge.

Each group begins work with members choosing a team role. These roles are facilitator, recorder, researcher, and presenter. On the wall, a poster illustrates the tasks of each team role. The learners are already familiar with this type of collaborative group work because Morgan conducts most of her lessons in small collaborative groups. The team approach serves to hone soft skills for employment and multiplies opportunities for language use.

Each team has stepwise directions to complete their project: brainstorm a list of foods or select foods from a picture dictionary, separate foods by type to store safely, create a table to organize the information by type of food, list a storing method for each food category, provide details on the methods to keep these foods safe, and summarize findings in a list of rules to post for the cooks. At any step, if the team members need information, they can ask questions. The role of the researchers, who have portable electronic devices, is to locate information on the internet to answer any of these questions.

Morgan circulates to assist each team. She tells the learners that they should build on what they already know, but they need to check their knowledge against online text sources. She also recommends websites where quality information on food safety is available on the researchers' reading level as well as in other languages. Although Morgan encourages learners to work mainly in English, she also supports learners' using all of their resources, including multilingual websites and electronic translations. She reminds the researchers to read carefully, select relevant information, and dictate slowly for the team recorder. The recorder asks for the correct spelling of words. The facilitator keeps checking that the information is transferred correctly from the websites to the group's food safety table of information. After the information is organized, they begin to create their set of rules. The group members carefully craft each rule together and critique and approve each sentence.

The group work results in three products. One is a table in which information is organized by categories of food, the appropriate storing method for each type, and specifics on keeping each type of food safe. The second is a list of sentences that summarize the rules of keeping foods safe. The third is a quick presentation of the table and the rules the group created. Based on the information each work team gathers, the learners compare standards of food safety for different situations and explore the main questions of the day: How do standards of food safety differ? Why?

Morgan's aims with this discussion are to support active listening to each other's presentations, to provide feedback to the groups on their work, and to promote higher order thinking by having students compare and synthesize information. During the conversation, Morgan models active listening and acts as the note taker. She repeats and captures the main ideas of the speakers on the board. When needed, she reformulates learner responses and models accurate English. To sum up the discussion, she groups, connects, and organizes the ideas visually on a sheet of poster paper to make the thinking process visible.

Morgan ends her lesson by asking each team to discuss what they have learned about today's content and language objectives. She also reminds learners to record two items in their journals: the learning strategies they applied that were helpful to them and the new words or concepts they used that they would like to take away from the lesson.

Advancing English Language Instruction for Adults

We write this book to share TESOL's vision for exemplary teaching of adults who are learning English as a part of their preparation for the workforce. Career and technical education opportunities today require English language and literacy in many countries. Adults who wish to be successful in today's workplace need complex language and literacy skills: clear verbal and written communication, problem solving, collaboration, higher reading levels, and digital literacy. English language teaching for these adults must evolve to meet the demands of the 21st-century workforce.

When adults pursue learning English, often their long-term goals are better paying jobs and economic self-sufficiency. They view the English language as a means to reach those goals either because the jobs they seek require communication in English or because proficiency in English gives them access to education and training in their desired field of employment. Indeed, countless workplaces worldwide use English for business, from trade and tourism to manufacturing and the service industry (British Council, 2013). It is important that we position English instruction in a way to serve adult learners' long-term goals and help them beyond learning basic communication and life skills (Parrish, 2015).

Critical thinking, problem solving, verbal and written communication skills, teamwork skills, and professional manners are the top-rated "soft skills" managers seek in employees (Wonderlic, 2016) and are suitable instructional targets for adult English language classes. Today's employees need to rapidly adjust to ever changing job demands, follow written directions, participate in discussions, produce written reports, or conduct electronic research to solve problems. In turn, these same skills can also allow adults to thrive in all areas of their lives, including successfully solving life problems, making informed decisions for their families, and cooperating with others to benefit themselves and their communities.

Learning English is an important part of the acculturation process for immigrants and refugees who settle in English-speaking countries. In these countries, there is growing recognition of the pressing need to advance English language proficiency targets in all adult education programs to assist transitioning to English-language secondary or postsecondary education and professional training programs. In these countries, a large segment of adult education program participants are immigrants and refugees who do not speak English as their primary language and who vary highly in their prior education and literacy.

For example, recent legislation in the United States has raised the proficiency goals in adult English language acquisition programs; the law defines English language acquisition programs that are fundable as programs which help English learners (ELs) achieve competence in reading, writing, speaking, and comprehension of the English language and which lead to the attainment of a secondary school diploma, its equivalent, postsecondary education, or employment (Workforce Innovation and Opportunity Act of 2014; WIOA). To further this goal, the new English Language

Proficiency Standards for Adult Education (U.S. Department of Education, Office of Career, Technical, and Adult Education, 2016) detail the English language skills adult learners need to successfully access college- and career-ready academic instruction. Likewise, the Canadian Language Benchmarks (Centre for Canadian Language Benchmarks, 2012) and the Australian Core Skills Framework (Australian Government Department of Education and Training, 2015)—which guide the instruction of adult ELs in Canada and Australia, respectively—also set demanding goals for proficiency, which include being able to comprehend and fluently produce complex texts and complex spoken communication.

The 6 Principles we present here are applicable to all contexts for teaching adult ELs. In this volume, we focus on adult English language programs and workforce preparation programs where participants are developing literacy and relevant content knowledge as they are learning to communicate in English. The vignettes we include describe a range of adult education programs: settlement programs, adult basic education, low-level literacy classes, workplace education, family literacy, integrated English and civics, and integrated English and career training.

The opening vignette in this chapter captured what we mean by rigorous English language instruction for adults with The 6 Principles. The teacher, Morgan, organized her lesson to focus on challenging content and language objectives. All of the lesson activities directly served the lesson objectives, as well as the personal goals of each adult learner in her class. The activities required team collaboration, problem solving, and higher order thinking; in other words, they entailed the soft skills necessary for employment and community interaction.

The students produced frequent and authentic language use through discussion, reading, and writing and were able to build on their prior knowledge and their full repertoire of language skills, including the strategic use of their home language when it supported their ability to solve problems and build content knowledge. They engaged meaningfully with a variety of text types and formats to develop their informational literacy in conjunction with their English language skills. Additionally, the students were able to hone language learning strategies, which will allow them to become independent language learners outside the classroom. The complex interactions in Morgan's class resembled the demands of today's work environment, where adult learners strive to succeed.

Diversity of Adult English Learners

Though not every ethnic and socioeconomic group in the world has equal access to English language instruction, an exponentially growing segment of the world desires to learn English to improve employment prospects either in professional fields or in those industries where English is gaining as the medium for conducting business. Among these are tourism, hospitality, the military, and now also the full range of service providers in health care, retail, shipping, transportation, and call centers (British Council, 2013).

An estimated 30 percent of the world's population (2.3 billion) speaks some English, although only five percent (388 million) acquired it as their primary language. The vast majority of English speakers (83 percent) have learned English as an additional language. Surprisingly, only four percent (71 million) of the world's English learners live in the six countries that linguists refer to as inner circle countries, or countries in which English

---

If the world had 100 English speakers . . .
18 would live in India
17 would live in China
13 would live in the United States
5 would live in Nigeria
4 would live in the Philippines
3 would live in the United Kingdom
2 would live in Indonesia, Germany, and Russia
34 would live in all other countries

(Crystal, 2019)

---

is spoken as the dominant language (i.e., Australia, Canada, Ireland, New Zealand, the United Kingdom, and the United States; Crystal 2019).

Adult ELs in the inner circle countries, although heterogeneous, are less representative of worldwide diversity. Immigrants, resettled refugees, asylum claimants, and temporary workers, who make up the majority of adult ELs, come from a smaller set of countries. Immigration laws, unique to each country, narrow which groups may be welcome, and the diversity also varies by immigration status (Organisation for Economic Cooperation and Development [OECD], 2018). Table 1.1 summarizes the country of origin of newcomers by their immigration status in five English-speaking countries.

Table 1.1	The national origin of newcomers by immigration status in five English-speaking countries based on 2016/2017 data				
	Australia	**Canada**	**United States (U.S.)**	**United Kingdom (U.K.)**	**New Zealand**
Where did the largest groups of **new permanent residents** arrive from?	India China New Zealand Pakistan Philippines	Philippines India Syria China Pakistan	Mexico India China El Salvador Guatemala Philippines	Romania Poland Ireland India Italy Portugal	China India Pakistan Philippines
Where did the most **newly naturalized citizens** come from?	India U.K. Philippines China South Africa	Philippines India China Pakistan U.S. U.K.	Mexico India Philippines China Cuba Dominican Republic	India Pakistan Nigeria South Africa Bangladesh	U.K. India Philippines South Africa Samoa Fiji
Where did **resettled refugees** mainly come from?	Iraq Syria Afghanistan Burma Bhutan	Syria Iraq Afghanistan Burma Bhutan	Democratic Republic of Congo Burma Syria	Syria Iraq Pakistan Sudan Afghanistan	
What were the sending countries of the largest groups of **new asylum claimants?**	Malaysia Iran Sri Lanka Afghanistan China Iraq	Haiti Nigeria U.S. Turkey Pakistan Mexico	El Salvador Mexico Guatemala China Honduras Venezuela	Iran Pakistan Iraq Bangladesh Sudan Albania	
How much of the total population is **foreign-born?**	28%	20%	13.5%	14%	25%

(OECD, 2018)

The number of new-arrival immigrants who are highly educated and English proficient is growing. For example, about half of the recent immigrants to the United States were college educated, and one-third were bilingual (Batalova & Fix, 2017), much higher than in previous decades.

Specific humanitarian efforts and international agreements govern the intake of refugees in each country; as a result, only a limited number of nationalities qualify each year. For example, in 2017, 94 percent of refugees represented just 15 nationalities (Refugee Processing Center, 2018).

In Canada and in Australia in 2016, resettled refugees came mainly from Syria, Iraq, Afghanistan, Burma, and Bhutan (OECD, 2018).

Refugee claimants or asylum seekers—those who petition for refugee status after they arrive in a country—are a rapidly growing segment of English learners, who outnumber by far the annual intake of refugees who are resettled through international agreements. As table 1.1 indicates, this group varies the most by origin for each receiving country (OECD, 2018).

Another large group of adult English learners are those who are seeking naturalization, which requires the demonstration of language proficiency as well as knowledge of civics. In 2017 in the United States, 703,000 individuals became new citizens. The prior year, 149,457 became naturalized citizens in the United Kingdom; 148,103 in Canada; 133,126 in Australia; and 32,862 in New Zealand (OECD, 2018).

In the inner circle countries, foreign-born individuals make up a significant portion of the population. The labor market of these countries relies heavily on English learners. English skills impact the employment opportunities and earnings of these workers (National Academies of Sciences, Engineering, and Medicine, 2015). For example, in 2016, one in six U.S. workers was born in a foreign country (Gryn & Walker, 2018), half of whom spoke English less than very well (Gambino, Acosta, & Grieco, 2014). Individuals with limited English skills were far overrepresented among low-skilled workers (29 percent; Bergson-Shilcock, 2017).

Profiles of Adult English Learners

To explore the differences among the students we have in mind when we refer to adult English learners in this book, let's think about the following profiles.

Mahmoud (58) is a father of five from Syria. He fled the country after their neighborhood was destroyed. Mahmoud's family lived under traumatic conditions for two years before they received approval to settle in Canada. He feels relieved that his children are growing up in safety. He is adjusting to the new life, although he often feels overwhelmed with worry for family members who are still under constant threat for their survival. After a year in Canada with daily English classes, Mahmoud can now communicate in basic English, and he is able to read short texts. He is interested in his children's education and would like to help them achieve their best.

Min (35) grew up in China, where she knew hard work from childhood. In her early twenties, she moved to Saipan in the Northern Mariana Islands, where she labored in the garment industry. After arriving in the United States, she became a restaurant worker and assisted in people's homes, interacting mainly within the Chinese community. She often works long hours and several jobs to help her brother with the care of their aging parents in China. Min would like to learn English so she can become certified as a home care aide, although she has very little time or support to pursue studies.

Acindina (25), a young mother of a three-year-old, relocated to the United States mainland from Puerto Rico. She has been trying to regain a sense of normalcy after a distressing experience losing her home. Although she was a clerk before, now she works through a temporary employment agency in warehouse and assembly jobs. Acindina recognizes the importance of developing her English skills to find stable employment, raise her child, and move to an apartment of her own.

Diba (41) is a widowed mother of six. She fled the Democratic Republic of Congo for Rwanda. Diba witnessed extreme atrocities while she was in hiding for months. She and her children spent miserable years in a Rwandan refugee camp before they could resettle in

Australia. Diba speaks Tshiluba and Swahili. Prior to starting English classes, she did not have any formal education, and she could not read in any language.

Tareq (26) is a guest worker in the United Arab Emirates from Bangladesh. He works as a mason. He has enrolled in English classes because he is interested in further training to become a maintenance or engineering technician for a hotel chain. He is excited about the opportunities that English skills may open up for him.

Our purpose with this book is to support the English language education of those adults who are resettling in a new country or who pursue language courses to improve their life conditions and employment opportunities, like the individuals above. We define adult learners as persons 18 years or older who are not enrolled in secondary education or university courses. Adult ELs are those who speak a language other than English as their home language and have needs to use English either socially or for work, but who have not yet developed a level of proficiency to be able to fully function in both spoken and written English.

These learners vary in their prior schooling. Like Diba, some have little to no formal education and they are learning to read and write for the first time in their life in English. Others partici-pated in K–12 education without attaining advanced proficiency in English, like Acindina. Some had a few years of schooling but did not complete high school, like Min and Tareq. Still others are highly literate in their native language but arrived with a low-level proficiency in English, as did Mahmoud.

Our examples throughout this volume highlight programs in English-speaking countries that mainly serve immigrants, refugees, and asylum seekers. However, The 6 Principles and the teach-ing ideas we recommend apply more broadly.

Adult English Language Programs for Literacy and Workforce Development

A broad range of agencies deliver English language instruction for adults. Local education agen-cies (e.g., school districts) frequently have adult English as a second language (ESL) classes as part of their adult education programs. Many community agencies serve ELs with the help of pub-lic funding and private sponsorship. Other programs are for-profit proprietary language schools. Whatever the type, TESOL recommends that adult English language education in literacy and workforce development programs demonstrate the following characteristics to be effective:

- Programs are responsive to learners' needs and goals.
- Curricula are rigorous and prepare learners for the 21st-century workplace or for secondary or postsecondary education.
- Curricula, instruction, and assessment build on available research.
- Learners' acculturation to a new country is supported.
- Learners' home languages and cultural knowledge are affirmed and respected.
- Learners are assisted in overcoming challenges to participation.

Table 1.2 provides an inventory of adult English language and literacy programs along with the list of agencies that usually offer them. Because public funding for the various types of programs depends on specific legislation, the types of programs that are available change as the laws and regulations change. For example, in the United States, program offerings are in large part a function of each state's WIOA plan, which has resulted in more funding for one-stop career training programs than, for example, funding for adult ESL classes and family literacy; this is a dramatic change from the recent past.

Even as the distribution of the different program types changes and not all kinds of programs are available in every region, the table (1.2) is a good directory for the different ways in which various agencies have successfully offered English language and literacy training. Our hope is that each agency involved in English language education will consider the possible options for instructing adult English learners and choose to offer the kinds of programs that best fit the specific adult learners they intend to serve.

Table 1.2 Types of adult English language and literacy programs	
Type of program	**Where to find them**
Public adult basic education programs	School districts Adult learning centers, usually at community colleges Refugee serving agencies Regional career and technical education centers Settlement programs
Workplace ESL programs	Places of employment, usually delivered in partnership with an educational agency
Family literacy programs	Public schools Publicly funded child development centers and preschool programs Libraries
Integrated English and civics programs	Social services agencies Libraries Community and civic organizations School districts
English literacy programs for institutionalized adults	Prisons Youth rehabilitative institutions Dedicated education facilities for institutionalized adults
Out-of-school programs	Homeless serving facilities Youth centers
Drop-in English language programs	Libraries Faith-based organizations Community centers Community schools Refugee camps
Career education programs	Job centers/employment service agencies Regional career and technical education centers Technical colleges and institutes
Fee-based ESOL classes	Privately owned language centers Online education providers

The 6 Principles for Exemplary Teaching of English Learners

The 6 Principles put forth in this book are not revolutionary or groundbreaking concepts in language learning. They are well-established guidelines drawn from decades of research in language pedagogy and language acquisition theory. The 6 Principles bring to life TESOL's core values. Though we present them in seemingly simple statements, they carry substantial weight because their effective implementation can make a significant difference for learner success. The 6 Principles must be taken together as a cohesive whole for them to be effective. One cannot know one's learners, for example, and then not use that knowledge when planning lessons.

Figure 1.1 provides a brief explanation of each principle, and later chapters show teachers of adult ELs how they can actualize The 6 Principles in their instruction.

Figure 1.1	The 6 Principles for Exemplary Teaching of English Learners

Exemplary teaching of English learners rests on the following 6 Principles:

1. **Know your learners.** Teachers learn basic information about their students' families, languages, cultures, and educational backgrounds to engage them in the classrooms and prepare and deliver lessons more effectively.

2. **Create conditions for language learning.** Teachers create a classroom culture that will ensure that students feel comfortable in the class. They make decisions regarding the physical environment, the materials, and the social integration of students to promote language learning.

3. **Design high-quality lessons for language development.** Teachers plan meaningful lessons that promote language learning and help students develop learning strategies and critical thinking skills. These lessons evolve from the learning objectives.

4. **Adapt lesson delivery as needed.** Teachers continually assess as they teach—observing and reflecting on learners' responses to determine whether the students are reaching the learning objectives. If students struggle or are not challenged enough, teachers consider the possible reasons and adjust their lessons.

5. **Monitor and assess student language development.** Language learners learn at different rates, so teachers regularly monitor and assess their language development in order to advance their learning efficiently. Teachers also gather data to measure student language growth.

6. **Engage and collaborate within a community of practice.** Teachers collaborate with others in the profession to provide the best support for their learners with respect to programming, instruction, and advocacy. They also continue their own professional learning.

A Look Back and a Look Ahead

The number of adults who are learning English increases every day. Teacher professional learning plays a critical role in advancing the outcomes of adult English language instruction. This book lays a foundation for the efforts to professionalize English language education for adults, provides shared language for instructional practices, and aims to improve career and education options for adult learners of English as a new language.

In this chapter, we have done the following:

- explained TESOL's rationale for identifying core principles for exemplary teaching of ELs and the pressing need for their implementation in adult literacy and workforce development contexts

- showed an example of a rigorous English language lesson that serves 21st-century workplace skills

- emphasized inherent challenges in instructing diverse learners who vary widely in their academic preparation and what they wish to gain from English classes

- outlined the types of English language programs various agencies make available

- introduced The 6 Principles, which are discussed in detail in Chapter 3. These principles help teachers create conditions in the classroom that promote language learning and plan and deliver lessons that keep learners' backgrounds, goals, and needs in mind.

Teachers of English learners need to understand that language development in adulthood is complex and that it does not always lead to full proficiency within the time frame available for instruction. Instructed language learning may be just one—albeit critical—segment of the journey toward proficiency in a new language for adults. Language instruction is formative for eventual attainment of advanced proficiency when it provides learners with the skills and strategies they need to continue motivated and self-directed learning outside the classroom.

Additional resources pertaining to this chapter are available at www.the6principles.org/adult-education

Acronyms Associated with English Learning

EFL	English as a foreign language
EL/ELL	English learner/English language learner
ELA	English language acquisition (in K–12 this refers to English language arts)
ELP	English language proficiency
ENL	English as a new language
ESL	English as a second language
ESOL	English speakers of other languages (refers to students)
ESOL	English to speakers of other languages (refers to programs)
L1	First language (also home language, primary language, native language)
L2	Second language
LESLLA	Literacy education and second language learning for adults (previously, low-educated second language and literacy for adults)
SLA	Second language acquisition
SIFE/SLIFE	Students with (limited or) interrupted formal education

Acronyms Associated with Adult Education Programs

ABE	Adult basic education
ACSF	Australian Core Skills Framework
CLB	Canadian Language Benchmarks
ELL-U	A professional learning network for adult English to speakers of other languages practitioners
ESL Pro	Resource collection for the instruction of adult English learners
GED	General Educational Development (refers primarily to a U.S. high school equivalency program)
HSE	High school equivalency
LINC	Language Instruction to Newcomers to Canada (program)
LINCS	U.S. national leadership initiative to support adult educators
WIOA	Workforce Innovation and Opportunity Act of 2014

2 WHAT TEACHERS SHOULD KNOW ABOUT ENGLISH LANGUAGE AND LITERACY DEVELOPMENT TO PLAN INSTRUCTION FOR ADULT LEARNERS

All around my new life is plenty of English words. There are many ways that my everyday life is immersed in English: shopping, business, and trips. I have American friends and I want to know more about them, and, of course, the only way is to listen and learn with them. My daughters are also a good influence too because they are learning English quicker than me in elementary school. They have good teachers who are interested in my daughters' education. My daughters and I exchange a lot of information about our new knowledge and about what we are learning. We read a lot of new books that we have located in libraries or purchased in stores.

(Ignacio Morrondo; Minnesota Literacy Council, 2017)

I was born in Burma in a small village. When I was ten years old I moved to a Thailand refugee camp with my parents. I went to school in the refugee camp a few years and then I got married early when I was in middle school. . . . My family had the opportunity to move to the United States. . . . Everything was new for my family, and it was difficult to do anything. I was very upset and wanted to move back to Thailand. One month later, I started going to school four hours a day, five days a week. Childcare took care of my kids every day when I was in school. At that time I studied hard and went to school every day to improve my English, how to speak, read, write, and listen in English. I had a problem memorizing the English I was learning during class. I wanted to speak English fluently and help my family and my neighbors by translating the English to the Karen language.

(Elizabeth Htoo; Minnesota Literacy Council, 2017)

This chapter addresses key knowledge teachers should have about adult language learning, second language acquisition, and literacy development in English. Chapter 3 explains The 6 Principles and helps you apply this knowledge as you design lessons to teach adult English learners (ELs).

Knowing how the language acquisition process works can guide teachers with their instructional decisions, both in their planning of a lesson and in their delivery of it. For example, if a learner makes an error in English, a teacher's response should be based on whether (a) the error is normal for the learner's level or (b) it indicates that the learner did not understand instruction or has acquired incorrect language forms based on mishearing or a misapplied analogy. Effective teachers hold reasonable expectations for ELs because they are aware of the time, effort, and practice it takes to learn a new language.

In this chapter, we provide foundational knowledge for language and literacy instruction.

First, we look at some distinguishing characteristics of adult learners, and, specifically, why and how adults learn differently from children. Next, we examine the essential conditions for language learning and discuss factors that may help or hinder progress. When teachers know which of these factors they can control, they can boost language learning. For example, when teachers know that language develops through practice and interaction, they can plan lessons that have students use language actively and negotiate meaning with conversation partners. When teachers are aware of how learners' home language literacy can serve as a resource for literacy in English, they can introduce strategies and learning materials that best suit their students. We explain that advanced English proficiency depends on literacy development and detail those aspects of literacy that challenge many ELs. Finally, we discuss the basics of English language functioning levels that teachers in different countries use to guide placement and instructional planning for adult ELs.

Why Learn English

Adult learners pursue educational opportunities for reasons that are integral to their everyday lives and personal goals. They come from vastly different life circumstances and with a broad range of prior knowledge. They have had diverse formal education experiences. Some have adequate resources for learning, while others have struggled all their lives with profound disadvantages.

However different in their background and preparation, adult ELs are like-minded in that they perceive opportunity in learning English. They don't usually (or initially) pursue learning English as an academic subject; rather, they see English as a practical tool to move toward a life goal. English can be a key to access additional training, becoming self-sufficient, advancing in a career, and improving themselves. It may be the code to expand their social networks and to integrate as members into a new community. When asked "why learn English?," most adults cite economic and self-esteem goals, such as *I need to take care of my kids* or *I need English for a better job*, *I'm tired and exhausted by the work I do now. With education, I could do better*, or *I came to this country with a dream to be someone and to help my family. I can do that if I know English.*

> Adult ELs don't usually pursue learning English as an academic subject; rather, they see English as a practical tool to move toward a life goal.

This means that teachers should become aware of learners' goals and rationales for pursuing English proficiency and explicitly connect these to instruction. The starting point for instruction is to recognize what tangible benefits learners are expecting to gain from knowing the language—because "knowing English" is likely shorthand for working toward a greater goal. It means access to those areas of life—jobs, further training, and education—that require career-ready communication skills and literacy in English. Consequently, instruction that these learners receive must be truly useful for converting opportunity into reality.

What Adults Bring to Learning

When designing instruction for adult ELs, we should start with what we know about teaching adults.

Every Adult English Learner Is Unique

Our adult learners represent more than one hundred ethnicities with dozens of different home languages; they differ in the quality and years of formal education they received. Some are better educated than their English-speaking peers, and others never attended school. They are accustomed to different traditions, cultural norms, religions, and ideologies. Some are still adolescents; others have already reached retirement age. Many have suffered trauma, which may have left them with physical and/or psychological scarring. They also have many varied responsibilities; schooling comes in addition to these responsibilities. Each learner brings a unique set of strengths and challenges that is important for educators to know.

Adult Learners Have Social Capital

Adult learners can derive resources from their immediate and extended family and their larger social networks. The utility of their social capital differs depending on their community's resources and their network's values and behaviors. Their social capital may hinder or facilitate their educational goals (Zhou & Kim, 2006). How a network orients toward English use in everyday life and the pursuit of education to integrate into English-speaking social networks influences learners' motivation and what resources they can generate to help them capture those goals. When teachers are aware of each learner's social capital, they can encourage students to draw on these resources, or they can explore with students the difficulties that may require supports from mentors in a new social network.

Adult Learners Set Their Own Goals

Adults have their own reasons for what and why they want to learn. They tend to weigh the value of participation in terms of costs (effort, time, self-esteem, and resources) versus benefits (Patterson, 2018), which are usually framed as social or economic goals (Appleby, 2010). Their cost-benefit judgments are ongoing, and if they experience diminishing returns or slow progress toward their goals, or if they perceive the costs to be too high, they often drop their studies. If learners are to stay in programs long enough to master the skills they need, they must experience a direct connection between what they are learning and their personal goals for pursuing the program.

> If learners are to stay in programs long enough to master the skills they need, they must experience a direct connection between what they are learning and their personal goals for pursuing the program.

Adults Are Autonomous Learners

Adults are self-directing in major areas of their lives; they expect this to apply in the area of education as well. Therefore, the atmosphere of the classroom should emanate mutual respect, trust, and collaboration. Educators should welcome adult learners to give their input about the course plan, the teaching approaches, and the evaluation of their own learning. Although self-directed learning is developmentally desirable for most adults, not all adults possess the aptitude to direct their own learning. Through modeling, coaching, and explicit strategy instruction, we can support adults who are inexperienced learners (Knowles, Holton, & Swanson, 2015; Merriam & Bierema, 2014).

Adult Learners Have "Funds of Knowledge" to Draw On

Adults are able to draw on their accumulated life experiences to support their learning. For the most part, prior experiences provide a rich resource for mastering new skills and content; however, prior experiences can also frame and limit how adults approach new learning. Because adults often define themselves by their prior experiences, teachers should not ignore or devalue these, but rather try to understand and build on them (Knowles, Holton, & Swanson, 2015; Merriam & Bierema, 2014).

One type of knowledge diverse adults can draw on is the historically and culturally accumulated knowledge essential for the functioning of their communities. This knowledge stems from traditional ways of life: farming, ranching, gardening, mining, manufacturing and marketing goods, constructing homes, practicing crafts, managing the household and cottage industries, or applying indigenous medicine. These funds of knowledge constitute cultural and cognitive resources, which can facilitate new learning for adults and which teachers can blend into instruction (González, Moll, & Amanti, 2005).

Adult English Learners Have Linguistic Capital

When adults learn a new language, they bring with them fully developed oral language ability in at least one language, or sometimes several languages. They have well-established neural pathways that make it possible for them to process that language automatically, and they may also have conscious awareness of language structures in their previously learned languages. Adults can name thousands of concepts, carry out communicative functions with language, and use language to support a broad range of cognitive tasks. However, adult ELs vary in how much of their linguistic capital they can transfer to their new language; this depends on how much their other languages overlap with English in terms of the sound system, vocabulary, linguistic structures, and writing system (National Research Council, 2012).

Adult Learners Are Resourceful with Language Use

Adult learners are resourceful with how they apply their knowledge of languages. They are often able to switch dynamically between their languages in purposeful ways that reflect their awareness of another speaker's language repertoire as well as the full communicative context.

This type of language behavior among bilinguals—known as translanguaging—serves as an expression of identity and group solidarity. Translanguaging can also be a very practical solution when individuals who are learning each other's languages try to communicate. For these reasons, translanguaging can play a role in instruction when teachers encourage learners to convey meaning using English when they can and switching to another language to fill gaps (García, Johnson, & Seltzer, 2017). For example, in the following vignette, a Spanish-speaking adult who is a beginner English learner is communicating with an English teacher who has some basic language skills in Spanish.

Teacher: Tell me about your job.

Student: My job. Drive truck. *Mi colega y yo entregamos muebles.*

Teacher: *Muebles?* Furniture truck? I get it. Furniture delivery.

Student: Yes, furniture delivery. *Entregamos muebles que la gente pide en línea.*

Teacher: Okay, *en línea.* Online orders.

Student: Yes, online they buy it. We put together. *Los muebles vienen en cajas grandes. Nosotros los armamos. Se llama* white glove delivery.

Teacher: Aha, you assemble the furniture.

Student: Yes. We assemble it. Desk, bed, *archiveros, libreros.* Everything. *Tenemos que leer las instrucciones y seguir los dibujos. A veces es muy difícil. Tiene que ser todo perfecto. No podemos equivocarnos.* Can't make mistakes.

Teacher: This job requires many skills.

The episode reflects solidarity between the two speakers and confident bilingual behavior from the learner, regardless of the imbalance in language proficiencies. When adult learners are allowed to apply all of their language resources to communicate their meaning, they gain self-efficacy, courage to use the new language, and the ability to convey meaning beyond their current level of proficiency in the target language.

How Adults Learn Best

What adults bring to new learning affects how best to instruct them. According to the National Academies of Sciences, Engineering, and Medicine (NASEM, 2018), because adults only sustain learning that gives them a sense of growth and accomplishment, designing the right kind of learning experiences and building on their preferences are essential to keep them going. Instructional time in the classroom is usually very limited relative to the learning goals most adults identify, which makes it critical to spend that time wisely.

Adults learn best when their learning is relevant to their immediate needs and includes the problem solving and critical thinking that are part of adult functioning. For adults, learning happens both inside and outside of the classroom. Adults who are not used to formal classroom learning benefit from the guidance of a lifelong learning support system.

Adults Learn Best When They Experience a Pressing "Need to Know"

Children, for the most part, learn a variety of subjects in school. Adults, however, have pressing "need to know" as they ready themselves to take on specific new roles and assignments (Knowles, Holton, & Swanson, 2015; Merriam & Bierema, 2014). For example, seeking a new job, getting a job transfer, learning to drive, becoming a parent, buying a home, preparing taxes, applying for citizenship, and starting a business all create situations where the adult has an urgent need to learn quickly in order to apply knowledge right away. These changing roles and life tasks create authentic and compelling contexts for adult learning.

Problem Solving and Critical Thinking Are at the Core of All Adult Learning

Adults value troubleshooting and problem-solving skills. They want to make solid decisions based on understanding, questioning, making inferences, and evaluating information from various sources. Adults make important decisions daily for themselves and for others. The quality of their lives depends on having strong skills to support their decision-making. We serve our learners best with language and literacy instruction that also includes critical thinking and problem-solving tasks at every proficiency level (Parrish & Johnson, 2010).

For Many Adults, Learning Informally Can Be as Productive as Classroom Instruction

Much of what adults learn is not in classroom settings. Some adult learners have access to individual tutoring, online learning opportunities, and on-the-job apprenticing. Widening access to such options is important because they may fit the busy lifestyle of adults. Learning in nonclassroom contexts can be more immediately applicable, which supports both motivation and the retention of new skills. Because classroom practice is usually limited to just a few hours per week, learning language is especially difficult if that learning is not extended outside the classroom. Therefore, helping adults access informal learning opportunities and teaching them strategies for extending their learning are vital components of educating them.

Conditions for Second Language Learning

We would all like to know the best way to teach a new language to any learner. However, although an entire field of research—second language acquisition—is dedicated to examining this topic, we do not yet have a definitive answer. A dozen theories focus on the neurological, psychological, cognitive, and/or linguistic processes by which people learn languages other than their mother tongue. Yet these theories have not necessarily focused on ideal ways of teaching a particular variety of a particular language—in this case English—in a particular context (e.g., survival English or English for a specific occupation; Lightbown & Spada, 2014; VanPatten & Williams, 2014; Valdés, Kibler, & Walqui, 2014; Williams, Mercer, & Ryan, 2015).

Despite the range of theories, we have learned from decades of research findings that some conditions are essential and some conditions are beneficial for second language acquisition. Some individual variables play a role, too.

Essential Conditions

Essential conditions are those that must be present for second language acquisition to occur. Teachers can play a role in promoting some of these. Essential conditions include the following.

1. **Neurophysiological capacity.** Language is a complex neurophysiological function. It can be thought of as software that runs on the hardware of the brain (Anderson & Lightfoot, 2002). Second language acquisition is facilitated by the software of the first language. In other words, a learner's acquisition of his or her home language established neurophysiological processing that plays a key role in how he or she handles input in a new language. Normal first language development indicates that all is well with the learner's neurophysiology for acquiring additional languages. Given this, teachers should inquire about students' experiences with primary language development and view rich home language development as a strong foundation for learning new languages (Baker, 2014; Kohnert, 2013).

2. **Motivation.** Motivation is the force that prompts individuals to pursue and sustain an effort toward a goal. Avoiding pain is a human tendency, but language learning requires a great deal of effort over a period of many years. Either activities that lead to language learning must be inherently pleasurable or the eventual goals must be so positive that they are worth the struggle. Motivation cannot be successfully sustained externally, with threats and rewards. Therefore, teachers should work with each learner to understand and optimize internal sources of motivation (Dörnyei & Ushioda, 2011).

3. **Facilitative emotional conditions.** Learning cannot succeed if students are anxious, worried, or feel threatened or overwhelmed. Under negative emotional conditions, the learner shuts down and is unable to take risks with language or attend to language forms. In contrast, a welcoming, safe, and relaxed environment is indispensable for language learning. Managing emotions in the classroom and supporting each learner to overcome his or her anxiety or negative emotional responses are essential teaching responsibilities (Williams, Mercer, & Ryan, 2015).

4. **Usable input and feedback.** Input can refer to how teachers present information. The term is related to *comprehensible input*, which denotes language that is only one level above the language that the learner already knows (Krashen, 1985). Input beyond a learner's understanding can become usable when a teacher supports meaning through other means, such as by providing context, simplifying, or elaborating (as shown in Chapter 3, Practice 3B). Another form of input that is key to acquisition is feedback. Without feedback, learners cannot be certain that the language they produce is understandable in its meaning, form, or pronunciation. A large body of research exists on the many useful varieties and relative efficacy of different types of feedback (Ellis, 2017; Ellis & Shintani, 2014; Lyster & Saito, 2010; Nassaji & Kartchava, 2017). Some types of feedback are clarification requests, explicit correction, reformulations, metalinguistic signals, and recasts (explained in Chapter 3, Practice 5B). Prompting speakers to repair their own speech, also called elicitation of self-repair, is the most productive form of feedback.

5. **Deliberate practice.** Practice is the collective name of activities whose goal is to systematically develop second language skills (DeKeyser, 2007, 2010). These activities are not drills that demand imitation and repetition; rather, practice is a much broader range of activities that lead to fluency, accuracy, and automaticity of specific subskills. Knowing language rules cognitively is not the same as applying them in real time, fluently, consistently, and without conscious awareness. Language proficiency involves moving focused attention on basic skills into accurately executed, automatic processes. Mastering a second language requires a complex skill set that takes thousands of hours of systematic, deliberate practice to develop (DeKeyser, 2007, 2010).

The foundation of effective instruction is monitoring and ensuring that all of the essential conditions of second language acquisition are met and sustained for every learner.

Beneficial Conditions

Beneficial conditions are those conditions that contribute to second language learning and work to the advantage of learners who have access to them. Some beneficial conditions depend on the context of language learning. Some can be enhanced by instructional practices.

1. **Relatedness of the home language and the new language**. When we say that the first, or home, language is closer to the new language—in this case English—we mean that the home language and the new language have similar speech sounds and phonological features, have many cognates (words that have similar form and meaning), have the same basic word order, and use the same writing system. In such cases, learning the new language is significantly easier. Learning a new language that is quite different from the home language, such as learning Swahili when the home language is Bengali, is harder and typically takes longer.

2. **First language oracy and literacy skills.** Many first language skills are transferrable to the second language, including a large conceptual vocabulary (August & Shanahan, 2006). Although the names of concepts and related terms are different in the second language, understanding the concepts themselves can scaffold word learning in the new language. Other areas of language transfer include phonological awareness, understanding the meaningfulness of print, and use of cognitive and metacognitive skills. When learners have these skills in their home language, learning a new language is easier.

3. **Avid reading.** Being a motivated, avid reader in the home language helps in acquiring a second language. Practiced readers decode words automatically. They are able to hold their focus on texts for long periods of time. These skills are preliminary for being able to allocate working memory to the task of word learning by not struggling with the decoding task. Avid readers also read more, which means that they encounter more words and meet each word more frequently, which can result in a larger vocabulary and deeper word knowledge. Skilled readers may have mastered transferrable reading comprehension strategies in the first language, such as inferring the meaning of new words from context or quickly identifying main ideas and supporting details (Grabe, 2009).

4. **Prior foreign language learning**. If a student has experience learning a foreign language or is bilingual, learning English will be easier for him or her. Bilingual students bring to the learning process prior experiences, self-efficacy, and strategies that helped them succeed previously (De Angelis, 2007; Ó Laoire & Singleton, 2009). They are able to draw on the language that they consider to be closer to the target language. They do not necessarily "understand" the differences between the language (or languages) that they speak and the new language, but they draw effectively on their intuition, and they are ready to "give it a go" (Rutgers & Evans, 2015).

5. **Cultural knowledge and the ability to read social situations.** Language and culture are intricately bound together; communication depends on gleaning meaning from contexts and assumptions and on being attuned to nonverbal cues. Being able to process situations, gestures, or unarticulated intentions correctly is important for inferring the real meaning of messages (Lynch, 2011). Adult learners who already understand the culture or have teachers who serve the role of culture facilitator are at an advantage.

6. **Personality factors.** Research has identified a number of personality factors as facilitative for language learning, such as courage (shaking off fear, being willing to take risks), positivity (reacting with positive emotional responses to experiences), tolerance for ambiguity (experiencing partial understandings as "the glass half full"), and willingness to communicate in specific situations (Brown & Larson-Hall, 2012; MacIntyre & Doucette, 2010; Williams, Mercer, & Ryan, 2015). Although teachers have no control over a learner's personality, they can be aware of it when making instructional decisions about lesson activities; they can also model and reinforce actions that benefit learning.

7. **Regular access to competent speakers of the new language**. Although all types of interaction are useful for language learning, students gain more from interacting with teachers and proficient peers (Sato & Ballinger, 2016). Sometimes, teachers assume that learners have access to interaction with native speakers if they live in an English-speaking country; however, this is not always the case. Each learner's circumstances are different, and making broad generalizations regarding individual learners' actual access to competent speakers of the new language is not advisable.

8. **Having purposes and frequent opportunities to use the new language.** Having reasons and occasions to use the new language is closely related to the previous condition of having access to competent speakers of the language. But this condition matters even more than that one for language learning. It is also an achievable condition within most instructional contexts with careful lesson planning. Regardless of the educational context, lessons with collaborative learning tasks such as pair work, small-group work, and one-on-one coaching benefit most students.

9. **Integrative motivation in the speech community**. This is one type of motivation that deserves separate mention from motivation for language learning in general (Gardner, 1985). Students who identify with a speech community will work harder because of their desire to be a member of it (Pavlenko & Norton, 2007). This condition is powerfully supported by active measures to make adult ELs and their families feel included and integrated in the English-speaking learning community.

10. **High-quality instruction.** Effective instruction includes all the necessary conditions of second language acquisition, leverages beneficial conditions, and mitigates the challenging factors for language learning (NASEM, 2017). Adult learners benefit from direct instruction that helps them focus on language forms and develop language learning strategies (DeKeyser, 2018). Chapter 3 offers a wealth of ideas for providing high-quality instruction that facilitates learning English in adult education settings.

Additional Factors

Most of the conditions that we have discussed so far are within a teacher's or learner's control and can enhance language learning. Several additional factors merit special consideration. These factors potentially hinder second language learning, so teachers should recognize them and try to minimize their impact with specialized instruction and suitable interventions.

1. **Older learners.** The age at which a learner's exposure to the new language begins matters for the eventual outcome of language learning. Age effects have been the subject of much research since the 1960s. Ample evidence suggests that there are some limits on late-onset learners' development of native-like proficiency, particularly regarding

pronunciation and the automatic production of errorless grammatical forms, but that type of proficiency is not the educational goal for most adult language learners in literacy and workforce settings. Learners who begin to acquire English as adults have less time and much more to learn if they desire to attain the level of their fully proficient peers. Nonetheless, dynamic bilingualism—the ability to function with several languages skillfully—is achievable even for adult learners (Birdsong, 2016; DeKeyser, 2013; Muñoz, 2011).

2. **Socioemotional factors and special needs.** The challenges that socioemotional factors and special needs present to second language learning can manifest themselves in many forms, including trauma, posttraumatic stress, anxiety, depression, speech and language disorders, or learning disabilities. Effective teachers of adult learners are informed about the indicators of special needs, and they actively monitor their students. They consult with individuals discreetly about their needs for support. Where specialists are available to support learners with disabilities, teachers collaborate with them to design an inclusive learning environment where learners receive accommodations as part of the regular classroom routine (Delaney, 2016). Most importantly, effective teachers have a keen ability to recognize and validate learners' assets and to act from a strengths-based approach (Zacarian, Alvarez-Ortiz, & Haynes, 2017).

3. **Long-term beginner status.** Many adult ELs fail to achieve the language proficiency necessary for success in the skilled workforce, even after they have participated in instruction. Becoming a long-term beginner can be the result of many factors, such as incoherent or poor-quality instruction, transiency, or the challenges of adjustment to the new language and culture. This also occurs because many years of instruction are necessary to achieve proficiency, but not all adults can devote that amount of time. Additionally, not all adults can maintain the language skills they previously developed, especially when they do not regularly use the new language. Teachers should be aware of the consequential negative effects when learners experience difficulties with initial adjustment, have problems with attendance, or cannot access the supports they need to make significant progress (NASEM, 2017).

4. **Low literacy.** Adults with low education levels and a low level of literacy in their home language are at a disadvantage (National Research Council, 2012). Although they can develop oral language skills and "survival English," it is more difficult for them to compensate for age-related memory decline with strategies that literate adult language learners rely on (NASEM, 2018), such as note-taking, rereading, using dictionaries, or consulting texts. Background knowledge and reading level can make many language teaching materials and tools inaccessible or overwhelming for these learners. They require a variety of accommodations within the language classroom, as well as supplemental instruction with adaptive tutorial programs that can address the full range of their needs (National Research Council, 2012; NASEM, 2018).

When teachers pair their understanding of the conditions for second language learning with knowledge of each of their adult ELs' background, educational history, and personal characteristics, they can maximize the conditions that they control or shape. Chapter 3 explains in detail the process of designing instruction to optimize essential and beneficial conditions of second language acquisition and to limit the challenging factors to the extent possible within a specific teaching context.

Language Develops through Use and Interaction

Effective teachers understand that language development involves active learning. Students construct language; they learn to use language in the way that it is used when others communicate with them. Watching or overhearing speakers are not effective ways to learn language. Rather, through conversation, speakers establish joint attention with partners; they co-construct meaning, check their understanding, and ask for clarification. They can test their hypotheses about language forms and receive valuable, just-in-time feedback so they can make adjustments or learn something new (Mackey, Abbuhl, & Gass, 2012; Rex & Green, 2008; Swain & Suzuki, 2008).

Language competence is not an abstract skill or stored knowledge that may be useful some day in the future. This is particularly true for adult learners in literacy and workforce programs. Language competence is functionality—the tool for shared cognition, shared understanding, and cooperation. An individual's language competence is the accumulation of all previous language uses. The more frequent and varied learners' opportunities are for language use, the more functional, complex, and flexible their language ability becomes. This means that effective teachers prompt students to interact frequently, and they provide regular opportunities for learner to use language in varied modalities (listening, speaking, reading, writing). They also encourage students to use and build on all their language resources, including relevant and strategic use of their home languages (Echevarría, Vogt, & Short, 2017; Ellis & Shintani, 2014; Johnson, 1995).

Specific examples of how teachers promote language use in the classroom include the following:

- creating simulations and role-plays that mirror actual situations adults encounter on the job or through their many life roles
- encouraging pair work and small-group activities
- prompting learners to annotate texts with their own explanations and responses
- asking learners to notice language forms in texts and to make use of them in their responses
- assigning quick-writes to stimulate language use and to promote writing fluency
- reminding learners to discuss ideas and plans before they start a writing task

In short, effective teachers multiply opportunities for learners' active engagement with the material through frequent language use, speaking, writing, and active reading (Baker et al., 2014; Fairbairn & Jones-Vo, 2010; Gibbons, 2015; Short & Echevarría, 2016; Zwiers, 2014).

Literacy Expands Language Development

Full competence in English includes reading and writing skills. As teachers help develop the literacy skills of their adult ELs, they need to be aware of possible challenges to the process, such as an unfamiliar writing system, confusing and inconsistent spelling rules, a need for oral language connections, a lack of vocabulary knowledge, a low motivation to read, or a lack of background knowledge. These challenges merit individual attention:

- **Working with an unfamiliar writing system.** English learners vary in their knowledge of the English writing system, particularly if their native language uses an entirely different form of writing. Writing systems vary in the linguistic features of the language that they mark, such as vowel or consonant sounds, sound length, tone, or stress. Writing scripts vary from alphabetic (e.g., English, Russian, Greek, Korean) to consonants only (e.g., Arabic, Hebrew) to syllabic (e.g., Bengali, Gujarati, Thai) and to logographic (e.g., Mandarin). Harder than mastering the script itself is learning the specific language features that a writing system encodes. The English writing system, for example, demands attention to both consonant and vowel sounds but not to word stress, consonant length, or tone (Weingarten, 2013; Borgwaldt & Joyce, 2013).

- **Dealing with confusing spelling rules.** Because pronunciation often does not match spelling in English, students may struggle when learning to read. Consider the spelling variations for sounds that are the same (*you, do, threw, through, shoe, ewe, queue, flu, true*). Although English has many dialects in which pronunciation is systematically different, the spelling of words remains the same regardless. Consequently, recognizing letters of the alphabet is a very small part of learning to read in English in contrast to the much larger part that it plays in those languages where the sound-letter correspondence is more predictable. To read in English, learners need much practice in hearing and segmenting sounds (phonological awareness), mapping sound patterns to spelling patterns (phonics), and memorizing sight words. Teachers can provide better help to learners when they familiarize themselves with the phonemes and syllable types in their students' home languages and become aware of the phonological features of English that are likely to be unfamiliar or troublesome to them.

- **Building oral language to supports to understand texts.** For proficient English speakers, oral language serves as a scaffold for reading. If learners understand a text when listening to it, they will find it much easier to comprehend the text when reading it again on their own. However, if the text they are reading is beyond their oral language abilities, reading comprehension becomes an extreme challenge, even when they can decode the words with apparent fluency. Therefore, it is essential that teachers talk with learners about the content of texts before and after reading. In addition, by doing so, they will ensure that oral language and reading comprehension will develop simultaneously (Baker et al., 2014; Calderón & Slakk, 2018; Herrera, Perez, & Escamilla, 2014; Saunders & O'Brien, 2006).

- **Coping with too many unknown words in texts.** An important element in the readability of texts and second language literacy development overall is the vocabulary coverage — that is, the number of different words in a text. Research indicates that comprehension of text read independently depends in large part on how many words a reader knows in the text (Nagy & Scott, 2000). For example, knowing 80 percent of words in a text might seem reasonable; yet, reading comprehension is virtually impossible at 80 percent of vocabulary coverage. For minimal reading comprehension, a reader should know 90 percent of the words, and for adequate comprehension, 95 percent. To be able to learn vocabulary or content information from a text, the typical reader needs to understand 95 percent of the words. For unassisted reading for pleasure — the most sustainable and rewarding reading activity — most readers should have 98 percent vocabulary coverage (Nation & Webb, 2011). These facts have important implications for teachers of ELs:

  — To learn *language* through reading, adults need texts in which they know almost all words, with very few exceptions. Their language development is best served when they read books with few unknown words per paragraph or a single word in every third line. To achieve this high level of vocabulary coverage, teachers need to make available for adult learners modified texts that are suitable for their age and interest but are not overwhelming in the number of unknown words (Jeon & Day, 2016; Nakanishi, 2015; Nation & Webb, 2011; Schmitt, Jiang, & Grabe, 2011).

— When assessing the percentage of unknown words in a text, teachers need to recognize that ELs are often able to sound out words fluently without knowing the meanings of those words. For language learners, being able to decode—that is, sound out—text is distinctly different from comprehending it. Some teachers have students read aloud, but a better way to gauge their vocabulary coverage is to ask them to read shorter passages in the beginning section of the text—say, 100 words—and have them mark unfamiliar words. If more than ten different words are unfamiliar, alternative texts or additional supports are needed. Teaching students to preview texts to identify and gauge the ratio of unknown words when they select books for independent reading is also useful.

What to Do If There Are Too Many Unfamiliar Words in a Text

Ask a learner to read a short passage of about 100 words at the beginning of a text and to mark any unfamiliar words. If the number exceeds 10, consider doing the following:

- Mark the key passages for the learner to focus on rather than the whole text.
- Find alternative readers with controlled vocabulary.
- Supply bilingual editions and mark strategically the sections to read in either language.
- Elaborate texts by inserting brief, comprehensible explanations of unknown words.
- Simplify texts by replacing some of the unknown words and sentence structures.
- Provide a bookmark that glosses the target vocabulary in the text.

- **Managing texts that are too difficult.** Some readings adults have to manage are too difficult for their English language and literacy levels, yet they need ways to make sense of them. Texts that might fall into this category are business documents, contracts or leases, application forms, medical and safety instructions, and compliance-related documents. An important component of bilingual literacy is being able to assess when translations are needed, being able to generate rough translations with software (e.g., Google translate), and knowing how to obtain translation services through qualified providers.

- **Kindling the motivation to read.** Teachers should provide adult learners with a diverse selection of high-quality reading materials, including bilingual texts, and teach them strategies to select books according to their interests and vocabulary knowledge. Students should learn to become strategic about the choice of language, the fit of the texts for their background knowledge, and their own purposes for reading. Sparking adult learners' motivation to read and kindling their self-efficacy with reading widely are among the most important contributions that teachers can make to language development (Hadaway & Young, 2010; Grabe, 2009; Herrera, Perez, & Escamilla, 2014; Turkan, Bicknell, & Croft, 2012). The Center for Study of Adult Literacy offers a large collection of web-based texts on lower reading levels about topics that most adults find useful and interesting (http://csal.gsu.edu).

- **Building on existing background knowledge.** Background knowledge refers to the information and conceptual understandings or schemas that readers bring to their comprehension of texts. Studies have shown that second language learners' content familiarity can compensate for linguistic knowledge at most proficiency levels. Conversely, lack of schema and relevant background knowledge will impede reading comprehension even for advanced language learners or for seemingly fluent readers. When teachers know what learners are knowledgeable and passionate about, they can match them with texts that enable their prior experiences and existing background information to support reading comprehension and bootstrap language learning. Knowing learners better will also help teachers recognize when students are not be able to manage texts on their own or without additional support before, during, and after reading (Grabe, 2009; Herrera et al., 2014; Krekeler, 2006; Lesaux, Koda, Siegel, & Shanahan, 2006; Lin, 2002).

What Level of English Is Needed

As adults participate in language programs, they—and their teachers—want to gauge their progress. Many programs therefore use standards documents and curriculum frameworks that define functioning levels or proficiency levels. These standards documents also serve as the development structure for large-scale proficiency tests. The functioning or proficiency level adults may reach depends on their goals and on the time frame they have available for language learning. For some, achieving an intermediate level of English may be sufficient for their immediate needs.

Most programs assess adults periodically with tests that measure performance with different language skills. The results of these tests are useful to educators for placing learners in course sections and for documenting learning outcomes at the end of instructional cycles. However, the large-scale tests that aim to capture learners' English language functioning levels may be more important as an accountability measure of publicly funded programs and for designing a coherent multiyear curriculum than for informing adult learners of their true progress or for providing them with a credential of their language achievement.

Table 2.1 shows the standards documents that define English language functioning levels for adult learners in the United States, Canada, Australia, and the European Union. Teachers can refer to the document applicable to their context to obtain detailed descriptions about learners' expected performance at each level. These performance descriptors are also useful for creating lesson objectives for high-quality lessons (as shown in Practice 3A in Chapter 3). In Chapter 5, we demonstrate the use of several different frameworks for English language proficiency that instructors use in the United States, Canada, and Australia.

There is seldom a need for teachers to compare levels across the different adult English language proficiency standards that different countries use. The tests that measure these levels contain assessment tasks that are substantively different from each other. In general, tests based on these standards measure test takers' performance in listening, speaking, reading, and writing in English and employ progressively complex texts and tasks. These assessment tasks start with the more practical and contextually supported and move toward the more abstract and cognitively demanding. We include here a basic description of the functioning levels, which can help teachers identify the current level of their students, but which is basic in comparison to the detailed standards documents teachers have available to guide their instruction.

Table 2.1	English language functioning levels and the documents that define them	
Standards document	Levels	Reference
Educational Functioning Level Descriptors for ESL (United States)	6 levels: Beginning ESL Literacy, Low Beginning ESL, High Beginning ESL, Low Intermediate ESL, High Intermediate ESL, Advanced ESL	U.S. Department of Education, Division of Adult Education and Literacy, 2017
English Language Proficiency Standards for Adult Education (United States)	5 levels: ELP Levels 1–5	U.S. Department of Education, 2016
Canadian Language Benchmarks	12 levels: Stage I CLB 1–4, Stage II CLB 5–8, Stage III CLB 9–12	Centre for Canadian Language Benchmarks, 2012
Australian Core Skills Framework	5 levels: ACSF Levels 1–5	Australian Government Department of Education and Training, 2015
Common European Framework of Reference	6 levels: Basic User A1–A2, Independent User B1–B2, Proficient User C1–C2	Council of Europe, 2001

Beginner Levels

On the beginner levels, students rely on context to interpret meaning; they manage short and simple texts about familiar topics. They perform concrete tasks and communicate basic messages and produce short phrases and sentences with repetitive patterns. They possess a small vocabulary, which consists of high-frequency words and memorized chunks of language. High-beginners can understand and form longer phrases and sentences that connect ideas. Their vocabulary grows to several thousand words, which allows them to begin reading abridged texts that contain a clear organization and controlled vocabulary.

Intermediate Levels

Intermediate learners can succeed reading texts that have a clear structure and familiar contexts and contain a broader range of vocabulary, that is, a few thousand words. Intermediate students can handle conversation about most topics related to their daily life and work. When listening to others, they can identify the main topic and important details of a conversation. They can perform tasks with familiar steps. They are able to gather information to learn about new topics, and they can write a simple paragraph about a familiar matter that contains a main idea and supporting details. At the high-intermediate stage, learners can manage a range of texts independently. They can read for different purposes. They are able to participate in a variety of social interactions and express themselves in multiple, related sentences. Intermediate learners can provide explanations and descriptions; they can compare and contrast. Their accuracy and fluency with language is improving, as is their ability to produce a broad variety of sentence patterns.

Advanced Levels

Advanced learners easily manage routine texts, even ones that contain some technical and specialized vocabulary. They know enough words to independently read unabridged texts of lesser complexity. They still have difficulty with idioms, fixed expressions, and figurative language. They can formulate a reasoned argument, explain a position, and cite textual evidence. They can write a report about a problem or construct a basic position essay. Their writing demonstrates coherence and growing accuracy with a broad range of grammatical forms. They show awareness of the audience by switching register as appropriate. They can converse naturally and fluently about most topics.

Proficient Levels

Proficient individuals can handle complex texts in a broad range of subjects. They can analyze and critically evaluate the reasoning of writers and speakers. They can write out a detailed explanation or a reasoned argument and carry out a research project to gain new knowledge. In their writing, they can treat abstract topics by explaining, evaluating, and synthesizing information. They are able to explicate information from graphs and data tables. They can edit and proofread their writing because they have good control of the subtleties of grammar, idiomatic expressions, register, and genre. Proficient individuals can express themselves at length in clear, fluent speech, and they can participate in formal discussions on complex issues.

Table 2.2 shows an estimated equivalence of functioning levels based on the main standards documents that educators of adult English learners use in different countries. The alignment is based on the level descriptors in each document; actual testing data to establish equivalence are not currently available.

Table 2.2	The estimated equivalence of functioning levels from standards documents used to guide the instruction of adult English learners in different countries			
Functioning levels	**Beginner**	**Intermediate**	**Advanced**	**Proficient**
Educational Functioning Level Descriptors for ESL (United States)	Beginner — L1 | L2 | L3	Intermediate — L4 | L5	Advanced — L6	
English Language Proficiency Standards for Adult Education (United States)	Level 1	Level 2 | Level 3	Level 4	Level 5
Canadian Language Benchmarks	Stage I — CLB 1 | CLB 2	Stage I — CLB 3 | CLB 4	Stage II — CLB 5–8	Stage III — CLB 9–12
Australian Core Skills Framework	ACSF Level 1	ACSF Level 2	ACSF Level 3	ACSF Levels 4–5
Common European Framework of Reference	Basic — A1	Basic — A2	Independent — B1 | B2	Proficient — C1 | C2

An Important Caveat

Research shows that participating in adult literacy education for 100 or more hours has significant lifelong benefits (Reder, 2012). However, the caveat with adult learners is that they are usually unaware of how long it takes to develop English language and literacy to a level that allows them to function on a par with proficient English-speaking peers. They don't expect to participate in an English language development program for many years, and this mismatch of expectations and reality can lead to tension and disappointment.

Adults come to language programs to meet their needs. The resources required by them for participation are high, and they generally cannot sustain years of attendance. The best approach to adult language education is to begin by informing learners about the time needed to achieve advanced functioning, offering them (as quickly as possible) language skills they can put to immediate use, and equipping them with useful tools and strategies, so they can continue their learning independently outside the classroom.

A Look Back and a Look Ahead

Chapter 2 explores what teachers should know about English language and literacy development to plan effective instruction for adult learners. The chapter highlights the following ideas:

- Foundational knowledge for teaching adult ELs includes an understanding of how adults learn best. They tend to seek relevant knowledge that they can apply to their immediate needs. Teachers can best serve them by finding out what they wish to achieve and building on the strengths and prior experiences they bring to their language learning.

- When teachers know the necessary conditions for second language learning, they can assure that the classroom environment they facilitate meets all of those conditions consistently. They

  — work with learners to sustain their internal sources of motivation,

  — manage the emotional conditions of the classroom to lower anxiety and boost positivity and engagement,

  — employ a variety of techniques to make input and feedback to learners both comprehensible and useful, and

  — create frequent practice opportunities to make sure learners don't just learn about language but they develop skills that are increasingly fluent and automatic.

- Individual variables influence the outcome of language learning for adults, some of which are facilitative and can enhance instructional practices, such as first language literacy, avid reading, integrative motivation, access to competent speakers, and having purposes and frequent opportunities to use the new language.

- Literacy development is critical for achieving English proficiency, and some aspects of literacy development require altered instruction for those who are developing reading and writing skills while simultaneously learning English as a new language. For reading comprehension, ELs need oral language support; systematic and intensive vocabulary development; and strategies to compensate for linguistic knowledge, to manage unknown words, and to gain meaning from texts that are beyond their reading level.

Chapter 3 builds on these issues in greater detail by showing exemplary practices for The 6 Principles and sharing strategies that teachers can apply at every stage of their instruction.

Additional resources pertaining to this chapter are available at www.the6principles.org/adult-education.

3 TEACHING WITH THE 6 PRINCIPLES

his chapter focuses on The 6 Principles for teaching adult English learners (ELs). We build on information shared in Chapter 2 about learning a new language to help teachers make instructional decisions, define each principle, and present practices that put the principles into action. We elaborate each practice with several examples; these examples serve to show the kinds of steps teachers can take to implement these best practices and recommendations, which are drawn on expert opinion and well-established research findings.

Classroom vignettes show how teachers design and implement high-quality lessons for adult learners in different types of programs and highlight teachers' experiences with adult learners on various English language functioning levels. The learners in the vignettes represent the broad range of adult learners in English language programs in terms of their home languages, prior education, and goals for learning. Instructional suggestions are abundant throughout the chapter in the forms of handy charts and practical lists.

Although this chapter serves to paint a full picture of the scope of practices exemplary teachers engage in, the best use of this text is not to read through it quickly. The 6 Principles taken together capture an instructional process: from getting to know learners to creating lessons that serve their learning goals to evaluating their progress. In fact, this process is recurrent and dynamic, requiring the teacher to revisit each step constantly.

In that same spirit, we hope that you keep coming back to each principle to gain more from the practices as you continue to reflect on and improve instruction. We also hope that you find the framework of The 6 Principles to be a useful schema for new practices you encounter in your professional learning. This collection of useful practices is not exhaustive and is intended to supplement and complement those practices you already use—for example, ways in which you assess the needs of learners, ways in which you structure lessons, ways in which you give useful feedback. The framework of The 6 Principles has a fitting place for those practices that you already use successfully, and it does not require that you change them. What the framework offers is a way to pinpoint where your own instruction may need additional support and fresh ideas to improve learner outcomes. The 6 Principles is an open, live framework for continuous professional improvement.

The 6 Principles for Exemplary Teaching of English Learners and Recommended Practices

1. **Know your learners.**
   1a. Teachers gain information about their learners.
   1b. Teachers embrace and leverage the resources that learners bring to the classroom to enhance learning.

2. **Create conditions for language learning.**
   2a. Teachers promote a supportive learning environment, with attention to reducing learners' anxiety and developing trust.
   2b. Teachers demonstrate expectations of success for all learners.
   2c. Teachers plan instruction to enhance and sustain learners' motivation for language learning.

3. **Design high-quality lessons for language development.**
   3a. Teachers prepare lessons with clear outcomes and convey them to their learners.
   3b. Teachers provide and enhance input through varied approaches, techniques, and modalities.
   3c. Teachers engage learners in the use and practice of authentic language.
   3d. Teachers design lessons so that learners engage with relevant and meaningful content.
   3e. Teachers plan differentiated instruction according to their learners' English language functioning levels, literacy levels, needs, and goals.
   3f. Teachers promote the use of learning strategies, problem solving, and critical thinking.
   3g. Teachers promote self-directed learning.

4. **Adapt lesson delivery as needed.**
   4a. Teachers check comprehension frequently and adjust instruction according to learner responses.
   4b. Teachers adjust their talk, the task, or the materials according to learner responses.

5. **Monitor and assess student language development.**
   5a. Teachers monitor student errors.
   5b. Teachers provide ongoing effective feedback strategically.
   5c. Teachers use effective formative assessment strategies.
   5d. Teachers involve learners in decisions and reflections about summative assessments.

6. **Engage and collaborate within a community of practice.**
   6a. Teachers are fully engaged in their profession.
   6b. Teachers coordinate and collaborate with colleagues.
   6c. Teachers utilize publicly available instructional resources for adult English learners.
   6d. Teachers participate in community partnerships.

Principle 1. Know Your Learners

After several ice breaker activities, Logan asks students to write two paragraphs, one in English about what they would like to achieve in class and another in their home language about themselves and their life goals. The paragraph in English helps Logan gauge the new students' English language and literacy level, and the one in the home language shows how literate and educated they are. Even if Logan doesn't understand the language, she can see how much and how fast they write. The handwriting usually indicates whether they are fluent, practiced writers. Logan also has other information to go by: the results of the placement test and an intake interview, which program staff conduct at registration, when they arrange to have interpreters present at least in the home languages of learners they typically have.

Unlike children, adults are not "the captive audience" in school. When they pursue education, they do so for reasons of their own, take classes as they wish, and usually overcome challenges to be able to attend school; they could be working or tending to other important tasks in their lives. Getting to know them personally and what they expect to gain from instruction is essential for their participation.

Basic information to gather about learners includes the correct pronunciation and spelling of their name, language skills in any language, educational and occupational history, life goals, and, of course, what they expect to achieve in the course. Figure 3.1 indicates areas for teachers to explore when getting to know a new learner and designing a learning plan for him or her. Although lots of other facts may be useful for educators, we should always exercise care with collecting any potentially sensitive information. Adult learners should be able to withhold anything they consider private. It is important to be aware that adult learners' rights to privacy and to the confidentiality of their personal data outweigh the educational benefits of sharing particulars about themselves. Therefore, teachers must exercise caution with any questions that may be perceived as sensitive, such as immigration, residency, or refugee status; country of origin; disabilities; or traumatic experiences. It is possible to get to know learners on a personal level without documenting sensitive information about them.

The way to gain useful information about adult learners is by asking the types of questions that are fitting for job interviews:

- Tell me about your education.
- What would you like me to know about you?
- Are you able to attend classes regularly? What could be a problem?
- What was the most important job you've had?
- What languages do you speak/read/write?
- How have you learned these languages?
- Tell me about a big challenge in your life.
- Name some things you love to do.
- What would you like to be doing in five years?
- Why is learning English important to you?

Learning about students' cultures and home languages is a wise move for every teacher. Fortunately, many excellent sources are available for this purpose. For example, the Cultural Orientation Center website (www.culturalorientation.net) provides in-depth introductions to major refugee groups in the United States in the form of briefs, videos, and image libraries. The Government of Canada also maintains an archive for researching every ethnocultural immigrant group in the country (www.bac-lac.gc.ca/eng/discover/immigration/history-ethnic-cultural/Pages/introduction.aspx).

FIGURE 3.1 Characteristics to know about adult English learners

What teachers may find relevant to know about their learners' background and resources

Home country

Home language

Linguistic features of the home language

Cultural background

Home language literacy level

Educational background

Employment history/status, work schedule

Skills in additional languages

English language proficiency in the four domains (listening, speaking, reading, writing)

Purposes for learning English

Literacy practices

Personal goals

Life experiences, possibly including trauma

Learning preferences based on prior experiences

Digital literacy and access to technology

Access to resources, esp. social supports

Cultural knowledge

Interests, gifts, talents

Job skills and employment experiences

Technical and career training

Sociopolitical context of home country

Cultural adaptation experience

Special needs (physical and mental health, disabilities)

Situational challenges (basic needs, transportation, work obligations, childcare)

Dispositional challenges (behavior, anxiety, time, value on education)

PRACTICE 1A   Teachers gain information about their learners.

Teachers collect information about their learners' lives, home cultures, languages, and academic preparation. They engage learners in exploring the uses they have for English, the opportunities that are already available to them, and opportunities they may create to practice their English skills. They inventory and analyze tasks that learners need to perform in English. Teachers gauge the challenges to learners' attendance and continued participation in classes, personal hardships, and disabilities, which may require supports and proactive measures.

Examples of Practice 1a

Teachers follow an intake protocol. Many programs have a protocol in place to collect information from learners who are applying and registering for classes. They may employ several different data collection methods, from filling out forms to interviewing learners either in English or in their home languages. They may administer several quick placement tests as part of the intake process. Teachers can collaborate with administrators to assure that the data collected capture what is useful to know about learners for keeping them in the program and helping them succeed. They can also create procedures for disseminating these data to teachers in a form that they can easily use for instructional planning.

Teachers conduct a needs assessment. Different programs are able to address different needs. For example, a workplace ESOL (English to speakers of other languages) program typically addresses a combination of employer needs and participant needs. An integrated civics and ESOL class addresses governmental requirements for citizenship and the personal learning needs of those participating in the class. When they know learners well enough, effective teachers create a bridge from what individual participants need to what other stakeholders (employers or program funders) expect them to gain from the program.

A needs assessment typically involves multiple sources of information and multiple methods (Long, 2005). Data collection methods can include the following:

- observations (e.g., of the learner and peers engaged in job tasks at their workplace)
- interviews
- checklists and inventories
- questionnaires
- tests
- diagnostic analysis of learners' writing and oral reading

The following may be sources of information:

- learners
- peers of the learner with more advanced English language skills, such as coworkers
- supervisors and human resources staff
- photographs and videos (of work places and contexts in which the learners use English)
- audio recordings (messages, phone calls, interactions)
- documents (collections of learner writings, job descriptions, forms, schedules, memos, manuals)

A workplace education site team at a hospital was planning English classes for housekeepers on its staff. The team consisted of five members: two managers from the hospital's Environmental Services and Customer Service Departments, a supervisor from Housekeeping, and two ESL teachers from the local community college, Nessa and Cullen. The hospital staff served as advisors for the needs assessment, which the teachers carried out. They had three goals for the needs assessment:

- *collect samples that represent the language housekeepers use to perform their tasks*
- *capture the wants and needs of prospective students*
- *identify the priorities for improvement from the perspectives of hospital staff*

The ESL teachers toured the hospital and met with the staff to document the specific issues the hospital wished to address with the workplace English classes. They also held a recruiting event to connect with the prospective students informally.

After the meet-and-greet, Nessa and Cullen conducted observations of the housekeepers on two different shifts. Each teacher had unstructured interviews with several housekeepers from different departments. While observing, the teachers took notes of the types of exchanges that occurred between housekeepers and the people with whom they interacted: supervisors, nurses, visitors, and patients. Cullen recorded several daily briefings, which occurred between housekeepers and their supervisors at the start of each shift. He also collected various complaints, which were the usual subjects of the daily briefings. Nessa reviewed the videos that the hospital used for mandatory safety trainings. She asked to have copies of hazardous material incident reports, which housekeepers needed to write and found especially challenging. She also collected sample text messages after she learned that the housekeepers struggled to correctly follow the instructions in them.

When Cullen and Nessa assembled the findings of the needs assessment, they sought feedback from the site team. They wanted to check that they captured the information correctly and did not overlook anything crucial. This process really helped the ESL teachers connect with the learners and capture the learners' personal expectations as well as the communication demands of the workplace. Cullen and Nessa were able to determine what levels of classes they needed to plan and how they could sequence the content and skills that the participants desired to focus on in the English classes.

Teachers use interest and background inventories. With adult learners, it is necessary to balance the class learning goals with the personal interests and backgrounds of the learners. Adult learners spend many hours working, so anything that makes learning enjoyable and engaging is preferable. Any lesson can at least briefly address specific interests learners have. Teachers have many creative tools to learn what these are:

- funds of knowledge surveys
- board games in which learners answer questions about skills, hobbies, and experiences
- autobiography projects
- life story anthologies
- preference surveys of what topics should be taught
- inventory of learners' literacy practices
- inventory of learners' experiences with learning technologies and current access to electronic learning tools

Teachers monitor learners for challenges. Some adult learners who participate in these programs experience difficulties that are more persistent and burdensome than those of the average learner. Identifying these early and addressing them proactively are key to being able to retain these learners. We recommend using observation checklists and having discussions with individual learners in private settings in order to gain insight into the nature of their difficulty and the desired supports (Delaney, 2016). In Chapter 4, we discuss the signals that indicate challenges and present proactive steps for serving these learners successfully.

PRACTICE 1B Teachers embrace and leverage the resources that learners bring to the classroom to enhance learning.

Teachers tap their learners' prior knowledge purposefully in their teaching. Much of what learners bring with them is positive; they have life experiences and cultural knowledge to contribute, passions and work ethic to mine, and values to share. Be aware, however, that some adult learners may have unsuccessful educational histories, which may have turned them into hesitant students who are less than confident with what they have to offer. Part of our teaching has to be positioning our learners in ways that they can embrace their strengths and contribute their cache of expertise to the workings of the classroom.

Examples of Practice 1b

Teachers connect with learners' home cultures and languages. Culture is a lens through which we view the world. We take what we see for granted, not noticing that a lens, which is invisible to our view, defines our perception, the *what* and *how* we are able to see. Effective teachers recognize that knowing learners entails an engagement with their cultures, gaining firsthand knowledge of their cultural perspectives, which includes deeply held beliefs, values, norms, and attitudes. To establish shared understandings and common ground, teachers invite learners to introduce them to their lives, communities, histories, customs, and languages.

Adult students are usually happy to serve as cultural informants for their teachers and some are active members in associations whose purpose is to maintain heritage cultures. These organizations welcome members of the community to lectures, celebrations, commemorative events, and educational programs that serve to nurture their language and cultural identities. Becoming active in these societies is both informative and rewarding.

DeCapua and Wintergerst (2016) offer a treasure chest of activities that help teachers build their cultural competence and provide opportunities to gain insights into their learners' worlds. Here are just a few suggestions to try out:

- Sample proverbs from students' cultures and reflect together on the values these may convey.
- Play word association games to reveal deeper meanings of key concepts across cultures, choosing words like *friendship*, *family*, *time*, *pride*, *freedom*, *loyalty*, *community*, and *elders*.
- Collect photographs of people in ordinary daily activities in different cultures and discuss these to explore assumptions.
- Survey learners' responses to a list of value statements. Examine similarities and differences in everyone's priorities.
- Present critical incidents—situations that reveal cultural quandaries—and uncover everyone's perspectives and dilemmas.

The more teachers know about learners' home languages, the more insight they can have into the linguistic features that students need to acquire and the linguistic features that overlap between their languages and English. Learning and periodically using a few words and expressions in everyone's home language can also serve to delight your learners.

Teachers build on their knowledge of learners' prior educational experiences. Adult English learners often enter our language classroom with nervous anticipation. Nothing in their educational experiences may resemble the interactive, collaborative, and learner-focused classroom environment that exemplary language teachers facilitate. Teachers need to begin where learners are by understanding their educational background and dispositions, including what they have and have not learned regarding content, skills, and learning strategies. A variety of sources of information is available about the education systems of countries where adult learners come from, such as the websites of schools and ministries of education, classroom videos available on the internet, and, of course, the learners themselves. Flaitz (2006) provides a useful guide for the kinds of information about schooling around the world that teachers find especially informative. She presents synopses about many countries where recent refugee and immigrant students come from.

Teachers educate themselves about cross-cultural issues, including literacy practices. The language classroom is a natural setting for gaining understandings about cross-cultural issues. We can do the following:

- encourage students to open up about cultural differences and conflicts across cultures
- model curiosity, appreciation, respect, and productive conflict resolution
- help learners hone positive cross-cultural negotiation skills
- teach them how to recognize and overcome prejudice and stereotyping
- guide learners to seek common ground and to value collaboration and mutual awareness over indifference or conflict

Cross-cultural communication scenarios provide excellent prompts for language practice through group discussions, written commentary, role-plays, and problem-solving activities.

Principle 2. Create Conditions for Language Learning

My heart does hurt because I don't understand anything. I do feel lonely. No, I don't feel anything, but I can't go anywhere. I can't do anything.

(Durga Bahadur Adhikari; Center for Applied Linguistics, 2012)

I remember my first time at school. I was nervous because I didn't understand what they wanted from me. When someone said to me, "You will be testing," my heart began to beat faster and my hands started to shake, this is the first time in the U.S. I was testing . . . .

(Vitalii Fartushnyi; Minnesota Literacy Council, 2017)

I am going through a lot of things in my life. I have three jobs and I also come to school for English classes.

(Avimael Clara Molina; Minnesota Literacy Council, 2016)

It makes me feel excited and motivated to wake up early in the morning, take a fresh shower, and get ready for school. Another good reason [to come to class] would be to meet the classmates and also the teacher, who is very nice with all of us. I feel really happy enjoying those couple of hours with them in class. It is like being in a small party for me. I have too much fun during the class time, so it does not stress me at all.

(Miguel Chavez; Minnesota Literacy Council, 2017)

I like this class because it gets me interacting with other people and gets me out of the house. In class we wrote our personal learning goals so that we can strive towards getting them accomplished and to have a reminder.

(Klava Foreman; Minnesota Literacy Council, 2017)

When adult English learners describe their initial experiences returning to school, many evoke their shaky nervousness. They fear failure and losing face in public and that they may not be good enough to learn. Some feel insecure because they have not had much education, and many feel old for school. They worry that the opportunity which they were presented may go to waste because they are too overwhelmed to take advantage of it.

Mastering a new language is demanding enough for the young, for the academically experienced, and for those who are already fully literate in one or more languages. The chances of success diminish for the overwhelmed adult learner who is academically inexperienced, is wary of interaction, and faces a number of obstacles apart from language learning.

Effective teachers are aware of these understandable anxieties and create an environment where students feel welcome and safe to interact with one another, taking risks to grow their skills and being open about their needs.

PRACTICE 2A Teachers promote a supportive learning environment, with attention to reducing learners' anxiety and developing trust.

Teachers apply their knowledge of optimal conditions that promote language learning as they make decisions regarding the physical environment and the social climate of the classroom.

Examples of Practice 2a

Teachers welcome everyone and show respect to every learner. Showing respect to adults from diverse backgrounds may mean more than welcoming gestures and smiling. Cultures vary in terms of preference for physical proximity, eye contact, body language, conversational overlap, the timing of conversational turn-taking, and the topic of conversations. Some cultures have strict rules about the interaction between men and women, elderly and younger persons, supervisors and subordinates. Learners and their peers may serve as cultural informants for teachers about ways that people from their background perceive and demonstrate respect. Some cross-cultural basics include the following:

- Address learners in their preferred way.
- Learn about their lives.
- Focus on their strengths.
- Be sensitive to their feelings and concerns.
- Be mindful of cultural differences that can lead to misunderstandings.
- Value their contributions and expertise.
- Involve everyone.

Teachers conduct team-building tasks. Collaborative group tasks provide authentic opportunities for interaction and language practice; that said, group activities are much more productive when group members are caring and supportive of one another. To promote community, make sure learners have opportunities to get to know each other and to be involved in making decisions. Everyone should have a role in which they can successfully contribute. Hold team meetings, debrief group activities, celebrate achievements, and acknowledge contributions to constructive team work.

For team-building games for the adult language classroom, visit www.the6principles.org/adult-education.

Teachers invite learners' home languages and cultures into the classroom. Effective teachers encourage learners to build on their entire language repertoire, switching between their languages to best express themselves. They provide cross-linguistic references and explanations and make bilingual texts, glossaries, translated texts, and other teaching tools available.

See how the teacher engages the student about her home culture in the following conversation.

Teacher:	Esperanza, what a wonderful shirt you are wearing!
Student:	Thank you. It is from home, my town.
Teacher:	I like the flowers!
Student:	They are flores huastecas. I am from the Huasteca region in Mexico.
Teacher:	I like the geometric shapes.
Student:	The shapes of the flower are los cuatro puntos cardinales.
Teacher:	The cardinal points? Oh, the four directions. Right?
Student:	Yes, norte, sur, este y oeste. Los puntos cardinales they mean something.
Teacher:	What does the north mean?
Student:	El norte shows to the gods.
Teacher:	What about the south?
Student:	El sur means Mother. Babies come from. Plants grow. Fertilidad.
Teacher:	Sure. South is down. The soil is down. The soil stands for fertility. What does the east mean?
Student:	El este es el origen del fuego.
Teacher:	Oh, fuego, fire. Fire-sunrise. It makes sense. The sun is the origin of the fire, and east is where the sun rises. What about the west?

Student:	El oeste es el origen del dinero.
Teacher:	*Money? Where it gets dark? I would not have guessed that. Esperanza, your shirt is not only pretty, it speaks to us of your culture.*

Teachers create the physical environment for collaboration and interaction. They make full use of the classroom environment. Movable tables are ideal to accommodate active interaction among learners; these tables can be pulled together to form groups of various sizes, to create a larger conference table, or to set up stations with different tasks. Such configurations allow the teacher to move around the room to engage individual learners and small groups in order to differentiate instruction. Use the walls for displaying visual aids, such as posters, word walls, concept maps, and sentence starters. Bulletin boards are helpful for posting task explanations and passwords and for documenting the products of learning. Have a designated display area for each of the following: lesson objectives, key vocabulary for the lesson, and the daily agenda; also provide a "parking lot" for learners to post their questions. Have a dedicated area for role-plays and improvisations to inspire lively performances, especially if props and backdrops are also available.

Teachers provide orientation to new learners. Knowing what to expect and how to do well in a program can lower anxiety quickly. With most adult literacy programs having open entry and open exit policies, it is essential to be ready to provide orientation upon entry and have procedures in place to ensure that everyone feels welcome regardless of when they arrive.

Teachers maintain a line of communication with individual learners. Adult learners have many legitimate reasons for missing class. Without an open line of communication, it can be difficult for learners to return to class after a period of absence. A channel for private communication allows learners to share concerns about the class and the teacher to be in a position to provide a remedy. Many teachers have been successful with hard copy dialogue journals passed back and forth with learners. More recently, however, class social media sites and messaging applications have served this relationship-building purpose as well. An additional benefit to staying in touch is the authentic opportunity for learners to practice reading and writing frequently, in small bursts.

PRACTICE 2B Teachers demonstrate expectations of success for all learners.

Teacher expectations can affect how learners achieve, but teachers are often unaware of behaviors that reflect low expectancy. These may be as subtle as ignoring some learners, responding in a patronizing way, or interpreting students' actions in a negative light. Unfortunately, many low-literacy adult learners are accustomed to experiencing low-expectancy treatment and may have internalized it, and some hold negative assumptions about their abilities to learn at their age. Effective teachers convey high expectations for their learners; this may be a radically new experience for them and perhaps a source of inspiration and empowerment. Learners are less inclined to disappoint a teacher who believes in each of them, who picks up the signs of progress in everyone, and who seeks opportunities for every student to succeed.

Examples of Practice 2b

Teachers use a variety of approaches to appeal to diverse learners. When teachers create conditions for learning, they consider learner preferences and best practice based on language learning and literacy research. For this reason, they may choose from various group configurations or individualized approaches. They break down complex tasks into step-by-step procedures. They select from learners' topics of interest or allow learners to choose their own. They let learners work in alternative formats, such as video, simulation, demonstration, interview, poster, scrapbook, app, web-based collection, or exhibit. These choices serve learners' language learning needs, but they also tap into how individual learners perceive the usefulness of the task, how much enjoyment they may gain, how engaged they are, and how likely they are to succeed with it.

Teachers teach learners study skills and strategies to help them gain more from instruction. Many of our learners are new to interactive and collaborative instructional formats, which means that they need our support for gaining the most from activities. It is not always easy to remember what happened in class from one week to the next. Learners may need structured time in class to journal their learning, create records, review handouts, or get started with homework while the teacher is available to answer their questions.

Teachers guide learners to practice and extend learning outside the classroom. The amount of time adult learners spend in the classroom is a small fraction of the practice hours necessary to develop proficiency in a new language. The only way to reach the thousands of hours of deliberate practice needed for mastery is to continue learning between and beyond classes. The lives of adult learners vary in how much language and literacy practice they can engage in outside the classroom, but teachers are in a good position to help them see and create possibilities for more verbal interaction in English and for more regular opportunities to read and write.

Teachers help learners set challenging but achievable learning goals. When learners define their goals, they tend to use goalposts recognized in our society: *I want to get my GED*, *I want to get a degree*, *I want to know English*. Even more often, they think of *goals* as a synonym for *hopes and dreams*, an idea not needing a clear definition because hopes and dreams are held in the heart (Minnesota Literacy Council, 2016, 2017).

Goals that are achievable with classroom instruction, however, are much more narrowly defined and based on analysis of communicative skills and situations. Part of a teacher's contribution is to help learners plan a series of personally meaningful action steps that they can follow. For example, for a student who is also a parent, the steps that lead to "knowing English" may include sending emails to his or her child's teacher, reading to the child at home, being able to help the child with homework, and volunteering at school events. These are challenging but achievable goals that parents can experience as success. These goals entail English language skills that can be taught in the classroom and practiced in real life. They can be ranked and ordered to form a developmental path to personally meaningful English proficiency.

Because it is difficult for learners to identify specific language goals that are within their reach, teachers can offer questionnaires and checklists to facilitate goal-setting. An example is available on the website for this book (www.the6principles.org/adult-education).

PRACTICE 2C Teachers plan instruction to enhance and sustain learners' motivation for language learning.

As the research presented in Chapter 2 makes clear, motivation is one of the essential ingredients of language learning. It takes a very long time to achieve advanced proficiency in a language, and during this time learners must maintain both motivation and practice. The role of teachers is to kindle and sustain these and to equip learners with the motivational tools they need to succeed on their own.

Examples of Practice 2c

Teachers help learners form a self-image as a capable multilingual. Research shows that the best tool teachers can use for motivation building in learners is guidance—guidance to construct a clear and vivid image of their future selves as high-functioning English speakers (Dörnyei & Ushioda, 2011). Guiding daily actions by a strongly held vision can lead to positive affect; for ELs, such a vision should include images of themselves as individuals who are proficient in English. The product of guided visualization can take shape as a narrative or a collage, which learners can share with one another. An important part of the visualization process is to explore how each learner's particular mental imagery can direct learning. Guided imagery can also be the foundation for learners' goal-setting.

Script for Guided Visualization

Close your eyes . . . Get comfortable . . . Breathe in deeply . . . Imagine yourself in the future . . . You have studied English. You have practiced English. Now you can speak it well . . . See your future self . . . How old are you? . . . What do you look like? . . . Where do you live? . . . What makes you happy in life? . . . What do you love doing? . . . What job are you doing? . . . What does your workplace look like? . . . Who are you talking to? . . . What languages are you speaking? . . . How do people respond to you? . . . What kinds of things are you saying? . . . How are you using English? . . . How do you feel? . . . What makes you feel this way?

Reflect on how these guided visions may generate motivated behavior for language learning.

Subira

A young Ethiopian woman is considering her passions. She loves baking cakes and decorating them for special occasions. She pictures herself in a bakery, speaking to customers in English. She is taking orders for cakes. She can see herself telling them about the kinds of cakes she can make. She shows them her cake catalog. The guests at weddings and parties are delighted with her playful, scrumptious creations. She keeps a display of the photos her customers send her of their weddings and anniversaries. She runs a cake shop with employees and takes care of the business responsibilities on her own, reading, writing, and doing the math in English skillfully. Her relatives respect her because she can support herself with what she loves doing and makes so many people happy.

Ezequiel

Ezequiel, a father of three from Mexico, pictures himself as a supervisor at the school furniture manufacturing plant, where he has been working for years. As a supervisor, he reads manuals, writes reports, and completes many documents. He checks on the production line and talks to workers in English and in Spanish about solving problems. He participates in company meetings and speaks in front of managers. They plan training workshops together and discuss actions to improve safety. He can afford to buy a home for his family and takes his children to visit their grandparents in his native country.

Teachers make learning tasks relevant to participants' learning goals. Once interest inventories, goal-setting, and motivation-building guided visualizations are completed, teachers can ensure learning tasks relate to learners' defined purposes. Conveying the rationale for the learning activities and explicitly stating how the tasks serve learners' visions and goals and how the skills can be applied outside the classroom can help to make the connections clear to the learners themselves.

Teachers help learners overcome obstacles to learning. The gap between individuals' ideal future selves as proficient multilinguals and their current abilities may be too wide to close within the very limited instructional time available. Nevertheless, it is possible to lay down a long-term action plan for every learner to advise them on how they might be able to move forward with reasonable expectations. In Chapter 4, we detail actionable solutions for some of the most common challenges adult learners face.

Teachers make language and literacy learning enjoyable. We began the discussion of Principle 2 with learner voices. Miguel's statement was a reminder that the journey to proficiency can be filled with fun. It is easier to pursue years of language learning when the classroom feels like our community and when learning is experienced as a pleasurable activity worth pursuing for its own sake. One way to boost the pleasure of learning is to set aside time for spontaneous conversations where learners share their recent experiences, news, anecdotes, or life stories (e.g., Roberts & Cooke, 2007). When teachers build instruction on these genuine conversations, learning can feel more relevant and natural.

Laughter is another way to boost shared enjoyment. Good humor and playfulness enhance retention. The use of positive humor has been associated with a more relaxed learning environment, higher perceived motivation to learn, and greater enjoyment (Banas, Dunbar, Rodriguez, & Liu, 2011).

Teachers continually add to their repertoire of new teaching ideas that appeal to their students and select from it strategically to inspire learning. Some examples include game-like activities, friendly competition, simulations, experiential activities, storytelling, riddles, chants, rehearsed performances, and online learning games.

Principle 3. Design High-Quality Lessons for Language Development

Ethan teaches a low-literacy class, where each day attendance is unpredictable. He cannot use a sequential syllabus because the students progress at different rates, and most are not in class every day. Instead, Ethan structures classes around a set of learning activities that suit any topic the learners choose.

Ethan has a large library of photographs that depict people in various communicative and problem situations. He uses these photos to teach vocabulary, language forms, language use in specific situations, problem solving, and basic literacy. Each day, Ethan offers four to five relevant images to select from, and either learners break into groups based on the situation they want to study or, if everyone agrees, Ethan leads the whole class in the study of one topic.

The class always starts with activating background knowledge and prior learning. Ethan holds up the picture and gives learners about ten seconds to look at it. Then, students have a minute to recall everything they can about the photo and name objects, actions, emotions, and descriptive adjectives. After this, students exchange what they can remember with a partner. While they do this, Ethan circulates and listens to what the partners say, which indicates what each person already knows about the topic. Next, they describe the picture as a class, adding in everyone's ideas and building on each other's language. Some students offer words, some phrases, and some full sentences. Learners select a few useful key vocabulary items that they would like to practice during the lesson. Everyone's vocabulary selection is a little different; they don't all need to learn the same words. Ethan checks that the words they picked represent frequent vocabulary that is useful across a broad range of topics.

Ethan integrates choice with technology. Learners can use their preferred device to type word lists, translate with Google, or compose texts. They have several computer stations and a number of tablets for this purpose.

The teacher works with what the students offered about the picture and with the target words they identified to create a paragraph-length descriptive text about the photo. (He sometimes also features a target language structure.) The students use this brief descriptive paragraph for reading and writing practice, which they do in pairs. Each pair also writes a title for the paragraph that summarizes the main idea.

In the next step, they create a dialogue between the people depicted in the picture. Sometimes this is a social language dialogue (What's new with you? or How was your weekend?), but other times it is more concrete and technical (We have a problem. What is it? How can we solve it?). They read and write the dialogues and then practice and perform them multiple times. They may even expand this into a full role-play or improvisational theater for some fun. For example, they hold up cue cards, and the performers have to use the word or phrase on the cue card in their next turn. This provides opportunities to work with the target vocabulary and language structures in specific situations that the students themselves have selected.

High-quality lessons are those that lead learners to advance toward curricular goals as well as personal learning goals. They build on learners' existing knowledge and skills, stimulate internal cognitive-linguistic processes through learners' active engagement, and produce observable learner outcomes, which allow the teacher to make inferences about how the learners processed input and constructed new skills or knowledge (Mayer, 1992).

From the definition, it follows that high-quality lessons are carefully planned to meet certain criteria. They

- have clearly defined lesson objectives,
- have a mechanism to activate learners' prior knowledge and existing skills,
- provide learners with inputs that they can comprehend,
- engage learners actively in knowledge construction and skills practice,

- include focus on learning strategies and higher order thinking skills, and
- have a mechanism to make the learning outcomes observable.

PRACTICE 3A Teachers prepare lessons with clear outcomes and convey them to their learners.

For teachers, lesson objectives serve to assure that the lesson contributes meaningfully to a longer term learning plan. For learners, the objectives allow them to recognize the significance of the upcoming activities and to selectively focus attention on what really matters. Focusing on the relevant information enables them to organize that information in working memory to create and retain a coherent whole (Mayer, 1992).

Learning a new language is much more than information processing; it is the acquisition of a large set of skills that require regular practice over a long time (DeKeyser, 2007). Lesson objectives can serve as a means of cognitive coaching by drawing learners' attention to the skills or subskills they will be honing through deliberate practice.

Many teachers have lesson plans that contain objectives they do not share with learners because they consider them purely administrative, but unstated objectives cannot serve learners' purposes. A learner-friendly approach to lesson objectives is to present them in the form of "I can" statements and to have learners elaborate what the statement means and how it is useful to them.

Consider how sharing the lesson objective may serve instruction.

Teacher:	Today, we'll be working on discussing our employment histories. Look at the lesson objective on the board: "I can answer questions about my employment history." How is this objective useful to you?
Ayan:	I think when I go to immigration interview.
Zaira:	Maybe I can get a job.
Hao:	When I rent apartment. They ask me that.
Narek:	I think it's good to learn this. I know it, but I cannot say it.
Hiep:	I don't know "employment history." What is "employment history"?

Examples of Practice 3a

Teachers determine objectives based on standards. By using standards to guide curriculum planning, teachers create a pathway for adult learners to access secondary school equivalency and postsecondary training opportunities and/or align instruction with required English language proficiency exams. However, curricula can also be designed around learners' personal goals or from program curricula that serve specific purposes, as for example in workplace education, family literacy, or civic education classes.

Standards are the blueprint to guide instruction toward a defined level of performance. They break an end-goal into a specific set of observable performance levels. In programs that have adopted specific standards for instruction, placement tests serve to measure where participants' skills are in relation to the performance levels described in the standards. Teachers in these programs then draw their lesson objectives from the performance descriptors that are at or only slightly above their students' current level of performance.

You can organize standards-based lessons around learner-friendly objectives by following this process:

1. Select a particular standard the lesson will address. (*"Write narratives in which they recount a well-elaborated event or short sequence of events, include details to describe actions, thoughts, and feelings."*; Pimentel, 2013, p. 26)

2. Write a series of "I can" statements based on the standard. Include only one learning target in each statement. (*I can write about an event in the past tense. I can describe a character's actions. I can use different verbs to introduce what a character said. I can use signal words to indicate the order of events.*)

3. Select the statement that best suits the lesson. Use language that is comprehensible to learners at their English language functioning level.

4. Display the "I can" statement at the start of the lesson. Ask learners to explain in their own words what it means to them.

5. Allow time at the end of the lesson to revisit the "I can" statement. Have students comment on what they have learned. They can make a record of how they achieved the objective in their learning journal or portfolio.

Teachers contextualize learning objectives. Lesson objectives are more meaningful to learners when they are embedded in contexts that are relevant to them. In addition, connecting lesson objectives to specific contexts can reduce the learning load because the vocabulary needed to complete activities or readings may already be largely familiar. Table 3.1 shows how the same objectives may look like in two different contexts: an ESOL class for parents in a community school and a workplace ESL program.

Table 3.1	Pairing standards-based lesson objectives with specific contexts
Standards-based objective	**Sample contexts for objective**
I can identify the main topic in oral presentations . . .	**Parent engagement in school** when I listen to the principal's phone messages **Workplace education** when I watch training videos
I can give a reason to support a claim . . .	**Parent engagement in school** when I speak to a teacher about a problem **Workplace education** when I speak to my supervisor about a problem
I can introduce a topic . . .	**Parent engagement in school** when I talk with other parent volunteers **Workplace education** when we have a team meeting at work

Teachers integrate language and content objectives for their lessons. English learners are capable of learning content in English at the same time that they are acquiring language and literacy skills. Learning content and language simultaneously is one way to accelerate ELs' transition to other types of training available in English-medium programs. Content-based language instruction is a well-established learning design. Exemplary teachers design high-quality lessons by matching language and content objectives.

Let's assume that a large franchise would like to train bilingual employees for front desk attendant duties. They already have a manual for such duties and would like the English classes to use this manual as the content of language instruction. In this situation, the teacher would draw a set of content objectives from the training manual and a set of language objectives from the diagnostic tests and observations collected during the needs assessment (table 3.2).

Table 3.2	Matching language and content objectives
Sample content objectives	Sample language objectives
I can use the phone protocol for front desk staff.	I can read the phone scripts fluently. I can say two phone scripts from memory. I can pronounce the phrases clearly. I can provide a proper response quickly. I can ask for help when I cannot answer a question. I can ask the customer politely to repeat information. I can take a message.
I can handle transactions with money.	I can say aloud the amount of money the customer is giving me. I can count the change back to the customer. I can write a receipt. I can read a registration form. I can scan a registration form for missing information. I can ask the customer politely to provide the missing information. I can fill out the "Office Section" of the registration form.

Teachers allow learners to select the content they want to learn. Another way to integrate language and content objectives is to allow the learners to select the content for their language learning. In this way, the teacher contributes the language objectives and the learners exercise a degree of control over the topics. Sometimes this can be a utilitarian choice, especially in situations where attendance is not predictable or where classes are multilevel.

Observe how Ray motivates incarcerated adult learners by offering them choices.

The learners in Ray's classes have different education levels. Five are on grades 7–8 level, eight are on grades 9–12, and three have some postsecondary training. Mixed-ability grouping is typical in classes for incarcerated adults. The learners all have prison jobs, but their jobs do not require much in terms of literacy. At the most, they occasionally read instructions, a reference manual, a diagram, or a memo. These jobs offer little in terms of motivation to improve reading and writing skills in English. Most come to class for the change of scenery and not necessarily to achieve learning.

Ray has found two ways to fuel his students' desire for continuing their education while incarcerated: One is to follow their personal interests and make the learning experience inherently rewarding for them. The other is to help them envision themselves in new lives beyond their time in prison, to see themselves do well with productive jobs where they can perform successfully in English. Both of these ways require that the learners should be able to select topics and tasks for learning. Having choices is a perk in itself in the highly controlled prison environment. The choices with learning tasks also help mitigate learning disability issues, which tend to be common. Ray identifies subjects that his students are interested in and the learning tasks that they enjoy. He offers a menu of assignments and assessments that they can complete individually or with a select group of peers. This format allows Ray to conference with individuals and have in-depth interactions with learners in small groups.

PRACTICE 3B Teachers provide and enhance input through varied approaches, techniques, and modalities.

A fundamental task of the language teacher is to provide usable input, which we discussed in Chapter 2 as one of the essential conditions for second language acquisition. High-quality lessons are carefully planned for ways to make input usable. Comprehensible input occurs by design when teachers ask themselves questions regarding the implementation of the lesson:

- How will I convey the information to my students?
- Will they listen to it, read about it, research it, or discover it through an inquiry task?

- How can I support their comprehension with contextual clues and scaffolding?
- How can I build input to match the language that the learners can produce at this time?
- How will I know that they comprehend the input they are getting from me?

Examples of Practice 3b

Teachers plan ways to make their input to learners comprehensible. Comprehensible input has a primary role in language development. Many people associate comprehensible input with oral communication, but the concept also applies to other modalities of input that learners receive. Teachers scaffold language input in their speech, in the texts they use to promote language and literacy development, and in the teaching of content. There are five sets of techniques that are particularly useful for providing comprehensible input:

- techniques that convey meaning by providing context
- techniques that simplify the input
- techniques that make it easier to process the input by allowing longer processing time, directing the learner's focus, making it easier to pay attention and notice important features
- techniques that elaborate the input by adding in simplifications without removing the more challenging parts
- techniques that help with checking the learner's understanding

We use these techniques in various combinations. For example, in oral communication, we may point to an object (context) and supply a simplified phrase, like *Ah! Rain boots* (simplification). Then, we wait to give the learner a little time to process "rain boots" (ease of processing). If the learner then repeats *rain boots*, we may respond by elaborating on the learner's output by saying, *They are colorful. Nice rain boots* (elaboration). Then, we might glance to see if the learner has a smile, which we interpret as a confirmation that she understood our input (comprehension check).

Table 3.3 shows common ways we can make different kinds of input (talk, text, and content) more comprehensible to our students; though these techniques may look different across the types of input, they serve the same purposes (context, simplification, ease of processing, elaboration, and comprehension checks). For example, we make processing oral input easier by slowing down, articulating carefully, and stopping more frequently than we normally would. To simplify a text, we might limit the reading to just the first paragraph or a few highlighted topic sentences or focus on captions next to the photos. To make content comprehensible, we could, for example, create critical incident scenarios from an employee manual and have students discuss the critical scenarios in small groups before presenting their own role-plays and commentary.

Table 3.3	Techniques for planning comprehensible input for talk, text, and content learning	
Ways to make **talk** comprehensible	Ways to make **text** comprehensible	Ways to make **content learning** comprehensible
CONTEXT		
• Point • Gesture • Display facial expressions • Demonstrate • Act out • Draw • Show illustrations • Provide physical objects • Use props	• Add — photos — illustrations — diagrams — infographics — picture books — maps • Provide — short videos — bilingual texts — translated texts	• Utilize — demonstrations — experiments — observations — experiential activities — simulations — imitation — images — videos — personal experiences
SIMPLIFICATION		
• Use short utterances that are grammatically well formed • Repeat often • Build on the learner's talk • Emphasize key words and key language forms • Limit vocabulary to high-frequency words • Avoid idioms	• Shorten readings • Focus on — captions, headlines — table of contents — glossaries — outlines — lists — topic sentences — shorter sentences • Replace unknown words • Omit extraneous information • Use readers with controlled vocabulary • Use leveled readers	• Utilize — basic examples — stories — explainer videos — infographics — study guides — handouts — step-by-step instructions — posters — images with descriptive labels — slide presentations • Remove unfamiliar references
EASE OF PROCESSING		
• Speak with clear articulation • Speak with a slower rate • Provide pauses to allow think time • Pronounce words that are normally unstressed or contracted (*the, a/an, is/are, not, do, have/had*) • Use a few easy filler expressions to slow talk (*you know, the thing is that*) • Provide subtitles • Provide transcripts	• Use texts with — larger print size — more white space — key information highlighted — bolded text — bullets — hyperlinked translations — guiding questions • Activate background knowledge • Preteach key vocabulary • Provide chapter summaries	• Choose — familiar topics — remarkable content — content with clearly marked organization • Make brief presentations • Provide opportunities for immediate application • Provide clear task explanations • Utilize — game-like drills — periodic reviews — distributed practice — content presented in native language

(continued)

Table 3.3 *(continued)*

Ways to make **talk** comprehensible	Ways to make **text** comprehensible	Ways to make **content learning** comprehensible
ELABORATION		

• Embed explanations
• Give examples and nonexamples
• Convey the same meaning in different ways
• Make explicit what is normally assumed or implied
• Use signal words frequently
• Write down key information
	• Choose texts with
	  — embedded explanations
	  — embedded definitions
	  — marginal notes
	• Provide examples
	• Be redundant
	• Be explicit
		• Present in multiple modalities
		• Allow group processing
		• Utilize
		  — debriefings
		  — coaching
		  — peer tutoring
		  — reteaching

COMPREHENSION CHECKS		

• Monitor listener's facial expressions, noting the appropriateness of verbal or physical responses
• Ask the listener to
  — elaborate on responses
  — restate or summarize
  — rate comprehension with gesture
	• Prompt reader to evaluate readability
	• Include comprehension questions in the margins
	• Give mini-quizzes throughout reading
	• Provide prompts
	  — that reference the reading process
	  — for partner discussion and partner reading
		• Provide feedback on
		  — practice
		  — performance
		• Correct errors promptly
		• Provide tools for self-checking

Teachers use multiple modalities and sources of input. Another way to approach the planning for comprehensibility is to reduce teacher talk as the primary means of teaching and communicating information. When learners engage with other types of input and use language to accomplish tasks, their language and literacy skills develop faster. Minimize teacher presentations in favor of learner actions, such as the following:

- paired talk and partner reading
- small-group discussions
- peer tutoring
- using technology to research information
- learner-led discussions and multimedia presentations

In addition, effective teachers switch modalities to serve learner strengths or preferences. Rather than reading independently, learners may prefer to use audio books, taped texts, videos, or text-to-voice protocol on their electronic devices.

Teachers prepare clear instructions and task explanations. A planned activity may not achieve its goals if learners are not following the directions, and time is wasted if learners are not sure what to do. We can reduce the need for task explanations by having instructional routines that we introduce and practice early on, such as the introduction and review of learning objectives. Collaborative learning groups with assigned roles (e.g., facilitator, note taker, questioner, surveyor, encourager, presenter, quality controller) may be another classroom staple. A posted agenda that learners can reference any time also cuts down on the need for directions.

For all activities that are not routine, ELs need both oral and written instructions. Written directions eliminate the effort to have to remember procedural information that is not essential for language learning. It is also helpful to break down more complex tasks into shorter steps or to model each step by showing learners what is expected.

PRACTICE 3C Teachers engage learners in the use and practice of authentic language.

We cannot overemphasize the role of language use and interaction for language instruction. We expect adult learners to be talking, reading, writing, and problem solving in their language courses in ways that they can apply English in their lives outside the classroom. Contrived pedagogical exercises seldom result in skills that are useful for participating in genuine discourse in the community. Authentic practice means that learners are building skills that allow them to convey real messages and perform actual tasks in real communicative situations (e.g., Ellis & Shintani, 2014).

Examples of Practice 3c

Teachers create opportunities for active engagement with language tasks. Language is best thought of as a verb rather than a noun (Levine & McCloskey, 2013). As such, it is best learned while doing something with it—by being actively engaged with it as a listener, speaker, reader, and writer.

Some forms of classroom talk are more suitable for learning and practicing authentic discourse. *Accountable talk* is a type of classroom interaction that promotes active listening and genuine interaction among learners (Michaels, O'Connor, Williams Hall, & Resnick, 2013). Learners must exert effort to understand what is being said and to build on the output of others in constructive ways. Using accountable talk moves, the whole class can build shared understandings, process learning, and solve challenging problems as a team.

Teachers can assist in productive classroom talk by introducing learners to talk moves such as the following:

- Say more on that.
- So, you are saying . . .
- Do you agree or disagree with that? Why?
- Why do you think that?
- Who can add to that?
- Who has another perspective on this?
- What other ideas should we consider?
- What have we learned from this?

Encouraging learners to share their knowledge and ideas in their other languages lets them use that language as a resource for learning English, including them in discussions and problem solving even if they do not know the words yet in English. They can share their ideas while also being introduced to the unfamiliar English words or forms in a teachable moment.

Teachers group students strategically to support language practice. As mentioned previously and shown in several classroom examples, establishing collaborative grouping is another way to multiply opportunities for all learners to engage in conversation. Groups that are carefully constructed, with attention to gender, personality, language skills, and knowledge levels, can promote productive classroom talk. Some examples of tasks used in collaborative groups include the following (Finn Miller, 2010):

- solving real, open-ended problems
- discussing (ads, articles, books, movies, news clips, job descriptions, emails)
- preparing for a debate or a panel discussion
- collaborating on a plan (for a goal, a process, a procedure, an event, an application)
- developing a product (presentation, report, memo, video, ad, catalog, web page, business proposal, brochure, business card, logo, flyer, greeting card)
- creating something new (a jingle, tag line, poem, story, skit, play, book, concept)
- designing and carrying out a survey (to poll program participants or members of the community)
- producing a performance (a book reading, play, job interview, business negotiation, pitch, live reporting, news program, talk show)
- generating their own questions about a topic (Rothstein & Santana, 2011)

Elements that lead to successful group work (Gibbons, 2014) include the following:

- providing clear expectations
- establishing and modeling a clear outcome
- providing appropriate content
- requiring talk
- teaching group procedures and participation etiquette
- involving all learners

Teachers embed language practice into learning content. Many techniques assist teachers in providing variety to lessons and encouraging productive classroom conversation (Zwiers, 2014; Vogt, Echevarría, & Washam, 2015; Vogt & Echevarría, 2008; Kagan & Kagan, 2009). Different techniques are useful at various stages of a lesson, as illustrated in the examples in table 3.4. An explanation of the techniques is available in Appendix A.

Table 3.4	Language practice techniques throughout a lesson	
Starting instruction	• Anticipation chats • Journal jumpstarts • The insert method	• KWL chart • Word splash posters
Building instruction	• Formula 5-2-1 • Framed outlines • SQP2RS ("Squeepers")	• Research and share • Expert groups
Application of instruction	• Study buddy teaming • Jigsaw what you know • Chart and share	• Gallery walk • Sentence analysis
Concluding instruction	• Student-created cloze sentences • Quiz-quiz-trade • Learning journals for review	• Rubrics for self-assessment • Status update on class social media board

(Zwiers, 2014; Vogt et al., 2015; Vogt & Echevarría, 2008; Kagan & Kagan, 2009)

PRACTICE 3D **Teachers design lessons so that learners engage with relevant and meaningful content.**

Just as learning tasks should relate to learners' goals, so should the content of the lesson reflect relevance to their life experiences, allowing them to tap into a rich resource for their learning. They can see the relationship between what they are learning and their everyday lives. It is worth investing the effort to adapt relevant, high-interest materials rather than using materials intended for young readers.

Examples of Practice 3d

Teachers collect resources that are relevant and meaningful to the learners. It is more feasible to offer choices about topics and content when we have a collection of suitable materials on hand. These do not have to be in the form of worksheets and textbooks. The best materials lend themselves to open-ended tasks that prompt genuine discussions and problem solving. Consider building a materials library with some of the following:

- photos of people in a wide range of communicative and problem situations
- problem-solving prompts
- incident scenarios with multiple perspectives, including cross-cultural issues
- picture dictionaries
- teacher- or student-made picture dictionaries of actual workplaces
- high-interest texts on different reading levels for self-selected reading
- graphic organizers
- infographics on a variety of topics
- home language books and magazines
- collections of life experience stories written by adult learners
- brief videos that simplify explanations and show practical examples

Teachers use information from needs assessments to identify what is relevant. The findings of needs assessments and the themes collected from learner interviews can guide lesson planning. For example, if learners have migrated from other countries, then learning to discuss the geography of those regions may provide context for language practice. If they did a lot of cooking growing up and learned about the preparation of traditional dishes, then they might value writing and publishing a cookbook. If they experienced oppression and violence firsthand, then they may find it empowering to develop their reading and writing around a theme of dealing with oppression and violence in our society (Freeman, Freeman, & Mercuri, 2002).

Teachers integrate technology use. Adult literacy in the 21st century includes digital literacy; adults need digital literacy to be able to communicate with their children's teachers, get a job or a promotion, or participate in education or training. As technologies evolve, adults need a flexible mindset to be able to solve problems in digital environments.

Some learners will have strong digital literacy skills in their non-English languages, while other learners may see technology as a barrier to their participation. Many elements of digital literacy we tend to take for granted may be entirely new to them, such as how to do the following:

- locate, download, save, and edit documents
- use features like copy-paste, spell check, text-to-voice, scan-to-translate

- locate and follow tutorials
- create, edit, and publish videos or multimedia presentations
- make purchases or pay bills online
- participate in social media
- evaluate the credibility of online sources
- stay safe on the internet

Digital skills are best taught in the context in which they are used, such as filling out an online form for a medical appointment, finding and evaluating information for a research project, sending a text or email message to a teacher, or using a map program in a unit on transportation. As our learners develop digital literacy, opportunities to extend their learning outside the classroom will multiply for them (Harris, 2015).

PRACTICE 3E Teachers plan differentiated instruction according to their learners' English language functioning levels, literacy levels, needs, and goals.

Differentiated instruction is an instructional model that provides multiple pathways to learning and offers differing challenges to a diverse learner population. Adult English learners' needs vary by all the characteristics we detailed in figure 3.1; however, this does not mean that serving them in the same class is impossible. Teachers who differentiate instruction are mindful of the ways that individual learners are the same or different, and create flexible assignments, adapted texts, and dynamic groupings to allow every learner to participate meaningfully on the level of their current abilities. Differentiated instruction requires that teachers scaffold instruction for student success rather than hold some learners to lower expectations or reduce their learning goals (Tomlinson, 2014).

Examples of Practice 3e

Teachers offer a menu of reading assignments and allow learners choices of texts. The readability of texts depends on three factors:

1. Features of the text itself (quantifiable and qualitative text features)
2. The preparedness of the reader
3. The way the reader needs to use the text (the reading task)

Texts are easier to read when they are shorter and have less complex phrase structure, fewer unknown words, more text cohesion, familiar subject matter, clear organization, and a great deal of context (as detailed in table 3.3). Reading tasks are easier to when they have lower cognitive demand, for example, locating information versus analyzing it. Learners are better prepared when they are highly motivated to read, are interested in the content, are familiar with the topic and the genre, and know all but a few words in the text, and when the sentences are comparable to the sentences they can produce themselves (e.g., Pimentel, Copeland, Shaw, Lakin, & Whealdon, 2011; Mesmer, 2008).

To differentiate readings, teachers can offer texts of different length and complexity for learners to select from. Learners can complete different tasks with the texts they read, such as answering different questions. Teachers can allow social supports to complete the tasks, such as a more competent peer for a reading partner, and they can provide the same information in a different format, like video, recorded text, or slide presentation.

Teachers allow learners to work in expert groups and complete jigsaw tasks. Jigsaw activities refer to a collaborative structure in which learners divide a more complex assignment into manageable pieces. In this case, the tasks can be differentiated to match each team member's abilities. After each learner completes the assigned part, he or she synthesizes the information to enable the group to wrap up the whole assignment as a team. The complex task that the whole team completes can vary and can include solving problems, reading a longer text in smaller chunks, and researching a topic. The goal is to ensure that regardless of abilities, each team member can play a vital role in providing at least one piece of the puzzle.

In one variant of jigsaw tasks (shown in table 3.5), learners move between two types of groups during the lesson: their base group, which is a mixed-ability group, and an expert group, which is a group with members on the same skill level (reading level, English language functioning level, or content knowledge). Learners begin the assignment in their base group, where they can discuss what they already know, what they expect as an outcome, and what each member will contribute. Then, team members regroup with their expert group to develop their expertise by reading or researching together. They then reunite with their base group, where they share the information everybody gathered in their expert groups, and finally solve their problem, create their presentation, or complete a data table they started when they began the assignment. This type of task organization allows differentiation to become a classroom routine. (Walqui & van Lier, 2010)

Table 3.5	Differentiation in a multilevel classroom with the jigsaw lesson plan
Starting instruction in base groups	• Learners receive the assignment. • They complete an anticipation guide. • They discuss background knowledge. • They assign tasks/sections to each team member.
Building instruction in expert groups	• Learners read text or research on their skill and knowledge level. • They collaborate to complete answers/notes. • Teacher checks product and provides feedback.
Application of instruction in base groups	• Learners take turns sharing their answers/notes from their expert groups. • Learners record answers/notes based on everyone's presentations. • They compare and contrast information based on what everyone shared. They summarize findings, draw conclusions. • They revisit the anticipation guide and record responses.
Concluding instruction	• Base groups report their summaries and conclusions.

(Walqui & van Lier, 2010)

PRACTICE 3F **Teachers promote the use of learning strategies, problem solving, and critical thinking.**

Teachers explicitly teach learning strategies, problem solving, and critical thinking skills so that adult learners can develop the ability to sustain learning outside the classroom. These are tools adult learners need to manage on their own to control and direct their own learning. Research bears out the role of learning strategies for success in second language learning (Oxford, 2017; August & Shanahan, 2006; O'Malley & Chamot, 1990), and critical thinking is the foundation of good life choices (Merriam & Bierema, 2014). All three components are indispensable for high-quality lesson plans for adult language learners.

Examples of Practice 3f

Teachers introduce and practice learning strategies. Over time, teachers introduce learners to a range of learning strategies that they can apply as needed when they are trying to figure out meaning, complete an assignment, or review material. Language learning strategies are classified by domain:

- **Cognitive strategies** help construct our thoughts. They help us keep information in working memory and connect it in meaningful ways. Examples of cognitive strategies include using our senses to remember, activating prior knowledge, making connections between ideas, connecting details into a storyline, and predicting what comes next. (Oxford, 2017)

- **Metacognitive strategies** regulate our thinking processes. They help us direct how we approach our thought construction. Examples of metacognitive strategies include paying attention to our actions, details, or to others' points of view; prioritizing tasks; organizing our learning space; seeking our practice opportunities; and setting up a study plan. (Oxford, 2017)

- **Motivational strategies** regulate our motivation to accomplish a goal or task. Examples of motivational strategies include giving ourselves consequences or rewards for achievement, practicing positive self-talk (*I can do this. This is important.*), turning learning into a game, and attributing success to what we can control (e.g., effort or perseverance rather than innate talent). (Oxford, 2017)

- **Metamotivational strategies** help consider, evaluate, and change our motivation. Examples include imagining our ideal future multilingual self, planning for ways to get ourselves motivated, monitoring our motivation level, and reducing distractions and off-task behaviors. (Oxford, 2017)

- **Affective strategies** help learners regulate their emotions. Examples include taking actions to make us feel smart and confident, like going to the library or meeting with a study group; doing breathing exercises to calm our nervousness; interpreting situations with positive emotions; and talking and tweeting about beautiful things we enjoy and appreciate. (Oxford, 2017)

- **Social strategies** direct us to pursue behaviors that support our learning, such as cooperation, respect, empathy, and exploration. Examples include seeking out a mentor and conversation partners, engaging with friends on social media, taking turns in conversations, and showing interest in the lives and cultures of others. (Oxford, 2017)

- **Language learning strategies** are specific to developing language skills. Table 3.6 provides a sampling of these.

Table 3.6	Language learning strategies	
Strategy type	**Strategies**	
Listening	• Reading the whole situation • Noticing cues • Listening selectively for key words and chunks of language	• Concentrating • Redirecting attention • Note-taking • Asking clarification questions
Speaking	• Planning • Rehearsing and self-talk • Using notes • Self-monitoring • Using formulaic expressions and filler phrases	• Repairing communication breakdowns • Seeking out conversation partners • Engaging in activities that require speaking
Reading	• Selecting "just-right" texts • Activating background knowledge • Using common text features • Skimming for main ideas • Identifying relevant details	• Asking questions about the text • Checking comprehension • Summarizing with graphic organizers • Annotating • Using context cues to guess meaning
Writing	• Brainstorming • Analyzing and following models • Using sentence starters • Outlining	• Reading aloud • Seeking feedback on draft • Learning from teacher commentary • Checking grammar and spelling
Vocabulary	• Key word method ("sounds like") • Analyzing word parts • Notecard method • Noticing parts of speech • Using dictionaries	• Vocabulary notebook • Building word families • Creating word maps • Guess and replace • Using word lists, glossaries

(Oxford, 2017; Echevarría, Vogt, & Short, 2017; Nation & Webb, 2011)

Teachers organize language tasks around problem solving. Employers indicate that the two skills they need the most from their employees are critical thinking and problem solving (Association of American Colleges and Universities, 2013), followed by oral and written communication. Teachers can build language skills around problem-solving tasks, which are useful for any phase of a lesson (starting instruction, building instruction, applying instruction, or concluding the lesson; table 3.4). These tasks can also extend over an entire lesson, and they fit well with collaborative jigsaw tasks (table 3.5). Teachers can frame virtually any discussion prompt as a problem-solving scenario. Consider these examples:

- It's raining hard. Water starts dripping on the floor from the roof.
- You walk into a restaurant to apply for a job. The manager gives you an application. He wants to interview you right away.
- Your supervisor asks you to stay for three extra hours. He will pay overtime. You need to pick up your children from school. You may be able to work longer if you can find a solution.
- You have a coworker you cannot trust. When you give him a task, he always says, "Sure. No problem." Sometimes he doesn't do the task, but he doesn't tell you about it. This can get you into trouble. You want to change this situation.

To infuse problem solving into language practice, teachers can provide these steps (Adelson-Goldstein, 2015):

1. Describe the situation in your own words. Give all the important details.
2. State the problem.
3. Brainstorm possible solutions.
4. Evaluate each solution for difficulties and consequences.
5. Decide the solution you would choose. Explain the reasons why that is the best solution for you.
6. Apply the solution. Evaluate the outcome.

Teachers use techniques to make thinking visible. Teaching thinking skills is challenging because we cannot directly observe the thought processes in learners' heads. Our learners have the added difficulty of struggling to say in English what they think, though they may think in another language. They rely on concepts that may only partially overlap with concepts conveyed by English words. Teachers can help learners capture their thinking processes by having students record them in images or in words and then imposing on them some form of organization with a chart, concept map, or graphic organizer.

T-charts lend themselves to capturing several thinking processes, such as observing closely (It looks like – It sounds like), asking questions (What I know – What I am wondering about), considering different viewpoints (What I see – What my partner sees), and making connections (Causes – Effects; What I thought before – What I think now). Venn diagrams are especially suitable for uncovering complexity (Unique qualities – Shared qualities); tables are a tool for analyzing multiple cases (Relevant features – Features of case A, B, C, D) and noticing gaps in the information we have available to us; and concept maps help with generating ideas, making detailed observations, elaborating with examples and supports, and connecting and categorizing features.

Teachers ask questions that prompt critical and analytical thinking. The vast majority of questions teachers ask are not challenging; they are rhetorical questions, display questions, yes/no questions, and ultimatum questions (those that prompt a choice between two alternatives). These types of questions do not require substantive thinking or elaborated responses that show students are analyzing and examining their ideas closely. Exemplary teachers ask productive questions that prompt learners to go deeper, to supply justifications for their opinions, and to support their ideas with evidence. They encourage learners to examine the ideas of others and to critique both evidence and reasoning. Good thinking questions start with *how, how come, why, what else, what about,* or *what if.*

Teachers grow learners as thinkers by asking questions like the following (Ritchhart, Church, & Morrison, 2011):

- What makes you say that?
- What evidence can you provide for that?
- What are you basing this on?
- What does that tell you then?
- Why do you think it happened that way?
- What else could it be?
- What might another person think/know/notice about that?

- What makes you doubt that claim?
- How does this change your interpretation?
- What do you conclude/predict?
- How could you best represent the essence of that idea as an image/symbol/headline?

PRACTICE 3G Teachers promote self-directed learning.

As mentioned previously, achieving advanced proficiency in a new language independently requires sustained motivation and effort over many years and regular interaction with proficient speakers. Achieving advanced literacy requires daily reading and writing in that language. Ingredients of self-directed learning are similar across all content (Andrade & Evans, 2013), including a new language, and exemplary teachers promote these practices: setting goals, regulating motivation, managing time and the learning environment, practicing good study habits, giving self-instructions, applying learning strategies, keeping a learning journal, monitoring learning, and using what was learned.

Teachers also promote the following additional requirements, which are necessary for and specific to advanced language proficiency through self-directed learning:

- Reading widely across a broad range of topics
- Paying attention to and collecting new words all the time
- Writing regularly and receiving feedback on writing
- Engaging in interaction with proficient speakers frequently

Examples of Practice 3g

Teachers foster in learners a habit and passion for reading self-selected texts. To read broadly, one has to become a curious, passionate reader. Reading must become a habit. Habits take much longer to establish than a few lessons. They require persistence and nurturing over time. Teachers provide learners with texts that turn them on to reading and allow them to experience pleasure and joy in the activity. This requires a fresh approach with each developing reader. Miller (2009) made an ardent case for how adults might find their inner reader, and suggested the following action plan:

- Set aside a little time and commit to reading every day.
- Choose books on topics that interest you.
- Read more books for children to experience the happiness of child readers.
- Take recommendations from your colleagues and children.
- Investigate the books recommended for you by the book industry.
- Keep your own record of what you have read in a notebook.
- Reflect on your reading, and talk to others about your favorite reads.

Teachers kindle in learners a curiosity and love for collecting vocabulary. The vocabulary size needed for independent reading of fiction and newspapers is around 9,000 word families. Movies require around 7,000 word families, and television interviews 3,000–6,000 (Nation, 2006). Although it is never too late to learn new words at any age (Hellman, 2011), the scope of word learning is an enormous challenge for the adult English learner. To ease this, teachers provide them with word lists that help them determine the relative frequency of words they encounter, to judge whether or not a word is worth memorizing. Teachers may also provide lists of technical words that are useful in their areas of interest and employment along with vocabulary learning strategies (table 3.6) and various techniques to aid their memory: word journals, vocabulary cards, sticky notes, and photos they take (Hellman, 2018a, 2018b).

Teachers support writing outside the classroom. It is difficult for teachers to support learners' writing outside the classroom (Salva & Matis, 2017), which is why they explore with students writing opportunities. One form of meaningful written communication is journaling about new words, books read, and other learning that occurred through daily interactions. Teachers ask learners to reflect on questions like *How do I learn best?*, *How do I enjoy learning?*, and *What have I done to manage a situation?* Teachers also encourage learners to participate in social media. On many social media sites, translanguaging is a preferred form of communication among bilingual friends, which can be energizing to developing writers. Teachers encourage developing writers to correspond with a mentor, who can validate their learning and support them with constructive feedback. Community volunteers and faith-based groups are in good positions to serve learners in that role.

Principle 4. Adapt Lesson Delivery as Needed

Seth teaches adult citizenship education for high-beginner ESL students. He follows the lesson plans available from the Citizenship Resource Center (uscis.gov/citizenship). Although his students are on the same English language functioning level, they are profoundly different in their background experiences and content knowledge. A third of his students have no experience with some basic concepts, like governments, constitution, elections, or civil rights. The others do not need elaborate explanations of the fundamentals; they are ready for the specifics and for learning the English labels for concepts they already understand.

To teach the basics, Seth has collected supplementary materials: a set of infographics, which are easy-to-remember visual explainers. Whenever students need preteaching of main concepts, he already has well-designed, ready-to-use explanations.

Seth begins every topic by activating his students' background knowledge with some type of brainstorming activity. During this time, he carefully observes to identify who might need preteaching of key ideas. At times, he pulls learners aside for preteaching in a small group, and sometimes he assigns peer tutors to go over a main concept using an infographic from his collection. The brief peer-tutoring sessions benefit both partners because they provide one-on-one interaction and authentic language practice. Although they derail the lesson somewhat, the modifications are worth it for both language and content learning.

The success of instruction depends on more than a carefully crafted lesson plan. When we interact with learners in a lesson, we may encounter a number of obstacles. Learners might lack knowledge we had assumed they had. They might show staggering differences in content knowledge or in language skills. They may lack key vocabulary, or the lesson may be too easy for them. They may not be progressing with the material at a similar pace. Teachers often must decide to adapt a lesson within seconds, and they are prepared for this.

PRACTICE 4A **Teachers check comprehension frequently and adjust instruction according to learner responses.**

Teachers need to know in real time that they are being understood and that every learner is mentally engaged in relevant tasks. They check whether learners have understood instruction throughout lessons to detect misunderstandings promptly and help learners get right back on track.

Examples of Practice 4a

Teachers use techniques that allow learners to comprehend auditory input. Processing spoken language is a demanding activity for language learners. Everyone varies in how long they can pay attention to speech that is only partially comprehensible and in our tolerance levels for what we do not understand. To avoid learner anxiety and disinterest due to partial comprehension, teachers can prompt learners to quickly debrief after every few minutes of instruction and actively monitor them while they do so. Some ways to debrief include the following:

- jotting down notes in their learning journal
- talking with a partner about what they understand
- teaching a partner what they have just learned
- writing a clarification question on an index card or on a mini dry-erase board
- sending a text message to the teacher
- leaving a comment on a class response board (hard copy or electronic)
- rating their level of comprehension with a hand signal

Teachers reteach in small focus groups. Based on the results of comprehension checks, teachers can gather small groups to revisit lesson concepts or to slow the pace of instruction for some learners. This activity does not have to take instructional time from other learners, who can proceed with lesson activities. During these reteachings, teachers can employ comprehensible input techniques, concentrate on what is the most important, spend extra time in practice activities, or add in just-in-time teaching of concepts that they previously did not make explicit.

Teachers make use of instructional routines. They establish routines in the classroom as a practical way to improve comprehension. Teachers lower learners' processing loads by ensuring they are clear on how to complete tasks, what their roles are, and what is expected of them. Here are a few examples that indicate instructional routines:

- posted daily schedule
- posted lesson objectives
- timeline for projects with checkpoints and deadlines
- menu of choice activities
- poster showing roles for collaborative learning groups
- poster showing academic discussion moves
- step-by-step task explanations for common learning activities
- displays of the stages of the writing process
- task explanations for apps and software
- posted log-in information and password reminders
- to-do lists and checklists of tasks/skills

PRACTICE 4B **Teachers adjust their talk, the task, or the materials according to learner responses.**

Teachers employ many techniques to quickly modify task and materials difficulty levels. When seeing confused faces, teachers turn to the board to show what they mean with a quick sketch. They may simplify and limit the information to a few main points, cut longer readings to a single paragraph, or let learners utilize an electronic translation. They may interject a quick translation or elaborate by giving concrete examples. Teachers may assign a partner or a classroom volunteer. They may provide a think-aloud to model how they might go about completing a task. Teachers apply available modifications in a systematic way.

Examples of Practice 4b

Teachers use various forms of scaffolding. Scaffolding is a temporary support that enables the learner to perform a task with help. When learners can perform a task with some form of scaffolding, they are progressing toward mastery but are not yet independent. Teachers use the two main types of scaffolding: social supports and materials supports. Social supports involve assistance from a peer or someone more capable. Materials supports provide help with visuals, abstracts, outlines, or home language explanations. Additional examples of these supports appear in table 3.7. Exemplary teachers recognize the stopgap nature of scaffolding and gradually remove these supports to ensure that learners do eventually achieve independent mastery.

Table 3.7	Scaffolding types: Materials supports and social supports	
Social supports	• One-on-one with teacher • Teacher-led small group • Partner work • Home language partner • Peer-tutor • Classroom volunteer/tutor • Self-selected study group	• Small group with equally skilled members • Small group with mixed ability members • Collaborative group with assigned roles • Interpreter
Materials supports	• Illustrations • Graphic organizers • Infographics • Tables and charts • Outlines • Forms • Sentence frames • Models of completed assignments	• Glossaries • Home language texts • Dual-language texts • Picture dictionaries • Simplified texts • Texts elaborated with explanations and hyperlinks • Readers with controlled vocabulary

Teachers adapt tasks to learners' functioning levels. They know the functioning levels of their learners in the various skills and have working knowledge of the descriptors of functioning levels, which enables them to adapt tasks quickly and appropriately. Teachers may find it helps to have a reminder of the functioning level descriptors displayed in the classroom for quick reference. Different adult education programs utilize different functioning level descriptors, usually based on the standards or the assessments they use.

When adapting a task, teachers can change the length of the response they expect from learners: a word, a phrase, a sentence, a paragraph, a multiparagraph composition, or a two-minute speech. They adjust expectations for variety in vocabulary or phrase patterns. They can shorten or lengthen readings and add or reduce scaffolding. Additionally, teachers may change the product of learning so that learners can demonstrate what they know, for example, through an oral presentation rather than a paper, or through a project rather than a test.

Teachers take cues from their learners' output to adjust their language. In classrooms where teachers do most of the talking and students respond with a single brief turn, teachers are not matching their language to their learners' functioning level. The following classroom examples illustrate the difference between a classroom dominated by teacher talk and a classroom where the teacher builds on cues from the beginner learners and matches her output to their level.

Classroom 1

Teacher:	Last week, we discussed using the past tense for telling events that happened in the past. Like yesterday or last week or years ago. And we read a story that had a number of verbs in the past tense. Some of the past tense words ended in *–ed*, but some of the past tense words did not. Do you remember what we called past tense verbs that ended in *–ed*? Omar?
Omar:	Wanted.
Teacher:	Yes. *Wanted* is a good example of a past tense verb that ends in *–ed*. But how do we call verbs in general that form the past tense with the *–ed* ending? Margret?
Margret:	Waited.
Teacher:	Yes. *Waited* is another example of this type of verb. We call these regular verbs. We form the past tense of regular verbs with *–ed*. Like *want-wanted, wait-waited, cry-cried, dance-danced*. So what are regular verbs, Fartun?
Fartun:	Danced? No danced.
Teacher:	Yes, *danced* is a regular verb. It is a regular verb because we spell it with an *–ed* in the past tense. It doesn't sound like *–ed* when we say it. It sounds like *t*. The *–ed* can sound differently when we say it. It can sound like *d*, or *t*, or *–ed*. It's a regular verb if we spell it with *–ed* regardless of how it sounds when we say it.

Classroom 2

Teacher:	Here is our story. We wrote this story last week. Let's read the story again.
Students:	[*reading with a partner*] We lived in Pakistan. We wanted to come to Australia. We waited for a visa. We received our visa after five years. We celebrated with our family. I cried because I was happy. I danced because I was happy. I wanted to come right away. We took a plane. We arrived in Australia last year.
Teacher:	Read the story again. Find the verbs in the story. Make a list with the verbs.

Partners reread the story aloud and list verbs. The teacher listens in on the pair work to assess how they are doing and engages them in pronouncing the final sound clearly in each verb. The teacher is careful to speak in short, simple sentences. She uses the same sentences multiple times: Where is the verb in this sentence? Say the verb slowly. What does it sound like? What is the last sound? Do you hear d, t, or –ed? She asks one question at a time, then allows wait time for the learners to respond. She provides feedback on what they say.

In the second classroom example, you see that the teacher used short, well-formed, simple sentences with controlled vocabulary and maintained a balance between her turns and the turns of her students. This style of interaction is much more suitable for her beginner learners than that of the first classroom.

Teachers model and scaffold academic language use. Although teacher talk should not dominate the language classroom, teachers are an essential language model. Many adult learners do not have access to comprehensible input that uses a formal register, which makes it difficult—if not impossible—for them to acquire it. Without academic language, learners cannot develop advanced proficiency in English.

When teachers notice students using everyday language instead of academic language, they may call attention to preconstructed phrases, which are associated with various rhetorical moves. They may point to charts displaying these formulas in the form of sentence frames to remind students how they can express various cognitive-academic functions. Table 3.8 shows an example of a classroom poster that models academic language for beginner to intermediate ELs. Teachers can grow this repertoire to include additional cognitive functions, such as inferring, comparing, contrasting, deducing, and evaluating (Fisher, Frey, & Rothenberg, 2008).

Teachers make learners aware of suitable learning strategies. If students struggle during instruction, teachers draw their attention to learning strategies that may help them succeed. Look back to Practice 3f for the types of strategies to bring into focus. Interjecting just-in-time teaching of specific strategies can be more effective than teaching the strategies explicitly in an isolated way. Teachers can also highlight when they notice some learners using a strategy productively and have them share a quick reflection on how the strategy has worked for them.

Table 3.8	Academic language poster for beginner to intermediate adult learners	
Function	**What am I thinking?**	**How can I say it?**
Agreeing	I think the same.	I agree that . . . You are right about . . .
Adding	I have more information.	I would like to add to that. Here is another example for that.
Clarifying	I don't understand well.	Do I understand you correctly? Are you saying that . . . Can you tell me more about that? Would you mind explaining that idea differently?
Asking for feedback	I want to know what you think.	What is your perspective on this? What feedback can you give me?
Affirming	I like this.	I appreciate your input. Thanks for raising that point. That's an excellent suggestion.
Disagreeing	I think differently.	I disagree with . . . because . . . My thinking on this is different in that . . .
Explaining	I want you to understand me.	What I mean by this is that . . . Here is an example that will show you what I mean.
Justifying	I know why I think this.	The reason for this is that . . . The evidence for this comes from . . .
Analyzing	This has parts.	This consists of . . . The most important element of this is . . . There are . . . parts to this. One is . . . . The second is . . .
Sequencing	This needs steps.	Please follow this process. The first step is to . . . The second step is to . . .
Summarizing	This is what I take away.	Here is the gist of what we decided. These were the main points of our discussion. The text was mainly about . . .

Principle 5. Monitor and Assess Student Language Development

Toni's learners have interrupted formal education. She teaches a low literacy class. Part of what she teaches is how to make the most of learning in schools. Toni's students use a portfolio to learn to reflect on what they have studied, what they can do, and what they need to tackle next. The class works on the portfolios as a group. Toni is teaching them about the value of review, self-assessment, and reflection.

She begins each unit by introducing the theme and a related big question. For example, one of the units is "Community." The big question for this unit is: How can we find services in our community? Students learn about the location of services, how to write addresses, and how to locate places using an address with a paper map and an online search tool. The class visits several service locations and writes a simple story about each: the library, city hall, a bank, and a community center. They use a bulletin board to document learning throughout the unit. The bulletin board displays the big question and the key vocabulary. This way, they create a display about each place with photos, realia, and the stories that they write about each visit.

At the end of the unit, the learners reflect on each display by writing "I can" statements. For example, "I can find the children's room in the library," or "I can write an address." They also write statements about what they want to learn. They share "I can" statements with each other and display these on the bulletin board. At the end, Toni takes photos of the displays, and they collect these into their portfolios. By the end of the year, learners have a complete book to show what they have achieved. They can review the big questions, all the key vocabulary, the stories, and the "I can" statements. They present these portfolio photos as part of the slideshow at the end-of-year celebration, which is always a source of accomplishment and delight for students and their guests.

Adult English learners who participate in basic education, literacy learning, and workforce development are often less sure of themselves than other learners. They tend to expect much faster progress and may not anticipate the years of preparation it takes to achieve advanced proficiency in English and to be fully literate. They make progress in varied ways and at differing rates. For these reasons, the role of assessment in adult education is different than the role of assessment in K–12 education.

Teachers conduct assessments to answer critical questions in a systematic way: Are my learners progressing toward their learning goals? To what extent have they achieved the objectives? Are they ready to move to the next level? Are there weak spots in their performance that we should work on? However, with adult learners, some other questions may be equally important in terms of their eventual attainment in English. For example, are they motivated to continue? Do they have the skills to continue learning independently? Teachers of adult learners approach assessment with the main aims of keeping them motivated, building their self-confidence, and helping them experience the results of their effort.

PRACTICE 5A Teachers monitor student errors.

An important way to assess our learners is to interact with them in English. We acquire a great deal of information about them both when they produce language freely and when they produce language in controlled ways (e.g., responding to prompts). The more language students produce and the more varied language tasks they practice, the faster they learn. The types of errors learners make in their output can indicate their current understanding of language forms and vocabulary. We might also notice misunderstandings related to their workplace, child's school, and the like. Though it is informative to monitor errors, we should be thoughtful with how we respond to them.

Examples of Practice 5a

Teachers note errors and decide how to best respond to them. Teachers understand that errors in their learners' output are normal and complex. They can be

- due to memory limitations during language processing;
- developmental, indicative of partial understandings;
- representative of forms in the learner's previously learned languages;
- the effect of mishearing; or
- a misapplication of an analogy (e.g., if "let's do lunch" is correct, then "let's do sandwich" should be fine also).

Teachers know that learners who do not make errors may not be at an advantage because they could be avoiding forms that they are uncertain about.

Teachers attend to errors that interfere with meaning-making and those that are persistent but not too far beyond a learner's current level of understanding of language forms. In the case of adult learners, troublesome, persistent errors usually require more than error correction. These features can be addressed through form-focused instruction followed by extensive practice (Ellis & Shintani, 2014).

Teachers respond proactively when they detect incorrect understandings. Though most language errors are a normal part of language acquisition, incorrect understandings of content can be the effect of instruction. Teachers can address these with reteaching and additional practice. At times, the whole class may need a mini-lesson on what was misunderstood, or it may be better to gather with a small group of learners who need more support.

PRACTICE 5B Teachers provide ongoing effective feedback strategically.

Feedback is one of the important tools of language teachers. A large body of research exists on what makes feedback effective for second language acquisition (e.g., Nassaji & Kartchava, 2017). The tone and delivery of feedback matter for how learners receive it. The best way to determine what type of feedback may be viewed by learners as supportive and useful is to observe the learners: notice how they respond to various forms of feedback, whether they apply the corrections they received, and whether they are motivated to speak and write more in response to the feedback. Teachers can also explicitly instruct learners how they can respond to corrective feedback in their output, and they can survey learners on their preferences for different types of feedback.

Examples of Practice 5b

Teachers use a repertoire of oral feedback strategies. Without doubt, the most common feedback move of teachers in English-speaking classrooms is to tell their students, "good job." This is a positive but generic form of feedback that lacks the specificity to help learners improve either the content or the form of their answer. Exemplary teachers use a variety of specific, intentional feedback strategies.

Revoicing is a useful form of affirmative feedback in which the teacher broadcasts an individual learner's response to the whole class. The intended message is that "I have heard you. I would like the whole class to hear what you have just shared."

A slightly more corrective version of this is known as the recast. A recast is when the teacher repeats the learner response with some changes to make it better formed, but without giving any other indication—either with tone or expression—that there was anything wrong with the original answer. The message conveyed is "Yes, I accept your answer. This is my way of saying the same thing." The recast is one of the most basic feedback tools of language teachers because it is unobtrusive and does not have a negative charge, yet it provides a model that can be seen in contrast with the language form the learner has used. Many learners are able to notice the contrast between the teacher form and their own; they find the teacher offering useful and do not feel corrected before the class.

There is a full repertoire of feedback moves for corrective responses. Each interrupts the flow of communication to a different degree. The most effective are those that require learners to produce a self-correction as opposed to those where the teacher supplies the correction (Lyster & Saito, 2010). Explanations of oral feedback strategies are included in figure 3.2.

FIGURE 3.2   Types of oral feedback

1. **Revoice.** The teacher repeats a learner's response for the whole class without corrections.
   Teacher: What can you do when your child is absent?
   Student: I call the school. I call the office.
   Teacher: Estela says, "I call the school. I call the office."

2. **Recast.** The teacher repeats a learner's response but reformulates some part to make it better formed, grammatically correct, or correctly pronounced.
   Teacher: What can you do when your child is absent?
   Student: I call sku office.
   Teacher: Right. You call the school office.

3. **Explicit correction.** The teacher indicates to the learner that an error occurred, and the teacher supplies the correct form.
   Student: I call sku office.
   Teacher: We say, "I call the school office." Remember to use *the. The* school office.

4. **Prompts for self-repair** are various signals to learners to alert them that an error occurred, which they should try to correct.

   a. **Repetition.** The teacher repeats the learner utterance with a question intonation.
      Student: I call sku office.
      Teacher: I call sku office?

   b. **Nonverbal clues.** The teacher makes a facial expression to indicate that something is wrong, and some form of repair of communication is in order.
      Student: I call sku office.
      Teacher: [Teacher shows puzzled look.]

   c. **Clarification request.** The teacher responds with a phrase that indicates the message was unclear.
      Student: I call sku office.
      Teacher: Say again, please?

   d. **Metalinguistic clues.** The teacher responds with a gesture or expression that references an error type.
      Student: I call sku office.
      Teacher: Remember? The article *the*? Say it again.

   e. **Elicitation.** The teacher repeats the learner response up to the point where the error occurred, which the teacher would like the learner to correct. This is the oral equivalent of a fill-in-the-blank task.
      Student: I call sku office.
      Teacher: Again. I call [*lengthens word* call *and pauses midsentence*] _____.

   f. **Open-ended questions.** The teacher asks a question to prompt the learner's focus on a language form.
      Student: I call sku office.
      Teacher: How can we say this more clearly?

Finally, not all error types can be treated with oral feedback. Local errors are more suitable for error correction than global errors. For example, it is easier to correct the ending on a noun from singular to plural in a single instance (a local error) than it is to prompt the learner to recognize that there is a class of nouns that are noncount, which cannot be used with the indefinite article—for example, *a rice*, *an information* (a global error). Global errors lend themselves to explicit instruction.

Teachers align their feedback strategy to learners' functioning level and individual preferences. Although feedback is an important tool of language teachers and research supports its use, it only makes sense for adults in the form that they like to receive it and can make use of it. This applies to both oral and written feedback. Some teachers come from a tradition where they do not think they have completed their job until they have thoroughly proofread and marked up every error in students' written work. Not only is this wasted effort, but it can be demoralizing to learners, who are developing their ability to express their ideas in a new language. Teachers ask adult learners what goals they are working on and what specifically they would like feedback on. They find time to meet with students one-on-one to help them clarify the ideas they would like to express, which can be much more beneficial than giving them corrections on their sentences.

Teachers educate students about the use of commentary on their writing. Experienced teachers usually have a set approach for responding to their students' writing. However, their commenting approach may be problematic for adult learners from diverse schooling backgrounds where they may not have had many formal writing assignments or where teachers evaluated them differently.

Teachers reflect on their approach to commentary. They clarify what they do and what they would like their commentary to achieve, and then they bring it in line with their learners' goals. Teachers also record their approach in a way that learners can comprehend it, with a goal of having a system for commentary that is both educative and teachable. The full cycle of a sound feedback approach is formed by teaching the system to learners explicitly, practicing with them how to apply commentary, and reflecting on the usefulness of the feedback system (Goldstein, 2005).

Teachers give specific, actionable, just-in-time feedback on assignments. Evaluative comments that students receive long after they submitted assignments can rarely be constructive. Learners find feedback much more valuable while they are actively working on the task, especially when the feedback is encouraging and specific to aspects of the work they can understand and still change. Rather than delaying feedback until the product is finished, teachers can embed feedback checkpoints into assignments, when learners are highly motivated to attend to guidance and to act on the teacher's recommendations.

PRACTICE 5C Teachers use effective formative assessment strategies.

Continuous interaction with learners about the learning process is essential to making headway. Both the teacher and the learner need to know whether their actions are bringing them closer to their learning goals. Information gained from formative assessments can help steer them in the right direction. This process also helps learners develop understandings of their learning, which benefits them beyond the classroom by building their capacity for self-regulation and independence.

Formative assessment is ongoing and occurs as teachers gather information about student learning during the instructional process. Its purpose is to guide teachers in making instructional decisions. Most formative assessments are informal and occur on the spot (Echevarría et al., 2017). Other formative assessments are conducted to evaluate lesson objectives or performance on assignments. They may be graded, marked on a checklist, written as anecdotal notes, recorded as voice notes, or collected through short quizzes, writing tasks, and presentations.

Examples of Practice 5c

Teachers dialogue with learners about the usefulness of particular learning tasks and assignments. Giving students opportunities to discuss which activities are working is a way to share ownership of learning. When learners have control over how they practice, they gain responsibility for their knowledge and skills. This dialogue can occur in a more formal way with a teacher-made survey and a discussion around focus questions, or it can be more open-ended and exploratory. Learners can identify instances where they felt they were really learning and explore why the task, activity, or teacher feedback was especially helpful.

Teachers employ self- and peer-assessment activities. Self-assessment is a life skill that can be taught in the classroom. Teachers can ask students to examine their own performance in relation to models and criteria. Students can describe the qualities of their work and the changes they notice from one assignment to the next. They can take inventory of skills that they have developed and skills they need to keep working on. They can explore opportunities that can help them close the gap between their current performance and the model they would like to reach.

Teachers use rubrics to align assignment expectations with their assessments. Particularly useful tools for formative assessment are analytical rubrics. Analytical rubrics separate relevant components of an assignment and describe each component with performance levels. Because each component is detailed separately, the rubric provides guidance for completing the assignment. Learners know what matters and what to pay attention to. They are able to focus on one component at a time. They can compare their work to the level descriptors and see how close or far they are from the criteria that describe excellent performance. An analytical rubric can double as a diagnostic tool and shows learners the steps toward success (O'Malley & Valdez Pierce, 1996).

PRACTICE 5D Teachers involve learners in decisions and reflections about summative assessments.

Summative assessment, in contrast to formative assessment, is usually conducted at the end of a longer period of learning (a semester or year). Standardized testing and program-wide tests are examples of summative assessment. Publicly funded adult education programs use such assessments to report on their participants' progress, mainly to provide funders with a measure of program performance. Programs may also use tests to present students with proof of English language proficiency at a specific level of performance or with a recognized credential earned through their coursework.

Regardless of use, standardized tests do not provide a full profile of the learning that individual students accomplish. Teachers should consider other forms of summative assessments, which are better for evaluating the outcomes of learning. Adult learners benefit from having control over end products that show what they have gained from instruction and can help decide what types of formative assessments they will take. In turn, these products of learning also provide teachers with valuable information for improving their teaching practice.

Examples of Practice 5d

Teachers give learners choices to demonstrate their achievements of learning goals in multiple ways and engage them in reflection. There is no limit to what artifacts may serve as evidence of learning. Learners can construct a story of their learning in any number of ways. When given a choice, it is unlikely that most individuals would tell that story by showing quiz grades or standardized test scores. The construction of a personal learning story takes searching and reflection. Alternative summative assessments can help learners answer authentic questions, such as the following:

- What have I written, and what is my writing mainly about?
- What can I read?
- How did I feel about having conversations at work when I started this class, and how do I feel now?
- What was my journey from not comprehending a word of television and radio programs to being able to understand TED talks?
- How did I go from reading wordless books with my child to reading chapter books with her?
- What were those learning activities that really grew my vocabulary, and what is the size of my vocabulary now?

Questions like these are worth contemplating because they can motivate continued learning.

Teachers allow their adult learners to define their own preferences for the assessments that are meant to evidence their learning, in part to help their learners develop the self-assessment skills they need on a lifelong language acquisition journey. Table 3.9 lists alternative assessments that learners can select from to present their learning narratives.

Teachers help learners share the products of their learning in meaningful ways. Adults are not seeking grades, but they value when their stories are read, their compositions appear in anthologies, and their blogs or video channels have subscribers. Being involved in the community is especially meaningful. Adult learners can be invited speakers at community events, or they can organize and create their own program for a speaker series. They can produce handbooks for future program participants based on what they would have liked to know from the start of the class. Adult immigrants can add their life stories to historical archives and digital collections (e.g., the Minnesota's Immigrants collection), which validates the importance of their lived experiences. Inviting the community to recognize these achievements serves to motivate learners to continue their education.

Teachers use feedback from learners to make improvements to their instruction. One of the main questions that assessments should answer is to what extent the learning needs of individuals are being met through the activities in the course, whether in or outside the classroom. We can probe this question informally through dialogue with learners, and we can collect this information systematically through surveys and open-ended reflection prompts.

Surveys are convenient because even preliterate students can rate their perceptions of various class and home learning activities. Teachers can also study learners' artifacts to decide whether particular tasks were productive. Learners' preference to include certain artifacts in their portfolio may also be a good indication of the value they attribute to those learning products.

Effective teachers respond to feedback they receive from learners through surveys and summative assessments by adjusting their instruction in ways to better engage learners on their functional level, to provide them with opportunities that are meaningful to them, to help them make deeper investments in the learning process, and to guide them to overcome barriers.

Table 3.9	Alternative summative assessments that can reveal learning	
Skill	**Assessment**	
Listening	• List of audiobooks finished • Sample of radio broadcasts/podcasts listened to • Recordings of online discussions (e.g., Zoom or Voice Thread) • Dictations • Information gap tasks • Response log of listening activities	• Channel created of favorite YouTube videos/TED talks viewed • Outlines or notes taken of talks/recordings • Favorite song lyrics • Journal entries about listening comprehension successes
Speaking	• Homework videos over time • Recorded presentations • Recorded role-plays, discussions • Recorded storytelling • Voice notes, videos	• Extemporaneous talk • Rubrics completed by teacher of speaking observations • Evaluations of speaking assignments
Reading	• Selection of "can-read" texts • Log of readings completed • Reading response journal • Summaries, outlines, graphic organizers of texts • Display of favorite books	• List of books read with children • Oral review of favorite reads • Graph of pages read • Chart of reading improvement • Record of benchmark assessments • Live reading of self-selected text
Writing	• Selected writing assignments • Evaluations of writing assignments • Multiple drafts and rewrites • Dialogues written • Journal entries • Emails, personal and formal letters	• Text messages, comments, notes • Blogs, social media pages • Photos of completed forms • Presentation of best sentences • Portfolio and reflection
Vocabulary	• Personal word lists • Words mastered from high-frequency word lists and the academic word list • Inventory of word parts known • Labeled diagrams and picture	• Learner-made picture dictionary • Vocabulary notebook • Glossaries • Results of vocabulary size tests

Principle 6. Engage and Collaborate within a Community of Practice

Teacher: *In class we have been practicing a strategy that helps with being able to assess the readability of a text. This is important for choosing texts that a reader can manage. The gist of it is that the reader previews the text for background knowledge and interest, and then examines paragraph-length selections for the ratio of unknown words and for sentence length. I think that the students understand the strategy. I'd like to know if they find it useful and whether it actually works for them. Is this something you could work with during tutoring?*

Tutor: *Maybe I can help with that, although I don't know much about readability. Can you share with me what you taught in class?*

Teacher: *Of course. I have a handout, and we created a poster that shows the steps. They select several paragraphs randomly, each about 100 words in length, and either they highlight or make a list of the words that are unfamiliar. More than five different unknown words per paragraph indicates that the text may be too difficult to read without needing to consult a dictionary constantly, which is very disruptive to reading comprehension and to the pleasure of reading.*

Tutor: *I think I get it. So how do you want me to find out if the strategy is working for them?*

Teacher: *First, see if they understand it. Have them tell you the strategy.*

Tutor: *Okay, so I'll say, "Show me how you select a good book for you. Show me your strategy."*

Teacher: *Exactly. So, you note whether they know how to use the strategy. They may have a completely different way.*

Tutor: *Okay, next, I think I should have them use the strategy to select a just-right text. I'll say, "Select from these books the best one for you." I'll give them some time to apply the strategy and to choose the best book from the pile.*

Teacher: *That's good. When they've made their choice, you ask them how they made the choice and why this is the best book for them.*

Tutor: *I'm writing these questions down. How did you choose this book? Why is this the best book for you? Next, I should give them some time to read the book. On their own.*

Teacher: *Yes, allow them five or ten minutes of reading on their own. You can pick up a book yourself and read along. Then, after some reading, you ask: How is your book? Did you choose the right book? Why or why not? How did the strategy work? Do you think the strategy needs to change?*

Tutor: *Okay. I have a lot of questions on my list now. And they require more than a "yes" or "no." They need to elaborate and justify their answers. Maybe it would be good for me to create a questionnaire, so I can record their responses. That'll help you answer your question, which was, Is the text-selection strategy working for the students?*

Teacher: *You're right. That would be a systematic way to collect the data. I think we'll learn a lot from that.*

The success of adult learners who are developing literacy and workforce skills at the same time that they are learning English as a new language depends on more than a single teacher can provide. Collaboration within a community of practice can enhance a teacher's expertise, multiply the productivity of a single educator's effort, and contribute to the sustainability of high-impact adult education programs.

Collaborators vary by program type. For example, teachers in workplace education programs typically collaborate with company representatives, supervisors, and specialists on writing curriculum, obtaining resources, and evaluating outcomes. Teachers in multilevel adult basic education programs work as a team on the continuous improvement of key elements of their program. In community-based language programs, teachers engage with volunteers, who serve in various roles. Professional organizations are another source of communities of practice for adult educators. Through them, teachers can join online study groups or carry out joint projects. Members can exchange materials and serve as mentors for one another.

PRACTICE 6A Teachers are fully engaged in their profession.

Although all teachers would like to feel fully prepared for the profession on the first day of their teaching careers, few of us really believe that we are. The more time teachers spend actively engaging with their students, the more they feel the need to develop and grow to help them achieve their goals and overcome unique challenges.

Examples of Practice 6a

Teachers engage in reflective practice to grow professionally. Dewey (1933) discussed reflective practice in his exploration of experience, interaction, and reflection and later, Schön (1990) enlarged on the notion by defining reflective practice as that process where professionals learn from their experiences and gain insights into themselves and their practice. Schön (1990) differentiated between reflection in action and reflection on action.

Reflection in action occurs when teachers reflect on a teaching or learning behavior as it occurs. Reflection on action involves reflecting after the event: reviewing, analyzing, and evaluating the situation.

Reflection in action asks for self-observation as we teach, monitoring of the choices we make, and then writing down notes upon completion of the lesson. This is the skill of critical inquiry. Some teachers use a journal for daily reflections. Others write anecdotally with the idea of sharing the experience with a peer.

Reflection on action requires that teachers have solitary time to think about the lesson and to reflect on what occurred, why it happened, how the teaching behavior related to theory or background knowledge, and what ideas it might suggest for future teaching situations. This is the skill of self-reflection. During this time, we examine our assumptions of everyday practice and evaluate them. The process can be distilled into three essential questions:

- What did I do?
- How did it go?
- What did I learn?

Reflective practice, sometimes called critical reflection, can lead to positive professional growth: "Unless teachers develop the practice of critical reflection, they stay trapped in unexamined judgments, interpretations, assumptions, and expectations. Approaching teaching as a reflective practitioner involves fusing personal beliefs and values into a professional identity" (Larrivee, 2000, p. 293). Teachers who engage in cyclical critical reflection become teachers who constantly test hypotheses about teaching and learning and experiment with these hypotheses in light of the context of the learning and the students who are affected. In this way, teachers are constantly renewed and steadily increase their professional competencies.

Teachers participate in continuous learning and ongoing professional development. The changes in the population of our learners and the quest for new learning outcomes, which reflect the demands of our society, press upon us to keep step with our profession. Our response to these challenges is to work continually toward professional involvement and lifelong learning. Initially, individual interest will guide our engagement in professional learning—our passion for theater or languages, our need to know more about literacy learning activities, an interest in particular cultural groups, or our perceived difficulty to manage a multilevel classroom.

Through personal learning networks, developed among teachers, administrators, grant implementers, specialists, and tutors in our programs, we can question, exchange experiences, share materials, design workshops, develop study groups, pursue online training, write curriculum units, and discuss our classes: *What I did today, and what I learned as a result.* These conversations are too rare in our overscheduled days, when we shuffle from one responsibility to the next. But they lead to the reflection and development that are so necessary to well-being in our teaching lives.

By participating in professional development associations, we can stay abreast of best practices. We can join a professional English teaching organization, like TESOL International Association or its regional affiliates, the Australian Council of TESOL Associations, or TESL Canada. We might engage in organizations that focus on specific learner populations, such as the Literacy Education and Second Language Learning for Adults and the Commission on Adult Basic Education. Those who work in special contexts, such as the military, correctional institutions, or workforce education may connect with a special interest group within the American Association for Adult and Continuing Education. We can attend and present at local, state, or national conferences or sponsored academies and symposia. We can also read and write for the publications of these organizations to get new insights and exchange ideas. Volunteering for these groups is also a rewarding way to form deeper bonds with our professional colleagues.

In addition, we can pursue learning options in specific skill areas related to teaching—technology, curriculum development, or assessment, for example. We can complete online courses and seminars, or apply for a grant, fellowship, or award to enhance our teaching or to pursue graduate education. The opportunities are almost endless; however, they require an investment of our time, and often our money. In exchange, we reap rewards not only in our own professional accomplishments, but also in the assurances that we have improved learners' lives by helping them move toward their desired version of themselves.

PRACTICE 6B Teachers coordinate and collaborate with colleagues.

When teachers practice in isolation—show up to deliver classes, plan on their own, hold the required office hours, and then leave—many opportunities are missed, and each person must reinvent solutions that another colleague may have already vetted (Honigsfeld & Dove, 2010). Adult educators often complain of the lack of resources to support their work, yet they forego the benefits that their immediate professional community can provide for them. From the perspective of administrators, teacher collaboration is a performance indicator of program quality. It signals that teachers share pedagogical resources and implement a shared vision with the intent to create improved conditions (U.S. Department of Education, Office of Career, Technical, and Adult Education, 2015). Collaboration is also a necessity for program sustainability, especially where programs are implementing rigorous, standards-based curricula that must have continuity over several years (U.S. Department of Education, Office of Career, Technical, and Adult Education, 2016).

Examples of Practice 6b

Teachers meet with colleagues to develop curriculum and to coplan. Teachers' schedules rarely permit lengthy meetings about curriculum planning unless they are specialists with designated time or they are serving in a formal role on a curriculum implementation team. However, it is possible for two or three teachers who share the same schedule to find time for brief, informal discussions where they can compare notes on instructional objectives, swap lesson plans, or exchange ideas for an interesting unit. With administrative support, teachers who are productive collaborators are in a good position to assume leadership for more comprehensive curricular planning.

Teachers share assessment results and make collective decisions about the placement and learning goals of individual students. There are three points in time where a meeting to discuss assessment data is the most consequential:

- When placement decisions are being made based on the results of intake assessments
- Midway through the semester to review how learners are progressing toward the desired course outcomes and what additional supports may be necessary to boost their performance
- Upon the completion of the course to evaluate whether the results of the summative assessments support that learners have met the course expectations and their personal learning goals. This is the right time to decide what adjustments may be needed to the coursework to advance the outcomes in future semesters.

In these conversations about assessments, teachers can serve each other as critical friends. Critical friends are in a trusted position to ask provocative questions, which let us take a step back to examine our data in earnest (Costa & Kallick, 1993). Critical friends know our context, our learners, the constraints, and the outcomes we wish to achieve; we can depend on them to be advocates for our work as well as for our students.

Teachers guide and apprentice tutors. They invest effort into training and coordinating with volunteers and instructional support staff in order to enhance their work with their invaluable services. In the vignette at the start of this section, the teacher and the tutor engaged spontaneously in an inquiry cycle to investigate the teacher's concern about the usefulness of a learning strategy, on which she spent valuable instructional time. The vignette suggests that even within brief conversations, the tutor was able to gain many insights into the curriculum, the desired learner outcomes, and the specific techniques used to achieve them. In turn, the tutor was able to extend the teacher's work and integrate the tutoring sessions well with the teacher's efforts in the classroom.

PRACTICE 6C Teachers utilize publicly available instructional resources for adult English learners.

Adult language and literacy programs are seriously underfunded relative to the per-pupil spending on other types of public education (e.g., the National Academies of Sciences, Engineering, and Medicine, 2017; Organisation for Economic Cooperation and Development, 2018, World Education, 2018). Given the limited funding, the cost of commercially available high-quality materials is high. Various agencies that support adult basic education have tried to ease this burden by making available free materials both for English language teaching and for teacher professional development. For example, in the United States, the LINCS resource collection is a major free online library of works commissioned through federal government funding. Here, adult educators can access online professional development and instructional toolkits and lesson plans. In Canada, the Centre for Canadian Language Benchmarks provides a large selection of free downloadable materials for students on every level. In Australia, the Adult Migrant English Program of the Department of Education and Training publishes free English teaching materials for volunteer tutors. Exemplary teachers of adult ELs have a solid knowledge base of and guide learners to free resources available via their government's initiatives to support the education of immigrant, migrant, and refugee populations.

Examples of Practice 6c

Teachers are familiar with and make use of free resources whenever available. Teachers who are mindful of adult learners' limited resources are careful about requiring the purchase of texts or apps, particularly when these are duplicative of free alternatives. They demonstrate and disseminate such resources via their learning networks. They involve learners in discussions about the pros and cons of open source vs. fee-based and subsidized vs. commercial materials, using these choices as teachable moments in problem solving. We include on our website links to lesson materials that are open educational resources (www.the6principles.org/adult-education).

Teachers keep abreast of new technologies for language learning. In our technology-driven world, the needs of learners are best served by teachers who can model for them the technologies they are expected to utilize for work, for communication and information gathering, and for lifelong learning. Our ability to do this depends on continually honing our own digital literacy. We also need hands-on practice with the learning management systems and the language learning technology tools that we expect students to use. Today's English language teachers may struggle to successfully integrate proprietary language teaching software into effective classroom instruction (Rosen & Stewart, 2015). Exemplary teachers approach such new advances as potential tools that can enhance both their students' efficacy with learning and the effectiveness of their teaching.

PRACTICE 6D Teachers participate in community partnerships.

There are innumerable ways in which partnerships can enhance the education of adult ELs. For example, many adult English language programs share space with agencies that provide services to the same population. Language programs may partner with refugee services, faith-based organizations, early childhood programs, community centers, libraries, and workplaces. Language programs may be just one part of one-stop service centers that provide comprehensive employment services. Adult literacy programs can be placed within other educational institutions that can help learners move through developmental coursework toward more advanced training in a streamlined fashion. Partnerships are more productive when stakeholders engage purposefully to achieve clearly articulated goals (Eddy & Amey, 2011).

Teachers and learners gain more from the partnership when they are aware of possibilities and when they are represented in the decision-making activities.

Examples of Practice 6d

Teachers advocate for students and program funding. The availability and quality of programs depend on the ebb and flow of funding in adult education. Resources are rarely commensurate with the demand for rigor and outcomes set by agencies that allocate budgets (Morgan, Waite, & Diecuch, 2017). Refugee and immigrant education in particular is subject to politics-driven decision-making, and budget cuts hurt those in our communities who are among the most vulnerable and who lack the means to advocate for themselves. Thus, advocacy for program resources falls on our shoulders. We are the ones who can help our learners tell their powerful stories, which communicate their hardships and personal victories. We are the witnesses who can provide our testimony that the transformation through adult literacy education is real and a superior return on our community's investment.

Teachers represent the interests of adult English learners in policy and decision-making. In addition to empowering our students through literacy and helping them lift their own voices, we can also work to ensure that laws and policies in our communities are favorable for our learners. We can express our concern where we notice discrimination or bigotry toward immigrants and refugees. We can promote cultural sensitivity and spread our passion for all cultures and languages. We can contact lawmakers about specific actions that they can take in support of our learners and their families. We can represent them on advisory boards or bring them with us to public forums where policies are being debated. We can join campaigns and take part in advocacy events.

A Look Back and a Look Ahead

The 6 Principles that Chapter 3 describes are the basic tenets that guide our profession. Some of these principles may overlap with the guidelines for other professionals in the adult basic education and adult foreign language teaching contexts. They concisely state what exemplary teaching of ELs requires teachers to do:

Principle 1. *Know Your Learners.* Teachers gather information about each learner's background, particularly those aspects that are consequential for instruction and their success. These include learners' home languages and cultures, their English language and literacy functioning levels, and all the factors that can support or hinder their language and literacy development in English.

Principle 2. *Create Conditions for Language Learning.* Teachers make their classes into spaces where students kindle their motivation to learn, practice, and take risks with language. Teachers work to secure all the essential conditions of second language acquisition, draw on beneficial conditions, and set high expectations for their learners.

Principle 3. *Design High-Quality Lessons for Language Development.* Teachers know what learners can do at their current level of functioning in English and what they need to learn next. Then, teachers determine lesson objectives, plan how they will facilitate comprehensible input, promote rich classroom conversations, decide on tasks that are relevant to learners' goals and encourage authentic language practice, and explicitly teach learning strategies, problem solving, and critical thinking skills.

Principle 4. *Adapt Lesson Delivery as Needed.* Teachers monitor their learners' comprehension, adjusting teacher talk or materials, differentiating instruction, and scaffolding tasks according to learners' English language and literacy functioning levels. In short, effective teaching of English learners requires decision-making during the lesson delivery on the basis of learner responses and actions and a solid understanding of the second language development process.

Principle 5. *Monitor and Assess Student Language Development.* Teachers gauge how well learners are making progress, note and evaluate the types of errors that students make, offer strategic feedback, and use a variety of assessment types to have learners demonstrate achievement.

Principle 6. *Engage and Collaborate within a Community of Practice.* Teachers understand that they can serve English learners better when they work with professional colleagues. Teaching ELs requires that teachers be part of a community of practice within their program and the broader educator community that affords them access to ongoing professional development.

Each of The 6 Principles calls for teachers of English learners to develop professionally. Chapter 4 builds on The 6 Principles described here, but provides additional examples of practice, which serve to accommodate learners who face specific types of challenges to their engagement and learning success.

Additional resources pertaining to this chapter are available at www.the6principles.org/adult-education.

4 ADDRESSING THE CHALLENGES WITH ADULT ENGLISH LEARNERS

"Inclusive, good-quality education is a foundation for dynamic and equitable societies." (Desmond Tutu)

As teachers, we want to reach every adult learner who would benefit from English language instruction and build their capacity and engagement within our classrooms and communities. We also recognize that building inclusive learning benefits everyone. We see the value and contributions that all people can make in our community if they are included rather than isolated.

Among adult English learners (ELs), many encounter intense, persistent challenges that are not possible to overcome without educators' and program administrators' active support. These learners are unlikely to succeed unless educators and administrators can find meaningful ways to include them. Some of these barriers to learning include poverty, cultural adaptation concerns, discrimination, gender inequity, precarious immigration status, mental health issues, disability and impairment, and literacy challenges. Although this list is not exhaustive, it is a starting point in highlighting some of the main difficulties that learners face in their language learning journey. These barriers to learning pose tangible challenges to what it means to be an exemplary teacher of adult ELs. Teachers see how these issues are interconnected and manifest in the classroom every day.

This chapter addresses some of the challenges and issues that educators of diverse adult ELs most often encounter. The particular topics reflect concerns the authors have faced in the role of teacher, trainer, community developer, and manager, working in many different types of programs and workplaces. Of these, the more persistent and intense challenges for the learners include attendance, cultural adaptation, literacy issues, disability and impairment, mental health issues (particularly trauma), and the concerns of special populations. There are challenges as well for teachers in adult community-based programs and in the workplace, including burnout and a lack of professional development opportunities and resources. The 6 Principles can provide a framework for considering inclusion and proactive measures to accommodate learners with such challenges. It can also help teachers feel more connected and supported in their work.

This chapter explores these challenges in various ways and suggests solutions in connection to The 6 Principles framework. However, in the discussion, this chapter highlights only those principles that apply most directly to each challenge.

Participation and Nonparticipation of Adults in ESOL Classes

By the sixth week of the term in your literacy class, one of your learners, Minh, has only attended about half of the classes, and last week he missed every session. You hear from other learners that he started working in construction to support his family and can no longer attend school.

Arguably, the greatest challenge we face in our language classes is the lack of participation of learners like Minh, who would benefit from English language instruction as well as from the social connections and community that English to speakers of other languages (ESOL) classes provide. Recent research indicates how broad the scope of this concern may be. For example, in the United States, Patterson (2018b) estimated that 90 percent of adults who could potentially benefit from adult education programs do not participate in any, while an "estimated seven million cannot read English well or at all" (p. 42). In English-speaking countries, adults need English language and literacy skills to work, parent, participate, and engage in the community and in civic affairs.

Factors that deter participation fall into three categories: situational, dispositional, and institutional (Quigley, 2006). Situational deterrents arise from an individual's life circumstances—from the many roles, responsibilities, and identities learners have in their lives. Dispositional deterrents refer to barriers that individuals have internalized about themselves; these are related to their self-perceptions and perspectives. Institutional deterrents include educational policies, procedures, and practices that hinder participation in programs (Patterson, 2018a; Patterson & Song, 2018).

Table 4.1 highlights some of the deterrents and the solutions for engaging ELs in adult education. By examining deterrents systematically, programs can design solutions that make participation more likely. These can include locating programs near other services where a supportive infrastructure already exists and publicizing the ways in which programs are equipped to help participants overcome their obstacles. To help programs create systemic solutions, teachers should communicate their learners' difficulties to decision makers and advocate for proactive measures to boost participation and attendance.

Table 4.1	Deterrents and solutions for boosting participation in adult education
Deterrents to participation	**Solutions to improve participation**
Life circumstances • Lack of transportation • Family care responsibilities • Work obligations • Lack of money • Lack of a personal support system • Lack of life skills to access services	• Integrate program with other services that have an existing infrastructure (schools, churches, community centers, early childhood programs, libraries, shopping centers, and social service providers) • Deliver programs where adults are located (workplaces, institutions, housing complexes, neighborhoods, shelters) • Make instruction available via personal electronic devices • Publish infomercials and infographics that teach life skills needed to access services • Engage peer-educators and tutors who can serve learners at alternative locations (their home, health center, or local library)
Individual dispositions • Health concerns • Disabilities • Behavior struggles • Lack of time • Lack of motivation • Low priority on education • Low self-confidence • Anxiety or fear • Limited educational or workplace experiences	• Conduct active outreach to enroll learners • Engage graduates of adult education programs as motivational speakers and role models to share their strategies for overcoming barriers • Create a network of sponsors or mentors • Organize support groups that focus on dispositional issues holistically • Partner with the leaders of learners' home culture community • Provide program orientation that is responsive to learners' concerns • Follow up promptly with students who are absent or stop out
Institutional barriers • Program costs • Lack of suitable programs • Lack of available seats in programs • Students have no knowledge of programs • Requirements for participation • Services not designed for those with limited English proficiency • Services not designed for those seeking academic or workforce skills	• Seek input on location, program design, and language supports needed from prospective participants • Identify sponsors and funders to make programs available free of charge or at reduced cost • Partner with employers, community agencies, and faith-based organizations • Make the program linguistically accessible for prospective participants • Publicize program information broadly • Engage translators, interpreters, and multilingual staff • Evaluate requirements for participation • Align program content with learners' wants and goals • Engage and train tutors to help teachers differentiate and customize instruction and supports for individual learner needs • Offer tutoring, access to computer lab, and self-paced content-complete online instruction while learners are on the waiting list

(Based in part on Patterson & Song, 2018)

Principle 1. *Know Your Learners* and Principle 2. *Create Conditions for Language Learning*

Table 4.1 illustrates the important connections to Principles 1 and 2. Principle 1 helps us identify the possible barriers to learning according to life experiences, including the dispositional and situational factors, and helps us respond to them in practical and meaningful ways. Principle 2 helps us better understand the institutional solutions we can create to deliver ESOL training, such as creating conditions for language learning that deter nonparticipation and that build responsive and engaged classrooms for our students.

Cultural Adaptation Struggles

Rosie is working with Ingrid, who has completed an intake interview. She has shared her feelings about living in Canada and the struggle she is having adapting. Her daughter is already proficient in English, but Ingrid is struggling to communicate. Although Rosie prepared a lesson on banking and budgeting for the class, Ingrid wants to be able to talk with her daughter's teacher and find out how her daughter is doing in school. Ingrid says she feels very nervous speaking to her daughter's teacher.

Rosie works with Ingrid to build her language skills to talk to her daughter's teacher in the next parent-teacher meeting. She creates a role-play and practices this dialogue with her.

Ingrid: *It's nice to meet you.*

Teacher: *I'm glad we're meeting today. Thank you.*

Ingrid: *You're welcome.*

Teacher: *I would like to talk to you about your daughter.*

Ingrid: *Is there a problem?*

Teacher: *No, your daughter is doing well.*

Ingrid: *That's great news.*

Teacher: *She is a wonderful student.*

Ingrid: *I'm so happy to hear that.*

The next session, when Rosie meets Ingrid, she tells Rosie that she was able to talk to the teacher. She also learned about a parenting group in her neighborhood.

Newcomers face struggles adapting to their new country, including struggles in their learning environment and workplaces. The transition to a new life in a new country in a new language is rarely easy for anyone. The process of cultural adaptation can take a long time, and the road can be bumpy. However, some of our learners experience acute difficulties with adjustment. Their living conditions, circumstances, and experiences (both pre- and postarrival) influence how well and how quickly they are able to adapt. Literacy issues can also impact the process of integration.

Some researchers view cultural adaptation as a three-stage process (Holder, 1999):

- Stage I is settlement: establish oneself in the new home and learn how to access basic necessities.

- Stage II is adaptation: engage with the new culture and adapt to the environment while seeking to keep some of one's own cultural identity.

- Stage III is the integration of biculturalism: become fully functioning members of the broader society through civic engagement, social connections, social bonds, safety, and stability (Ager & Strang, 2008). Integration is a two-way process, where both the newcomer and the receiving community positively affect each other's culture.

Principle 1. *Know Your Learners*

Monitor how learners are adapting. By engaging with learners, we can build their capacity to move through the stages of cultural adaptation. When we are getting to know learners, we can inquire about their level of optimism about their new life or workplace, what they may find troublesome, and how they feel about their new circumstances. We can try to gauge their social engagement and explore whether the new connections they are making are serving to buffer the stresses of change. We can provide support and encouragement to help them reach out and avoid isolation.

Become educated about adaptation issues. In Chapter 3, we discussed the importance of exploring cross-cultural issues with learners to understand where their difficulties lie with crossing linguistic, ethnic, and cultural boundaries. When these conversations about cross-cultural issues are open and genuine, they can provide insights into learners' struggles with adaptation. For example, when you see a student in the classroom who may be struggling with understanding the new cultural norms or practices, you might consider asking a support worker to join you to meet with the student and to see if you can learn more about the situation from the student's perspective.

> *Nelson holds a student-teacher conference with a high-intermediate learner. The student is a refugee from Sri Lanka and is the only Tamil speaker in the class. She tells the teacher that she feels very lonely. She thinks the other learners are not nice and feels she has nothing in common with them. She says she feels angry and complains about living in Sydney. She was expecting life in her new country to be easier.*

In the above vignette, by having a one-on-one conversation, the teacher gains insight into the student's life experience and challenges. Spending the time to get to know students pays off when we encounter these kinds of challenges. Our awareness of possible obstacles can help us develop informed learning strategies. This approach leads to more productive and inclusive classes.

Move toward a deeper understanding of culture. Becoming a culturally responsive educator is a long-term, ongoing process. It involves a frank examination of our own values, beliefs, and norms, which underlie our actions and ways of thinking (DeCapua, 2016). We can explore resources, which help us gain insights into the world views and culturally conditioned expectations and behaviors of our students. We can engage them in dialogue and self-reflection to develop shared understandings. The resulting deeper knowledge can become the foundation for introducing new content and curricula that reflect the interests and orientations of the learners in our classes. The work of Marshall and DeCapua (2013) on the mutually adaptive learning paradigm (malpeducation.com) or the work of Nieto and Bode (2018) on multicultural education can guide us with this process.

Principle 2. *Create Conditions for Language Learning*

> *Lila had a Burmese student in her class, Hayma, who was usually very quiet. When Lila planned a lesson about food, she purposely included in the lesson plan a Burmese fried rice recipe. Her Burmese student did indeed become very engaged that day. Hayma started talking about Burmese food and traditions, and she was using vocabulary that Lila did not know she knew in English. The other learners asked Hayma lots of questions and shared their own rice recipes. The class decided to have a potluck on the last day of the semester to share food from their home countries. Several students partnered to cook their dish together for the whole class.*

Promote a culturally responsive classroom. Lila, the teacher in the vignette, promotes engagement by encouraging learners to find commonality in their experiences and aiding learners in building relationships outside the class. Forming friendships in a highly diverse class can be difficult for some learners, and conflicts can arise. Here are some other suggestions to create a culturally responsive classroom:

- Include stories that represent the experiences of individuals and groups from a variety of backgrounds. For example, share accounts of the migration journeys of people from different ethnicities and circumstances; discuss the dreams immigrants and refugees have of a new life in a new land. Excellent resources are available from Passages Canada (passagestocanada.com) and the Immigration History Research Center (cla.umn.edu/ihrc /immigrant-stories).

- Listen actively and try not to judge if you feel learners are making assumptions. Be mindful of your own biases and assumptions and how they may impact your interactions with your students.

Build an appreciation and intercultural sensitivity for cultures.

Last week, Pierre taught a beginner class where he had the learners work in pairs. He grouped Maher and Zaynab together. He assumed their shared background would help their interaction; he knew that they both spoke Arabic and arrived to Canada recently from Syria. While he was working with another pair, he noticed that Maher and Zaynab were not working together on the assignment. When he checked in with them, Maher said he would feel more comfortable working with another student.

At the end of the class, Pierre asked Maher to stay in the classroom, so he could figure out what had happened. He learned from Maher that he didn't feel comfortable working with Zaynab because she was a single woman. He did not want to make her feel uncomfortable. Pierre listened to Maher's concerns and acknowledged them.

Later that day, Pierre spoke to Rasha, the Arabic-speaking support staff at his organization. She said that Maher came from a conservative family, which explained why he felt uncomfortable working with a single woman. Pierre realized he had never really considered gender and cultural expectations when grouping students. He was glad that Maher shared his concerns with him. During the next class, Pierre placed the students with other learners. Pierre did some reading about gender relations in different parts of the world and added a lesson on gender issues to the following instructional unit on family and relationships.

Building intercultural sensitivity in diverse classrooms takes constant planning. Begin by exploring the similarities and differences between the sending country and the country of settlement. The above vignette showed how students' values can impact interactions in the class. Teachers can engage learners in exploring different perspectives on issues, problems, and assumptions. We can teach learners about cultural practices, norms, and values in the new country and how these look both inside and outside the classroom.

Having regular conversations about intercultural issues becomes critically important for supporting students who are struggling to make a place for themselves in their new country. To mitigate problems of communication, we can learn about different communication norms of the learners' cultures and engage authentically with them. For example, Lisa was working with a group of newly arrived Syrian women in an employment program. She researched Arabic and learned it was a high-context language, so she prioritized relationship building in her first few classes. As we know, tensions can flare up between learners who hold different values or come from cultural groups that are in conflict with each other. Some of these intercultural or interethnic conflicts have long histories. Although we can't resolve them at will, we can learn to understand and recognize them. We can respond to tense interactions with compassionate and respectful dialogue.

Teachers need to build relationships with interpreters, settlement and outreach workers, cultural brokers, and leaders within the community. These individuals can improve understanding of learners' experiences and the adversity that they may be encountering.

Create a classroom agreement. Teachers can share classroom agreements at the start of the term to create a respectful environment and mitigate some of the conflicts that may arise. Here are some suggestions for how to approach this:

- Beginner learners can work with the instructor to name six ideas for the classroom that would allow them to feel safe, willing, and free to participate.

- Intermediate and advanced learners can create an agreement in small groups and then present it to the entire class. The class can combine and synthesize ideas to build a whole-class agreement.

- For reference, display the agreement as a poster in your classroom.

- Revisit and amend the agreement as needed, and in so doing create a learning opportunity to help learners better understand how classroom practices and expectations can help facilitate learning.

Each of us might need to think about what is vital to us as a teacher and negotiate these points with the group. Consensus building around these issues is a valuable learning objective. We should anticipate how we will manage disagreements and include the preferred approach in the classroom agreement (Ishiyama & Westwood, 2011).

Emerging Literacy Issues

Anosha comes from Afghanistan. She grew up under the Taliban. She entered an arranged marriage at the age of 16. Her husband was killed by a bomb in Afghanistan. She fled to Russia with her five children and then moved to Canada three years ago. This is Anosha's second year in ESL literacy classes. When she began, she was a true beginner in English and lacked the skills to read and write in any language.

Anosha is motivated to learn and attends classes regularly. She has expressed a desire to get a job in the future. Now, she speaks well and has already learned to write her address in the correct order. She really enjoys connecting with the other learners in the class. She needs a little more time in class to complete her work than the other learners. She writes very slowly and expends a lot of effort trying to avoid mistakes.

The teacher understands that Anosha's low literacy creates challenges for finding work. The teacher spends time taking small steps with Anosha and works with her on phonics and sight words. She points out the parts of the words that she spells correctly and isolates the problem letter-sounds in misspelled words. The teacher keeps the list of spelling words short—only about five words at a time. A word is considered "learned" when it is spelled correctly three times consecutively. The teacher frequently talks to Anosha about all the new words she has learned and how much she appreciates Anosha trying to come to class regularly.

Newcomers, like Anosha, arrive with mixed expectations for their new life. A large segment of newcomers (particularly refugees) lack formal education, or have limited or interrupted schooling. This can be a result of war, lack of access to education, gender disparity, or various other factors. Depending on how much education they have received, learners may be preliterate, nonliterate, or semiliterate. It is important to identify these learners and support them in different ways than other adult English learners.

Adults with low literacy have prerequisite skills to learn. We may need to demonstrate to them how to hold a pencil or teach them the meaning of common pictorial representations. These learners rely on memory and do not have the benefit of taking notes, so we may need to chunk our teaching, repeat information, and practice more. They need to develop background knowledge and learning strategies. Often, they have strong verbal skills, which can mask their struggles with reading, writing, and digital literacy.

There are many accommodations teachers can make in materials and lesson delivery for learners with literacy concerns. They can make learning materials accessible by choosing familiar fonts, enlarging texts, and reducing visual clutter. Adding more white space to the page can help new readers focus. These low literacy learners may also prefer experiential learning to text-based learning. This can require adding new kinds of learning tasks as well as social supports. The choice of texts is critical for novice readers because it is tremendously difficult to focus on decoding and comprehension simultaneously. Familiar language and content facilitate decoding, making a difficult task more manageable.

The issues of low-literacy learners tend to cluster. These learners are more likely to have trauma and health issues. The principles and practices in Chapter 3, including Principle 3 (Design High-Quality Lessons for Language Development) and Principle 5 (Monitor and Assess Student Language Development), highlight a number of proactive measures that can be used to engage learners with low literacy. These include enhanced input through varied approaches, techniques, and modalities. These practices are critical for supporting learners with limited literacy skills, like Anosha.

Principle 1. *Know Your Learners*

Understand how low literacy impacts learners' lives. As teachers, we can start by developing a more complete understanding of how low literacy can shape learners' behaviors and circumstances. In Anosha's situation, low literacy not only impacts her participation in class but also her ability to find work. Low literacy usually affects many aspects of functioning in learners' daily lives:

- Finances: Literacy can have negative impact on employability, income, and financial security.

- Poverty: Many learners with low literacy levels live in a cycle of poverty.

- Children: Parents with low literacy are less able to model reading and writing for their children, which can impact the children's own literacy and schooling.

- Exclusion and participation: People with low literacy skills are often marginalized and vulnerable because they are not able take part in many aspects of daily life, such as civic engagement, volunteering, or community involvement. They can become isolated, which may impact their health and well-being (Frontier College, 2017).

- Health, well-being, and safety: Low literacy may negatively affect these vital areas of life when people cannot search for and utilize available safety and health information.

Principle 2. *Create Conditions for Language Learning*

Find areas of strength and build on them. Students with low literacy often experience many systemic or situational barriers, which can impact their sense of self-worth. Teachers need to be generous with encouragement and consistent with positive feedback for these students. By recognizing and incorporating learners' background experience and "funds of knowledge" into lessons, teachers help build the students' confidence and self-esteem. We can recognize the strengths, capacities, and resilience that our students have and incorporate those into our classrooms and learning. We can work with our students to set goals and to recognize and develop their strengths.

Principle 3. *Design High-Quality Lessons for Language Development*

Start with working on oral language skills. Oral language has the most immediate effect on learners' ability to adjust to their new circumstances, access services, build community, and advocate for themselves and their families. Oral language is also a necessary skill for the development of literacy (Bow Valley College, 2018; Vinogradov & Bigelow, 2010). This is also an area where they tend to have strengths.

Beginner learners usually enjoy the Total Physical Response approach (Asher, 1969). Total Physical Response is a way to teach oral language skills by getting students to move and respond physically to various instructions. For example, to teach physical directions, get the learners to move right, left, forward, or backwards. Then, switch roles and have the students give each other directions. This method has evolved to teach more complex oral language skills, such as narratives, dialogues, and storytelling (Ray & Seely, 2015). We can use real objects, songs, dialogues, and interviews as well to help in the development of oral language (Bow Valley College, 2018).

Use a task-based approach. Teachers can use a task-based language teaching approach (Long, 2014) for adult learners with limited literacy. There are many reasons this approach is helpful. It emphasizes communication and using the language in a whole and relevant way. It focuses on authentic learning and on real-world tasks. It is also ideally connected to true need in learners' lives (Bow Valley College, 2018). Following is an example of task-based language teaching based on a group of learners on social assistance, who have identified as a need wanting to access the food bank.

Task: Interview Staff at the Food Bank to Learn about Their Services to the Community

Introducing the task: Today we are going to talk about going to the food bank. In a group, you will think of questions you might ask at the food bank.

Clarifying the task: Let's think about the questions together first. Who has a good example? (List and discuss the question form of examples. E.g., *Who donates to the food bank? Who gets food from the food bank? Do you have halal food here?*)

Completing the task: In small groups, work together to create a list of questions. (Students will use their list to get answers at the food bank.)

Wrapping up the task: Let's come back and get into a large group. Please share some of your questions.

Note: Guide the group to see and understand the strategies they use (e.g., questioning, asking for more information) and reinforce that they can use these to speak to staff at the food bank when the class visits the next week.

Build phonemic awareness. Research tells us that explicit instruction of phonemic awareness is important for emergent readers (e.g., Vinogradov, 2010). Literacy learners need systematic instruction to discriminate speech sounds correctly and to recognize letter/sound relationships. To develop these skills, it is best to use materials that contain language and content already familiar to students so they can focus on the new skills. Learners need ample practice with the following:

- hearing speech sounds correctly and distinguishing different sounds from each other
- recognizing which letter or letters represent each speech sound
- saying the sound while printing the letter(s)

Here is an example of teaching phonemic awareness to an adult learner.

Omar is working with Eduardo. Eduardo has been talking about activities he likes and dislikes. Eduardo says he likes basketball. Omar then writes the word basketball. Omar carefully says the word and asks Eduardo to listen carefully. He goes over other words that begin with the letter /b/. Omar then explains he is going to say some words and Eduardo should listen and tell him if the words begin with /b/. Eduardo circles all the words that begin with the letter /b/, and then Omar reads the circled words back to him. For a home assignment, Eduardo copies words that contain the letter /b/ from signs he sees.

Use learner-generated texts. Learner-generated texts immediately provide relevant, meaningful, level- and age-appropriate reading materials (Vinogradov, 2010). The Language Experience Approach is a useful tool for recording learner-generated texts (e.g., Wales, 1994). Teachers using the Language Experience Approach start by asking learners to tell a story, perhaps about how they got to class that day or what they did over the weekend. Learners dictate their story to the teacher or to a scribe, who records it word for word. The teacher can say each word as it is getting transcribed. It is important to keep the story short for learners with developing literacy so as to not to overwhelm them. The teacher reads the story to the learner without correcting the grammar or word choice, instead asking the learner if he or she would like to make any changes or additions. These texts become mentor texts for teaching reading (Vinogradov, 2010). Here is an example of this approach in action.

Judy has been tutoring Pedro for a month. After their sixth tutorial session, they started to work on their third language experience story. Judy had asked Pedro to tell her a bit about his work. As he spoke, she wrote everything down. They read it together several times. Pedro was still in the beginning stages of reading, so Judy read parts of it. She then asked him to circle the words he knew how to read. When she reread the story, she asked Pedro to identify the words that begin with /r/, /s/, /t/, and /g/, the consonants they worked on the previous week. At the end of the session, they read the story one more time.

Principle 4. *Adapt Lesson Delivery as Needed*

Pace the lesson activities mindfully. When working with literacy learners, good pacing is key to making headway:

- Be flexible.
- Take things slowly.
- Break instruction into small segments.
- Allow adequate time for practice activities.

The right pace allows students to process instruction and alleviates their stress. Teachers can reflect on their pacing by asking themselves, *Are the learners struggling to keep up or are they looking bored?, Do I need to break instruction into more or smaller segments?, Am I losing students' attention by going too slowly or too quickly?* The goal of this approach is to build learners' self-confidence and self-efficacy.

Offer alternative modes of learning. Teachers can take a more holistic approach to lesson delivery. We can engage the body and the mind through kinesthetic activities. We can offer learners art and project-based activities, which afford them creative and alternative ways for expressing themselves. We can bring emotion into learning by engaging learners in authentic conversations and recognizing the value of their stories (Gardner, 2017).

Principle 6. *Engage and Collaborate within a Community of Practice*

Recognize your own limitations. Teachers can seek out resources and resource persons to help and support them in their teaching of low literacy English learners. Educator groups exist that explore this area of teaching. For example, Literacy Education and Second Language Learning for Adults (www.leslla.org) and Bow Valley College (globalaccess.bowvalleycollege.ca/resource -finder/esl-literacy-network-resource-finder) offer valuable guidance for teaching learners with low literacy.

Disability and Impairment

Allam is a 28-year-old Kurdish man from Iraq with no formal education. During the war, he was a victim of a bomb blast. As a result, he suffered traumatic brain injury and injury to his eyes. He also has ringing in his ears. In spite of all this, he attends class every day and demonstrates a great eagerness to learn. He has very high oral skills. He likes working one-on-one with a teacher or in small groups. In a large class situation, he has trouble with background noise. He is also very sensitive to light and says he often gets headaches when writing and reading. He always sits beside the teacher at the front of the class. His favorite part of class is when he goes to the Digital Café, a computer lab, where he is able to control the background noise and light in the lab to better suit his needs. He likes to wear headphones and listen to the tasks the teacher has assigned him.

Refugees, like Allam, sometimes suffer from severe injuries and lack of access to healthcare and medical support. It is possible that many of the adult learners who are viewed as poor language learners are struggling because they have an impairment that impacts their learning. In many countries, disabilities are not recognized, and in some cultures those with disabilities are stigmatized.

The term *disability* encompasses many different conditions, including physical and developmental disabilities, mental health issues, and chronic diseases. These can include the following:

- pain-related conditions
- mobility problems
- mental illness
- hearing loss
- vision impairment
- learning disability
- memory loss

A wide range of indicators are related to disabilities. Teachers don't necessarily know if a student has a disability, particularly an invisible one, and may perceive problems arising from such a disability as a behavioral issue or lack of interest. Some occurrences or behaviors you may see that could indicate disability include the following:

- missing class frequently for health appointments
- struggling to stay awake or difficulty following instruction
- inability to focus or to remember
- performing inconsistently on learning tasks
- lack of practice outside the classroom
- avoiding certain tasks
- exhibiting low self-esteem or a lack of self-confidence

(Schwarz & Terrill, 2000; Root, 1994)

We can take proactive measures to include and support learners who we know have a disability or who may have a disability. All of the principles that follow can help us create an environment where students with disabilities are able to learn.

Principle 1. *Know Your Learners*

Knowing the student is absolutely essential if a teacher suspects there is a disability or related concern. We can engage family members and other important people in the learners' lives to help us understand what might be happening for the student, remembering that we need to ensure we have the student's permission to do so. We can assess further by using the following checklist, abbreviated here and developed by Delaney (2016, p. 23).

- Does the problem occur in every class and throughout the day or just in certain situations?
- Can the student interact and work well with other learners?
- Can the student remember and follow instructions? Is he or she easily distracted?
- Can the student work independently for long periods of time?
- Where does the student usually sit? Can he or she hear and see properly from that position?
- What types of tasks is the student good at and which does he or she actively enjoy?
- Does the student find activities too easy or too difficult? How do you know?
- Is the student able to ask for and accept help?
- Is there a noticeable difference between the student's spoken and written ability?

Principle 2. *Create Conditions for Language Learning*

Optimize the physical environment of the classroom. Many teachers already think about the physical environment of the classroom. When thinking about classroom space, we might consider ways to reduce background noise and remove distracting visual clutter. We should think carefully about lighting in the classroom and where we place ourselves in the room, so the learners can see our facial expressions. We should also consider the seating of the learners who have hearing and vision impairments and may need to sit closer to us.

Facilitate a positive emotional climate. Chapter 3 mentions the importance of drawing on learners' strengths, recognizing contributions, and acknowledging successes. This is key when we work with people who may have a disability and may have experienced discrimination and exclusion. Having a positive attitude toward all learners makes them feel valued and encourages them to learn (Delaney, 2016).

Make time for one-on-one support. On the first day, we can inform the class that anyone can meet with us privately to talk about needs that they might have for learning. We should let the students know when we are available to discuss their concerns. Administrative support may be necessary to ensure that teachers have paid office hours so they can meet with learners. Another solution may be to end classes early once a month for individual conferences.

Have open conversations about abilities while respecting individuals' privacy. Unfortunately, individuals with disabilities are often stigmatized and discriminated against. They may face stereotypes about their disabilities held by others and even by themselves. This can be a more complex experience for learners from places in the world where disability is stigmatized to a greater extent than in their new country. Having a classroom agreement and fostering acceptance of difference are important elements of creating inclusive classrooms. As teachers, we can create circumstances for one-on-one meetings and ask questions like, *How do you learn best? What do I need to know* *to help you learn best?* Teachers need to adhere to policies around disclosure; the disclosure of a disability is always the adult learner's choice.

Use stations to differentiate learning. Teachers can set up classrooms with individual learners in mind. Most adult classes are mixed ability, and learners with disabilities in multilevel classes can often feel overwhelmed with the pace. We might need to modify certain aspects of our teaching and support learners with disabilities by using learning stations (Delaney, 2016). Learning stations allow students to start with simpler tasks and content and build on their skills as they move to more complex tasks. Students work at their own pace and their confidence grows as they progress. Teachers can allow students to begin by choosing a station and then advise them that they can move to another station when they feel ready. As students work, teachers can assist them individually. This allows teachers to give extra time to those with impairments or other challenges.

Learning stations are useful not only for students with disabilities but also for those with emerging literacy. The learning station model allows students to work at the following:

- open-ended tasks, which can be performed on different levels
- the same task with different levels of scaffolding
- different tasks working toward the same skill
- different tasks working with the same target vocabulary
- different stages of the same task
- focusing on areas of need
- catching up on different work

(Bow Valley College, 2018, p. 167)

Here is an example of how a teacher has used learning stations in her classroom to support a student with a disability.

> *Diana sets up differentiated learning stations to engage learners by accommodating each of their learning styles and levels. She believes this activity helps students build confidence, which is a key for Jamal, who Diana thinks possibly has Attention Deficit Disorder. For a lesson on transportation, Diana sets up learning stations in four areas of the room. She encourages the learners to choose a station. Jamal starts with the first station because he feels confident about the first task of labeling the parts of a bus and he likes the kinesthetic nature of the activity. He then moves to an exercise on community using three-dimensional cardboard parts. Jamal works with another student on this interactive, hands-on activity. Finally, Jamal, feeling more confident, moves to the station on reading a bus schedule. From her observation, Diana notes information for an anecdotal assessment of Jamal.*

Principle 3. *Design High-Quality Lessons for Language Development*

Keep lessons well structured and highly organized. The following are some ways to structure the learning experience so as to pace teaching to meet learning capacities, make use of multisensory approaches and materials, reinforce the learning as the new is introduced, and instill organizational skills that assist learning. Although the following are discussed in Chapter 3, we highlight them here for their possible value when working with students who have disabilities or possible impairments:

- Post a weekly or daily agenda.
- Teach small amounts of information in a developmental sequence.
- Break information into smaller chunks.
- Use authentic or real-world material.

- Build on learners' prior knowledge and strengths.
- Repeat often.
- Teach ways to organize information (tables, graphic organizers, outlines).
- Support oral language input with nonverbal means (gestures, facial expressions, visuals, and demonstrations).

Use technology. Teachers can use technology as an aid when teaching people with impairments, but they must ensure this is in tandem with in-class instruction. Do your best to employ assistive technology tools, blended learning, and online programs designed to aid the learning of individuals with disabilities. Technology can also play a role in breaking isolation and allowing students who miss a class (because of a doctor's appointment, illness, or therapy session) to keep connected and continue to learn at their own pace. Teachers need to feel comfortable with the technology themselves, so start with something simple.

Explore the features of Universal Design for learning. Teachers can explore the principles of Universal Design (UD; universaldesign.ie/What-is-Universal-Design/The-7-Principles) to include and accommodate all students. These principles can help create a learning environment where accessibility is a main consideration and not an afterthought. UD features are helpful for all our learners, and particularly beneficial for learners with disabilities. For example, UD guidelines encourage formats where learners have a choice in tasks, and they can work at their own pace. The tasks don't contain unnecessary complexity, and the task explanations are clear and consistent. UD guides us to maximize clarity when presenting information, for example, by making it easily legible and arranging it in the order of importance.

UD can also help us better understand how the physical design of our classrooms impacts learning. A simple example of applying UD in your classroom would be to provide a quiet and uncluttered space where a student who is easily distracted by others in the classroom can work on tasks that require intense concentration, like an assessment. Another example is to dedicate space in the classroom for the use of assistive technology and for individual consultation with the teacher.

Principle 5. *Monitor and Assess Student Language Development*

Be flexible in monitoring and carrying out summative and formative assessments. Teachers can deploy alternatives to standard assessments to demonstrate learning. Individual portfolios can be helpful assessment tools: they allow teachers to collect students' work regularly, assess how persistent the individual student's challenges are, and evaluate which accommodations or techniques have assisted the learning (Schwarz &Terrill, 2000). Portfolios and projects can provide teachers with a selection of a student's work so that they can discuss what the student has learned and they can set goals for future growth (Ripley, 2013).

Mental Health Issues

According to the United Nations High Commissioner for Refugees (2018), "The forcibly displaced population increased in 2017 by 2.9 million worldwide." Every day, we meet learners who come to our countries and classes and who are part of this growing number of displaced people. Many of these learners arrive having experienced trauma through war, persecution, violence, torture, or other horrendous experiences. The effects of trauma often cause ongoing and even lifelong psychological challenges. Even immigrants and refugees who have not been traumatized in their country of origin may experience trauma through the process of upheaval in their lives that is migration and/or through the trials of living in a new country (Wilbur, 2016).

Many of the learners we welcome every day into our classes have experienced at least stress connected with immigration and resettlement. This may put them at higher risk for mental health issues, including anxiety and depression. Refugees and those with precarious immigration status are even more likely to have experienced trauma and to develop depression or anxiety, like posttraumatic stress disorder (Fazel, Wheeler, & Danesh, 2005). According to Clayton (2015), "Trauma has been shown to be a significant risk factor for resettlement success, with trauma 'load' as well as the trauma 'type,' particularly confinement, isolation, torture and rape, increasing the likelihood of [posttraumatic stress disorder]" (p. 5).

Refugees did not choose to leave their homes but were forced to; they might have lost or been separated from family, children, and friends. They may have suffered torture, persecution, or immense loss. They have unique needs that will require special attention as they adapt to their new lives (Jeffries & Wilbur, 2016). Teachers can offer support to learners but are not trained or equipped to be therapists. Therefore, it is critical that programs have connections to relevant services, such as social service groups, support workers, and counselors, who can step in to provide clinical support when needed.

Principle 1. *Know Your Learners*

Recognize the signs of trauma. Teachers want to know and understand how trauma impacts their learners and what they can do to support these learners in their classrooms. Trauma and mental health issues have some tangible signs, and it is important to recognize what the signs can be (Isserlis, 2009). The following are possible indicators of a trauma disorder or other mental health issue:

- irritability and anger
- sadness (quick to cry)
- hypervigilance (easily startled by loud noises or voices)
- memory gaps
- difficulty focusing
- demand for the instructor's undivided attention
- difficulty with planning and staying organized
- somatic (physical) health issues
- substance abuse
- exhaustion
- lack of trust (with peers and instructor)
- periods of absence from class

Seek information about the sociopolitical situations of learners.

A group of Yazidi women were accepted as refugees in Sara's community. Sara's workplace offered a professional development workshop on working with the Yazidi community. She learned about some of their experiences in Syria and the trauma they experienced during the war. Sara found that attending this workshop was helpful because when the women arrived, she had a better understanding of their physical, emotional, and mental health issues. She also understood some of the cultural norms and values they brought with them, and she learned about the kidnapping and sexual violence they had experienced. The workshop facilitator talked about some of the challenges and opportunities that might come up in a classroom environment for the Yazidi women. The facilitator spoke of the resilience of these women. Sara felt more prepared to support the new students. She recognized the level of compassion or care she would need working with these new students. She also learned about some of the concrete things she could do in her classroom to make the students feel more comfortable.

We will never know everything about the situations where learners have come from, but we can find ways, formal and informal, to learn more about their cultures to inform our teaching. We can try to gain some awareness of experiences and political situations that have led to the trauma of many learners, as Sara did. We don't want to risk triggering people's memories, but we can ask well-considered questions to better understand our learners and what they may have gone through on their journey. We can read and learn about trauma and how it impacts learning and, in turn, affects our classrooms and workplaces. With an understanding of the effects of trauma, we are better equipped to do our jobs. Insight helps us shape how we work with individual learners and allows us to create classrooms that feel safe for the learners, fostering trust (Jeffries & Wilbur, 2016).

Principle 2. *Create Conditions for Language Learning*

Create a calming physical environment. A positive environment is one key piece to supporting people who have experienced trauma (e.g., Bow Valley College, 2017). Strategies to reduce anxiety include the following:

- Reduce environmental stress and stimuli.
- Keep windows and doors open, if possible, to minimize any feelings of detention (Clayton, 2015).
- Seek input from learners on how they would like the space organized.
- Build roles and responsibilities for learners in the classroom (e.g., making tea).
- Provide a quiet space in your classroom or in your school so learners can take a break.
- Have the learners who have experienced trauma sit near the door or window, so they know they can leave the classroom at any time.
- Inform learners that they are free to step outside at any time they need a break.

Maintain an open disposition toward trauma and other mental health issues. Teachers should be compassionate when they suspect a student has experienced trauma. We need to be discreet when asking about personal histories and exercise caution when designing lessons around talking or writing about the self. We can respect learners' right to nonparticipation by offering alternative assignments, such as journaling, and by having an area of the classroom where a student can choose to work alone. Because we need to be prepared to deal with controversial or problematic topics when they arise (Clayton, 2015), we must learn strategies to support learners whose unusual sensitivity to certain topics or behaviors may trigger agitation, fear, or anger.

Gain awareness of the triggering of memories.

Pari's school requires her to follow a specific curriculum on the topic of policing and other emergency services. She invites a police officer to her class. The officer arrives in uniform and carrying a gun. One of the Burmese learners runs out of the class. Pari follows him, and he tells her he is afraid of the police. He was imprisoned in Burma. He no longer wants to participate in the class. Pari listens to him share his story. She then asks him to rejoin when he feels comfortable. He comes back to class after the police officer has left. The next time the police officer is to visit the class, Pari asks her to come in her civilian clothes and without a weapon. The officer is quite happy to do this, and the Burmese student stays in the class this time.

Certain triggers can bring on symptoms of posttraumatic stress disorder. The triggers—particular sounds, visuals, smells—may bring back strong memories and even flashbacks. Learners may feel they are reliving the trauma at that moment. Some triggers are obvious, and we can avoid them, for instance, by not asking learners to talk about their pasts until we know that it is safe to do so, or—like in Pari's case—not bringing uniformed officials as resource persons to the classroom. We can still help the learners who have trauma issues develop language without asking them to talk about their experiences.

Be sensitive to story sharing. Tensions may arise when refugee students decide to share their stories and the rest of the class is unprepared to hear them. When we ask learners to discuss personal information, we may find them sharing their stories of trauma with us. As teachers, we want our classrooms to be safe places for every learner. We must recognize the potential adverse impact of telling personal stories of violence in class. We need ways in which we can support our learners without further spreading the devastating impact of extreme trauma, even vicariously (Waterhouse, 2017).

Principle 3. *Design High-Quality Lessons for Language Development*

Indi teaches a class on feelings for beginner ESL adults. She wants to provide students with the language to identify, understand, and articulate feelings. Indi learned in a workshop she attended that the first step in managing and building a sense of control for students who have experienced trauma is being able to name and identify feelings. She is also aware that it might be helpful for students therapeutically if they have the accurate names for their feelings.

She identifies the vocabulary for eight feelings—sad, happy, tired, angry, afraid, worried, calm, and surprised. She introduces the new vocabulary by stating the words and miming the facial expressions associated with the emotions. Students repeat her words and demonstrate the expressions. She then draws eight faces with the eight feelings on the whiteboard and elicits the language. Next, she gives out a handout with blank faces and has the students read the feeling word below each face and draw the expression that represents the word. They then work in pairs—one demonstrates the emotion, the other states the word, and then they switch roles.

Include the topics that are relevant to learners' well-being. As teachers, we have an opportunity to provide real-world tools for our learners to help them build a better sense of well-being. To do this, we can begin by teaching the vocabulary for identifying emotions (Jeffries & Wilbur, 2016). Also, when we teach about the health system, we should not forget to add mental health services and the topic of self-care. We can talk about mental health issues and find ways to destigmatize them by explaining the "lived experience" of mental illness that real people have confronted (Jeffries & Wilbur, 2016). Our learners can read a life story or listen to an invited guest speaker. We can teach help-seeking behaviors and the communication skills needed to ask for help as part of language learning.

Principle 6. *Engage and Collaborate within a Community of Practice*

Belar in your class has a severely autistic son. She, along with her son and older daughter, came to Canada as Government Assisted Refugees. She said she spent eight years trying to get to here. She spent five years in Turkey, where life was very hard for her with two very young children. She has a lot of stress as a single parent with all the obstacles of the language barrier and caring for her children on her own. She often comes late or has to leave early because of her son. She often cries in the classroom because she misses her husband, who was killed in the war, and she says she feels overwhelmed.

Belar needs more support. The teacher meets with the settlement worker and Belar after class one day. He creates a plan with the settlement worker and Belar to get her more support. The settlement worker makes a connection with Belar's son's school and with an after-school program in the community for autistic children that her son can attend. There is also a Kurdish speaking counselor for her to meet with regularly and support her with her experiences of trauma.

We need to create community and relationship in the classroom, because these are key pieces to supporting learners who have trauma experience. We should also forge relationships with counselors, settlement workers, outreach workers, and other resource people to develop links with various services that can support us in our work and help us build the capacity to support learners like Belar. We need to advocate for our ESOL programs and build connections to mental health services so that there is known recourse for such learners. Moreover, as teachers, we need professional development on recognizing trauma and how to make referrals to mental health professionals.

Special Populations

A number of subpopulations of our learners have special needs or challenges. We focus on several populations in this section because they make up a significant or increasing number of our learners.

> *Pema, a student in George's class, left her two-, four-, and six-year-old at home while she attended her language class. George learned that the children were home alone when Pema told George she might have to leave a bit early that day because her children were sick. When George expressed concern, Pema said she didn't want to miss the class because she was afraid she would be kicked out of the program. She had already had six absences that month. George told her she needed to go home and be with her children. She agreed only because she received assurance from the school that she would still be able to continue her classes. George decides to meet with Pema the following day. George has asked his administrator to help Pema find some extra childcare support. He also learns about a new class starting up at his agency for women only. The class provides childcare, transportation, and food, and it is more flexible with attendance.*

Women

Refugee and immigrant women like Pema have distinct challenges participating in language learning and employment training programs. Women are often the primary caregivers within families with much responsibility. They may have to put their language learning on hold, or they may have to struggle with strict policies around attendance and punctuality in order to maintain eligibility.

Many refugee and immigrant women can't attend language classes because they don't have adequate childcare. Childcare fees are high, even for midincome families, and are usually not an option for refugee families. Many women remain in isolation for years without learning English or being able to contribute their skills to the workforce.

Having little or no competence in English limits the ability of a refugee or immigrant woman to take on roles in the community, engage as a parent in their children's schooling, make friends, or integrate into the host country's mainstream society (see Jeffries, Rahemtulla, & Wilbur, 2017). In many cases, mothers become dependent on their children or husbands for communication and financial support, resulting in a long-term negative impact on their lives stemming from a lack of integration.

As teachers, we can offer support to women through programming, lessons, and language that serves their needs. We can consider their multiple roles and how those play out in our classrooms.

Youth

Youth represent another group struggling to participate in language classes. What group the term *youth* refers to can depend on a variety of factors, including laws, policies, community values, or even family or personal values. In Canada, for example, 34 percent of all newcomers are under age 25, and these newcomer youth have specific needs and concerns.

Newcomer youth experience an enormous change when moving to a new country during a formative period of their lives. They may experience family separation, intergenerational conflict, increased family responsibility, or interrupted schooling. Some have to deal with family reunification after many years apart.

Adolescents should be in high school (typically up to age 18 at least). Leaving high school early has long-term adverse consequences. Young people who lack good guidance and social support are at risk of falling through the cracks, particularly between the ages of 16 and 25. As teachers, we want to encourage these youth to enroll in content-based instruction in traditional school subjects that leads to high school completion. We can build connections with schools, youth employment programs, community groups, and organizations to encourage youth to attend programs that might best serve their long-term needs and goals.

Undocumented and Precarious Immigration Status

Pedro keeps arriving late or not attending class at all. His teacher, Ming, asks him to stay after class to talk with him. Pedro seems quite nervous and scared. He tells Ming that he has a refugee hearing coming up and has been meeting with a lawyer. His wife is pregnant, but she is having trouble accessing health care. He doesn't want the rest of his class to know his situation. Ming realizes that she will have to reorganize her next lesson because she had planned to approach the topic of healthcare with the assumption that students either already have access or they are eligible. She now realizes she will have to develop the lesson to reflect the fact that not everyone may be able to follow the customary route to healthcare. She works with her manager to find out what is available for Pedro. She locates a clinic that will accept refugee claimants.

Migration movement is being transformed by globalization, and the number of people who are undocumented or arrive with a precarious status is growing in Canada, in European countries, and in many other regions around the world. Individuals with precarious status face multiple challenges, such as the lack of access to most publicly funded social services and most forms of employment. Access to social services and safe jobs is crucial to people's well-being and to their inclusion in their new society.

In Canada, for example, newcomer adults with precarious status aren't entitled to federally funded language programs. Community organizations, faith-based groups, and local governments have stepped in to offer language classes. However, many potential learners do not seek enrollment because of fear of deportation or being stigmatized. They may also lack transportation and other resources that would enable them to access language classes.

Pentón Herrera (2017) discussed some of the factors that impact the lives of this group of students, listing them as the following:

- immigration status (They fear for themselves and for their family members.)
- politics (They are subject to politically motivated actions.)
- problems in the household/income (They may lack a safe and healthy home, financial resources, and social support.)
- uncertainty about their future (They don't know where they fit or where they can be safe.)
- lack of opportunities for further education (They may not understand their options.)
- society (They experience discrimination in daily life.)
- individuals within their school system (They may be blamed for their difficult conundrums.)

Although each of these special populations is unique, there are many commonalities in how teachers can support them. In the following sections, we suggest some ideas.

Principle 2. *Create Conditions for Language Learning*

The Family Literacy Outreach (FLO) program services immigrant and refugee families with young children (birth to five years old) by bringing a learning environment into the home where mothers and their children learn together with a trained volunteer tutor. FLO focuses on mothers who are homebound because they live in poverty or have childcare needs, or they have health or transportation or other barriers. The participants in this program often fall below the radar of any other learning or education services. Tutors and families meet weekly for two-hour sessions.

Tutors in the FLO program informally interview their learners, determine needs, and cocreate with their learners sessions that are interactive and fun. The tutors follow guidelines, such as listen to the learner and ask yourself what they need, and then start with where the learner is. Be flexible and open to making changes to the session based on what you hear. In other words, bake the cake, don't just talk about it. Other guidelines include going outside and taking field trips. In this way, each learner leads the curriculum.

Make programs and topics relevant to the unique challenges of these learners. There are many ways we can tailor our programs and build content to meet the needs of specific groups. The example in the vignette of the FLO program highlights some of these important considerations. Teachers need to start by asking questions, working together to determine learning needs, and being flexible. Teachers also might need to go beyond the regular program structure, materials, curriculum, and resources. They can address specific issues or concerns when working with special populations. Here are some examples:

- If you are teaching immigrant and refugee women, consider running your program in an elementary school.

- If you are teaching a women-only class, consider creating a unit on women's health.

- If you are teaching youth, consider developing a listening activity using hip hop, country, or pop music.

- If your learners have immigration worries, consider teaching some lessons on the topic of sanctuary cities.

Be mindful and protective of the issues of these groups. We may take citizenship or legal immigration status—and the access that these provide—for granted. If we are working with undocumented learners or people with precarious immigration status, they may not have access to recreational programs, libraries, childcare, emergency shelters, public health, food banks, transportation, and police services. We don't want to put students at risk, so we may not be able to ask our students to disclose much personal information. We may not be able to invite a local police officer to class to be a guest speaker, or we may not be able to have students apply for a library card while visiting the public library on a field trip because they may not have a valid form of identification. We can, however, show our support by including these learners, by being sensitive to their struggles, and by creating conditions for safe and meaningful learning in our classrooms.

Principle 6. *Engage and Collaborate within a Community of Practice*

Advocate for program policies and decisions that specifically support the needs of these learners. We can ensure the learners have the following:

- solutions for child care and transportation
- connections with social service providers
- food
- flexibility (e.g., in terms of attendance and time of class)
- trained staff who understand the needs of the specific group

- classes available where they live
- other support services, as needed

The Additional Roles, Responsibilities, and Challenges of Teachers of English Learners

Carla works as a part-time language instructor. Through her teaching, she found that some women who suffered from past trauma didn't attend regular language classes. Carla wanted to ensure these women weren't left out of the opportunity to learn. This led her to pilot a class for women who had experienced (or were experiencing) trauma. Setting it up wasn't easy, though. She didn't know where to begin. Few of her colleagues had any experience teaching such students. She struggled to find resources for this new class. Eventually, she connected with the local health authority, and they formed a partnership, which made the class possible. She gained access to new resources and the tools she needed; the partners guided her learning on aspects of trauma that impact learning.

In this new class, students recounted their past experiences. Many of the shared stories revealed violence, loss, and isolation. Carla was deeply affected by them. Soon, she began experiencing burnout. She felt drained and tired. She was unable to watch or listen to the news. Some days, she did not want to go to work anymore because she felt overwhelmed and incapable of meeting the demands of the job. Recognizing that these feelings weren't normal for her and that they had drained her excitement for teaching, she sought help.

A counselor helped her work through these feelings. The counselor also encouraged her to find peers to speak with. When she reached out to other instructors, she recognized that she wasn't alone with her problem. Together, they organized self-care sessions, which turned out to be very helpful. She also joined BC TEAL (a professional organization in Canada for teachers of English), which connected her with others in her field. Additionally, she started taking daily lunch time walks with a colleague. With time, she began to feel like herself, again; her enjoyment of teaching returned.

Teachers have shared concerns and want to do what is best for students, but their work situations are not always ideal. Like Carla, we may struggle with a lack of resources or start to feel exhausted and drained because of the expectations of our jobs. In this section, we look at a few of the most prominent challenges that teachers face in their work. These include working in low-resourced programs, having limited professional development opportunities, and experiencing burnout. Even with these challenges, there are many proactive measures we can take to enhance and develop ourselves as exemplary teachers. We can advocate, collaborate, understand, ensure self-care, and create caring workplaces.

Unfortunately, the education of adult English learners is often undervalued and underfunded. We may be in work situations where our employment is precarious (as a result of being project based or dependent on short-term funding) and the prospect of full-time employment is bleak. We may not have the time or resources to support our learners. We may work in low-resourced programs where classroom materials and instructional infrastructure necessary to support learners with special needs or challenges are unavailable.

Teachers may feel frustrated by learners' lack of progress; they may feel discouraged and powerless. We may find that our paid time is insufficient to support certain learners in the way they should be taught. Teachers may lack the skills and preparation to support marginalized and vulnerable learners and feel helpless as a result of these failings (Wilbur, 2016). New teachers may not have the training or professional development opportunities to serve learners with challenges. Best practices and current research are not always shared with teachers on the ground. We can start to feel overwhelmed, overburdened, or ill-equipped to do our jobs some days.

Being a teacher of adult ELs is rewarding, provided we receive guidance and support along with the inevitable challenges. Our capacity to make a valuable contribution to learners' language skills and overall well-being depends on our dispositions as well as on access to resources that can sustain and enhance our practice. By building inclusive learning environments for our students (and ourselves), we are aiding intercommunication and laying the groundwork for students' meaningful engagement in their new communities. Teachers want to do their best and be exemplary professionals. They provide mentorship and support, and they share resources with students. Even though these extra roles, responsibilities, and challenges increase the workload several times over, teachers still take them on with passion and commitment in order to provide an educational experience that raises student capacity for social engagement.

Teachers recognize burnout, compassion fatigue, and vicarious trauma. As we engage with students who have endured difficult experiences and undergone enormous struggles, we cannot help but be affected. Teachers can experience burnout or vicarious trauma or suffer compassion fatigue. It is important for us to recognize what these conditions are and how they might impact us so that we can build our resilience.

Burnout is a state of chronic stress and exhaustion. Compassion fatigue is described as the cost of caring for others (Figley, 1995). Vicarious trauma occurs as a result of being exposed to learners' traumatic experiences (Horsman, 2000); it is the personal transformation during which we can begin to view and experience people, the world, and ourselves differently as a result of engaging empathetically with our students' traumatic experiences.

The signs for burnout, compassion fatigue, and vicarious trauma differ but also overlap. Consider the causes and seek help when these signs affect the way you function:

- exhaustion
- increased susceptibility to illness
- anger and irritability
- avoidance of learners
- distancing, as in avoiding friends and family, not spending time with colleagues in a social setting
- reduced ability to feel sympathy and empathy
- hypersensitivity or insensitivity to emotionally charged stimuli
- loss of hope

Be an advocate for yourself, your learners, and your programs. As advocates, we strive to ensure that the interests of adult English learners are represented in policy and decision-making. Teachers advocate for better teaching conditions, policies, and opportunities that give us the time we need to spend with our students and the resources and services we need to succeed in our diverse classrooms. Teachers might consider joining the local, regional, national, or international professional organizations where they find a forum for discussing the challenges that learners face. Teachers might consider other forms of civic engagement (e.g., writing op-eds or a position statement, joining a policy committee on the needs of special populations), and we might engage in research in the areas that need further investigation, such as supporting language learners with disabilities, trauma, and mental health issues.

Collaborate with others. Teachers are least effective when they work in isolation. We benefit from the connections we make with our colleagues, but many connections outside our profession may be equally helpful. We can liaise with service providers who have the know-how and capacity to support us with issues that we are not yet ready to handle ourselves. For example, we can connect with counseling services that can help support learners who have experienced trauma, or with disability advocates who can demonstrate to us useful instructional practices. We need to create links with settlement workers and outreach specialists who are available to meet the needs of our learners beyond the classroom.

Create caring workplaces. There are many strategies and approaches to prevent or mitigate burnout, compassion fatigue, and vicarious trauma. We highlighted some self-care strategies earlier in this chapter. Teachers also need flexibility and supportive managers who are open to looking at their workload and their job expectations.

Teachers can attend and advocate for ongoing professional development and build strong support networks within workplaces and communities. Administrators can offer professional development on topics related to trauma-informed care, cross-cultural competencies, and skill-building strategies. We can talk about our struggles and concerns with our colleagues, and we can talk to supportive and thoughtful managers.

Expand professional development opportunities. Teachers need a broad range of professional development and training to learn about methods to mitigate barriers, build language skills, and better support learners. Workshops sharing instructional practices are always welcome. Some programs have limited funds for teacher development, so we may have to seek out other opportunities. Membership in TESOL International Association and its affiliates provides access to networking and to low-cost and free online professional learning options. Building communities of practice in our local areas can help us collaborate with peers to gain the skills needed to lead students to success.

A Look Back and a Look Ahead

Learners come to our classes with their own stories, experiences, and migration journeys. It is critically important that we feel prepared to assist these learners and that we are supported in our work. In this chapter, we have examined a number of the challenges that teachers of English learners may encounter in adult ESOL and workforce development programs. These challenges are situational, institutional, and dispositional.

Some of these challenges are ongoing and some more profound than others. The chapter detailed the following:

- the impact of significant issues in teaching adult English learners, including cultural adaptation, literacy issues, disability and impairment vulnerabilities, mental health issues, and the concerns of special populations
- how *The 6 Principles for Exemplary Teaching of English Learners* can provide us with proactive measures to accommodate learners with such challenges and help us build our capacity to create inclusive learning situations
- proactive measures ranging from understanding why students don't participate in classes to promoting a culturally responsive classroom, and including understanding how low literacy impacts our students' lives
- how to recognize the signs of trauma in our students and burnout in ourselves, and how to seek help

The 6 Principles allow us to better understand how to support, promote, and advocate for our learners and programs in meaningful and effective ways, even in times of great change.

Chapter 5 describes how The 6 Principles apply to adult learners in five distinct adult education and workplace programs. Through this exploration, we see how The 6 Principles play out in practice and how we can implement them in our own classrooms.

Additional resources pertaining to this chapter are available at www.the6principles.org/adult-education.

5 THE 6 PRINCIPLES IN DIFFERENT PROGRAM CONTEXTS

Exemplary English language instruction occurs in many types of programs and with many types of students. Earlier chapters discussed student characteristics and classroom practices; this chapter describes how teachers in five types of programs apply The 6 Principles in English classes for adults.

Programs differ in several important ways that influence the instructional decisions teachers make and the outcomes of student learning (Condelli & Wrigley, 2006). In addition to language learning, some programs also focus on content (e.g., food safety, specific job skills, or information required for citizenship exams). Many programs follow standards and/or have required assessments that guide instruction. Though some programs rely on set curricula, others allow teachers to shape the curriculum. The resources available to programs (e.g., access to textbooks, the internet, and digital devices) differ widely as well. Programs also vary in the types of training required of teachers and tutors. In addition, instructional time differs: some programs meet every day for five hours, and others meet just once a week for one hour.

The 6 Principles for Exemplary Teaching of English Learners apply to all kinds of learners in all types of programs. They are a framework for designing or improving instruction, regardless of the setting. However, the application of principles varies by program type, and the principles will have different degrees of emphasis in each.

This chapter describes English language classes in five different settings:

- a U.S. workplace that partnered with a local literacy organization
- a Canadian employment preparation program
- an Australian government–funded employment preparation program
- a U.S. affordable housing organization
- an adult basic education English for Speakers of Other Languages (ESOL) program at a U.S. community college

Each of the classes is based on a real English language class in an actual program, although some details have been changed for anonymity (e.g., teachers' names, information about students, course specifics). Although we show these specific examples, many of the ideas are applicable to more contexts.

We invite you to read through all of these cases to see what the principles look like in each context and focus on the one that is the most similar to your own.

Learning at Work in the United States

Emery Gaines teaches English in a workplace environment in a small city in the western United States. The workplace manufactures clothing with many employees who are native Spanish speakers and English learners, so the employer invited a local literacy organization to provide English classes. Emery's class consists of 10 women, who all work in the sewing department. The students work four 10-hour days each week, Monday through Thursday. The class meets at the end of the 10-hour shift for 90 minutes on Tuesdays and Thursdays and is organized into 12-week terms. The employer pays the workers for 45 minutes of their time in English class, as long as they stay for the full 90 minutes. Attendance at the classes is very good. The literacy organization selects the textbook, which focuses on integrating English listening, speaking, reading, and writing for real-life needs.

The employer wants the employees to be able to use English on the job, including speaking with supervisors and staff in Human Resources (HR). Currently, most of the supervisors are bilingual in English and Spanish, and the employer would like to be able to hire supervisors who don't necessarily speak Spanish.

The students in Emery's program take the CASAS reading test and are placed into one of four levels of English classes at the workplace. Emery teaches the second of four levels, Beginning, for students whose CASAS reading score is between 185 and 200. She aligns her instruction to performance levels 2 and 3 of the Educational Functioning Level Descriptors for ESL (English as a second language; U.S. Department of Education, Division of Adult Education and Literacy, 2017). Table 5.1 shows the performance descriptors that Emery uses for planning.

Table 5.1	Performance descriptors for low beginning and high beginning English as a second language learners
Student level	**Performance descriptors for educational functioning level**
Low beginning (Student performance level 2)	Listening and Speaking: Can understand simple questions related to personal information, spoken slowly and with repetition. Can respond with simple learned phrases to some common questions related to routine survival situations.
	Reading and Writing: Can read numbers and letters and some common sight words. Can read and write some familiar words. Can write basic personal information like own name and address.
	Functional and Workplace Skills: Can handle routine entry-level jobs that require simple written or oral English communication and in which job tasks can be demonstrated.
High beginning (Student performance level 3)	Listening and Speaking: Can understand common words, simple phrases, and sentences containing familiar vocabulary, spoken slowly with some repetition. Can respond to simple questions about personal everyday activities, and can express immediate needs.
	Reading and Writing: Can read most sight words, and many common words. Can read familiar phrases and simple sentences. Can write some simple sentences with limited vocabulary. Writing shows very little control of basic grammar, capitalization and punctuation.
	Functional and Workplace Skills: Can handle routine entry level jobs requiring basic written or oral English communication and in which job tasks can be demonstrated.

(Source: NRS technical assistance guide for performance accountability under the Workforce Innovation and Opportunity Act: Exhibit 2.2 Functioning Level Table; U.S. Department of Education, Division of Adult Education and Literacy, 2017)

Emery is aware that the success of the program depends on whether she can unite the goals of all stakeholders. First, she meets with the employers to learn about their expectations and the parameters for the class. Then, as the lead teacher in the program, Emery coordinates with the other teachers on topics such as the following:

- student placement
- workplace topics to add to the textbook topics
- learning objectives
- tracking student progress in each level
- reporting test scores to the employer

Principle 1. *Know Your Learners*

The students placed in Emery's class all completed at least six years of education in their native country of Mexico, are native Spanish speakers, and have basic literacy in Spanish. Members of the class have been in the United States for an average of 15 years. They have a variety of comfort levels with technology; all of the students have cell phones, including several with smartphones, and use them to access Duolingo, a free language learning app.

When Emery first talked with the students about their English goals, they told her that they wanted to be able to use English with people at their children's school, with their doctors, and while shopping. They reported that they don't talk while they are working because they want to sew as much as possible. In addition, all of the supervisors are bilingual in both English and Spanish, so work-related needs can be met in Spanish. The students also reported that when they needed something from HR, they asked for the Spanish-speaking member of the department.

Emery designed a course that included the employer's goals and the students' goals. She planned units based on topics that students requested and also integrated employment topics in the curriculum. For example, in a unit on family, Emery added workplace topics such as filling out health insurance forms, talking about the jobs held by students' family members, and answering questions about who the employer should contact in case of an emergency (a form required by HR and also the school district). See the textbox below for Emery's selection of topics.

Sample Workplace Topics

Textbook topic	Associated workplace topics
Daily activities	Work schedule Being on time to work Paid holidays, vacation time
Transportation	Types of transportation to get to work Directions at work Nearby services (cash machine, gas station, hospital)
Health	Calling in sick Accident at work Family leave Parts of the body that are used at work (e.g., wrist, to prevent carpal tunnel)
Grocery shopping and money	Hourly wages or salary Reading pay stubs Depositing paychecks

Principle 2. *Create Conditions for Language Learning*

Because the students are tired after a 10-hour day, Emery works to make the class fun, engaging, and motivating. Each class period, the students take turns bringing food, and Emery and the class members spend their break eating together, making the group feel like a community. Emery also spends at least some time during each session getting the class up and moving around. For example, Emery moves the chairs and tables around to simulate a different environment, such as a grocery store or the HR office, for role-play activities. When the students are particularly tired toward the end of class, Emery has the class play vocabulary games, such as word bingo and letter/word guessing games.

To make the classroom a safe space for learners to raise their concerns, Emery is careful about what she shares with the employer. Information about health, family situations, and transportation problems, for example, always remain confidential. Emery shares information about attendance and language assessment scores with the employer, with the students' knowledge.

Emery is careful to use real-life scenarios to provide contexts that are meaningful and motivating to the learners. For example, the learners need to be able to communicate with people in HR at their workplace, so Emery designs activities in which students practice asking questions and giving information from interactions with individuals in HR. Emery helps the learners see that instead of waiting to talk to the only Spanish-speaking person in HR, they will be able to communicate with anyone in that department. This helps the learners to picture a future in which they will be successful using English in situations where they currently use only Spanish.

Principle 3. *Design High-Quality Lessons for Language Development*

Emery designs lessons that integrate both the topics students want for their daily lives and the language they need to succeed in the workplace. Table 5.2 illustrates how lesson or unit objectives can relate to both.

Table 5.2 Illustrative objectives	
Workplace use	**Daily life use**
I can ask my **supervisor** for time off, orally or by email.*	I can ask a **child's teacher** for a meeting, orally or by email.*
I can read and fill out basic **Human Resources forms** with personal information, both on paper and online.*	I can read and fill out basic **health or education forms** with personal information, both on paper and online.*
I can orally **report a problem to a supervisor** on the telephone or in person.	I can orally **report a problem to a landlord** on the telephone or in person.

*When using digital devices, Emery makes sure that students use the workplace wireless network so that they do not use their own cell phone data plan.

Consistent routines help learners know what to expect and what to do so that they can focus on new material. Emery has an established routine that she uses each class, and the students know the pattern (see table 5.3).

Section of class	Procedures	Specific example
Table 5.3	**Emery's class routine**	
Review	The teacher starts the class with a review by asking the same questions that ended the previous class. Sentence strips: The teacher hands out a sentence strip with the same questions that she modeled written on it to all learners. The learners walk around and ask each other the review questions. The students get out their textbooks and Emery leads them to go over the homework from the previous lesson.	In a unit on family, Emery reviews the previous topic by asking several students, "Are you married? What is your husband's name? How many children do you have?" She hands out a strip of paper to each student with the same questions. The students interview each other, reading their questions from the paper strip.
Textbook lesson introduction	The teacher introduces the lesson objective for the class.	The lesson objective is "You will be able to ask someone to be your emergency contact and complete an emergency contact form for the Human Resources Department." As a prereading warm up, the class discusses the kinds of emergencies that can happen at work and what to do when there is an emergency.
Reading passage	The routine for a new lesson always starts with a reading passage. First, Emery reads the passage aloud. Second, all of the students read chorally. Third, student pairs read aloud to each other. Reading the passage three times affords learners time to comprehend the reading and practice saying and hearing the passage. It also avoids creating the anxiety that reading aloud in front of a group can cause.	The reading in the textbook for this lesson is related to forms, but Emery wants to talk about forms specific to the workplace, so she has written a short paragraph about a person who has a small accident at work and whose employer wants to call an emergency contact to come and pick her up.
Comprehension questions in writing	Working collaboratively, pairs of students discuss and answer comprehension questions about the passage before writing their answers.	The students fill out an emergency contact form for the person in the reading passage. The whole class goes over the information in the emergency contact form.
Break	The class eats together.	
Role-play	The students perform a short role-play that mirrors the reading passage. Students are randomly assigned roles and groups rehearse the dialogue, which each group performs for the class. Rehearsal builds fluency while creating the opportunity to practice in a low-anxiety way, in an activity that is more enjoyable than a drill and creates the opportunity to improvise and use props.	The students perform a role-play in which they ask someone to serve as their emergency contact person and collect contact information from him or her.

(continued)

Section of class	Procedures	Specific example
Vocabulary game	Students play a game to practice the lesson vocabulary (e.g., word bingo, guess the letters and word).	The students practice key vocabulary (*emergency, contact, reach, accident, pick up*) by drawing, labeling, and sharing a picture.
Home learning	The teacher assigns homework. To support students who want to study more, Emery creates digital flashcards so that students can study their vocabulary independently on their digital devices.	Students will complete their workplace's emergency contact form. Students can practice key words and phrases related to emergency contacts with digital flashcards.
Exit ticket	Emery asks a question from the day's lesson. Each student has to answer the question orally before leaving. This question serves as the review question for the next class.	Emery asks each student as they are leaving class, "Who will be your emergency contact? How can you get their contact information?"

Table 5.3   Emery's class routine (*continued*)

Principle 4. *Adapt Lesson Delivery as Needed*, and Principle 5. *Monitor and Assess Student Language Development*

Emery builds in daily formative assessment to gauge learners' progress. During the review question at the beginning of class, she circulates among the students, allowing her to hear each student's question production as well as their answers to their partner's question. Emery's strategy for giving feedback is to recast the sentence or phrase that contains the error, slowing down slightly and emphasizing the part with the correction. Usually, the student will notice the change and repeat the correct answer.

The formative assessment helps Emery know if the class should revisit the lesson from the previous class or if they are ready to move on to the next lesson. If students need more review and scaffolding, Emery can provide more vocabulary practice opportunities, break the task into smaller parts, or give the students a fictional person to use for the emergency contact form.

Emery knows that some students prefer not to talk about themselves. She does not expect every student to demonstrate mastery of all the material every time; she knows that errors are a necessary part of learning, and she gets a sense of how well students are working with the new material.

Emery also uses an oral "exit ticket" to assess how well the students understand the new language from that day. As an oral exit ticket, Emery individually asks each student to answer one or two questions from the class that day. For example, "Who is your emergency contact and how can you get their contact information?" If Emery feels that the students are ready, she could also ask for the completed emergency contact form as a written exit ticket.

Principle 6. *Engage and Collaborate within a Community of Practice*

Emery has a community of practice in her program. Emery and her colleagues discuss curricular topics, objectives, assessments, and more. She and all of her fellow instructors have been through the training provided by the literacy organization. In addition, Emery has created and delivered specific workplace English training for them. They meet biweekly to discuss issues that have arisen, student progress, what has worked, what has not worked, and ideas for classroom activities to work toward meeting both the students' learning goals and the employers' goals.

Preparing for Hospitality Careers in Canada

Preparing for Hospitality Careers for Women (PHCW) is a 12-week program in which students learn workplace skills and gain Canadian work experience. Run collaboratively by a community college and a nonprofit community-based organization, PHCW offers the opportunity for immigrant women to learn safe food handling, cleaning, and hospitality skills to prepare them for entry-level work in the hotel, restaurant, and senior care industries. Students attend classes Monday through Friday, from 10 a.m.–1 p.m. for 10 weeks, and then participate in two weeks of a practicum work experience. While in the program, students earn an industry-recognized food handling certificate.

The program operates in a cohort model that integrates English language instruction with occupational skills that are specific to the hotel, restaurant, and senior home care industries, as well as with the soft skills required for work in the Canadian context. The purpose of the program is to help students build a foundation for entry-level work with a potential for higher level training in the future. Pamela Reyes teaches each cohort, along with the practicum coordinator, Niu Zhou. Experts from various fields come in to teach specific subjects, such as food safety, cleaning, and sanitizing.

> In contrast to technical skills, soft skills include competencies like interpersonal, oral and written communication, critical thinking, and problem-solving skills (Bartel, 2018).

Students are recruited from agencies that serve immigrant and refugee communities in western Canada. To be eligible, students need to be at least a 4 or 5 on the Canadian Language Benchmarks (CLB) in listening and speaking, and at least a 2 in reading and writing, as described in table 5.4 (Centre for Canadian Language Benchmarks, 2012).

Table 5.4		Sample performance descriptors based on the Canadian Language Benchmarks
Listening	CLB 4	The listener can understand, with considerable effort, simple formal and informal communication on topics of personal relevance.
	CLB 5	The listener can understand, with some effort, the gist of moderately complex, concrete formal and informal communication.
Speaking	CLB 4	The speaker can communicate information about common everyday activities, experiences, wants and needs.
	CLB 5	The speaker can communicate with some effort in short, routine social situations, and present concrete information about needs and familiar topics of personal relevance.
Reading	CLB 2	The reader can understand individual words, simple learned phrases and some very short, simple sentences related to immediate needs.
Writing	CLB 2	The writer can write basic personal identification information, words, simple phrases, and a few simple sentences about highly familiar information related to immediate needs.

CLB = Canadian Language Benchmarks
(Centre for Canadian Language Benchmarks, 2012)

Principle 1. *Know Your Learners*

At an initial information and intake session, students complete a questionnaire and have an interview with program staff. The instructor and practicum coordinator work together to collect information on students'

- educational experience,
- work experience,
- interests,
- childcare needs, and
- English language level.

The teacher, practicum coordinator, and program administrators use the information to help the learners understand what to expect in the program, to plan instruction that fits learners' interests and needs, and to start working on appropriate practicum placement. After the initial information and intake session, the students start the course as a cohort.

One of the main goals for the first week is to build rapport within the cohort of learners. The cohort is essential because it builds a system of support for the learners. Many have complex lives caring for children and other family members, attending multiple medical appointments, searching for permanent housing, and/or undergoing legal processes related to immigration. The PHCW program gives learners the opportunity to meet in a supportive environment with other women who are in similar situations. Pamela conducts team-building tasks in which the students learn each other's names, greet each other by name daily, and engage in social small talk.

As part of the program design, in addition to mutual support, the class activities model workplace soft skills. For example, when students learn to greet each other by name and engage in small talk, it models appropriate workplace communication, a soft skill that is required in Canadian work environments.

Workplace communication is also a course topic on its own. The teachers create activities on the topic of respectful communication. They discuss what respectful communication looks like (e.g., eye contact, turn taking, and forms of address) and compare and contrast the definition of respectful communication in Canada with their countries of origin. This helps the teacher know the students as well as to create conditions for language learning by inviting learners' home languages and cultures into the classroom.

Principle 2. *Create Conditions for Language Learning*

Though developing the protocols for respectful communication in Canada is crucial for learners, it is also important for teachers to respect the communication practices that learners use in their own families and cultures. In the class, Pamela does not frame communication practices as right or wrong, but as a particular coat that is suitable to wear for certain occasions. For example, one puts on a lab coat when working in medical settings and a "mom coat" when doing activities with children. Although they are different coats, both are useful and valuable in their context. This way of talking about language skills helps learners imagine themselves as capable multilinguals who can use their different languages in different situations.

The learners provide considerable support to each other as each person faces her own challenges. That others in the cohort group have faced similar issues can be reassuring. To help reduce anxiety and develop trust, each class starts with a daily check-in. During this activity, Pamela asks each student, *How are you doing? How are you feeling?* The students can choose to name their emotions, and cohort members offer support.

The program and teacher also demonstrate expectations of success for all learners. For example, like at a workplace, Pamela expects the students to arrive on time and be ready to work. However, when that does not happen, Pamela engages the student to understand the causes and to develop a solution.

One of the goals of the PHCW program is to build employability, and Pamela weaves activities with this theme throughout the curriculum. The learners have diverse work histories, some that are interrupted or problematic. An employment theme in the program is the concept of core values. Activities start with learners exploring their strengths using statements starting with *I have*, *I am*, and *I can*. Learners use these sentence starters as they explore their own core values, leading them toward confidence in talking about themselves. Being able to talk about one's strengths and core values is important in the interview process, but talking positively about oneself can be difficult for learners in this program. The next activity in this theme is to explore the core values of various Canadian companies, including those who participate in the program's practicum experience. Both sets of values—the students' and the companies'—are seen as important, but perhaps different. After learners gain confidence in talking about themselves, Niu conducts mock interview activities to build language skills for a real interview.

Principle 3. *Design High-Quality Lessons for Language Development*

Instruction in PHCW integrates English language instruction with instruction in workplace concepts related to safe food handling, sanitation practices in kitchens, safe handling of workplace hazardous materials, and principles of customer service. The syllabus is challenging and full for a 12-week course. Each day, Pamela starts the class by telling the students the language and content goals for the day. Announcing the daily goal helps the students know where they are in the class schedule of course topics and where they should keep their focus.

During week 1, in addition to teaching workplace communication skills, the teacher begins to introduce language and concepts related to the FOODSAFE program (www.foodsafe.ca/index.html), training that the government of British Columbia recommends for anyone working in the food service industry. It includes topics like the following:

- the causes of food-borne illnesses
- how to safely receive, store, prepare, and serve food
- how to clean and sanitize food preparation surfaces, tools, and dishware

The textbox on the next page shows a day in Pamela's class during this unit.

A Day in a PHCW Class

Pamela starts the unit with activities that determine what students already know about the topic. She asks students to think about what causes people to get sick from food. Working together, the students generate 20–30 questions about concepts and vocabulary related to food-borne illnesses, which they put on poster paper around the room.

The focus of the day today is on the pathogens in food that can cause people to get sick. In the previous class, the students had learned about some of the pathogens. Today, Pamela puts two or three questions on the board for review; one of them is: *Describe five pathogens in food that can make people sick.* Students work in small groups with others who share the same first language to provide answers to the questions. When the focus of the activity is on important concepts, Pamela generally asks students who share the same first language to sit together. The students are free to work in any language. When the focus is on social language and workplace communication that is likely to occur in multilingual or English settings, Pamela places the students into mixed-language groupings and asks them to communicate using English.

After the review, the class focuses on new concepts and vocabulary. To determine the vocabulary that students already know, Pamela puts the new vocabulary on the board and students work together to define and erase the words that they know, leaving only the new vocabulary. Pamela breaks the remaining words into component parts, many of which the students are already familiar with, such as the following:

Word	Related word with word parts
safe	un-safe
proper	im-proper
appropriate	in-appropriate
biology	micro-bio-logy

Pamela and the students use online resources to define the word parts and the words. Students create vocabulary cards, adding information about the word parts, the word meaning, a translation, and a visual representation of the meaning (Adelson-Goldstein, 2015). In this activity, students not only learn the meaning of these specific words, they also acquire vocabulary-learning strategies.

The next part of the class focuses on new concepts. Pamela employs multimedia as much as possible, including video, pictures, and slide presentations to share information on the concepts in a way that students can comprehend. She introduces the concept of the day today with an animated video on microorganisms. After the video, the students ask questions to help them comprehend the video, after which Pamela and the students discuss the information in the video, breaking it down into parts. Then, they work with the questions they put up at the beginning of class on the poster paper around the room to determine how the new information answers some of the questions. Pamela uses questioning strategies to elicit student output so that students have language practice with the new content in English. Students can then put the jointly constructed answers in their notes, which they will use to study for the FOODSAFE exam that they will take in several weeks.

When they are finished working through the information from the video, the students take a break. The program provides healthy snacks and tea. The break offers them an opportunity to have social time to talk and build further bonds of mutual support.

Pamela devotes the last part of the class to finishing any incomplete work and to activities that prepare students for the two-week practicum at the end of the course. The class finishes with announcements of upcoming events, such as guest speakers. As in a workplace, students are learning how to keep track of the class schedule, including changes to it.

Principle 4. *Adapt Lesson Delivery as Needed*

Pamela uses a variety of techniques to ensure that students comprehend the language they hear. In the example, Pamela has students reformulate the new information into answers to questions that they have asked. This gives students time to consider what they have heard and discuss it, collaboratively making sense of it. In observing those discussions and reformulations, Pamela gathers information about which students are struggling, and she takes steps to revisit the information with small groups of students who need more processing.

Pamela is intentional about modeling learning strategies that students can use in the class as well as in their learning beyond the classroom after the course has ended. For example, the students take notes and ask comprehension questions as listening strategies and use formulaic expressions in their social language/workplace communication activities.

Principle 5. *Monitor and Assess Student Language Development*

Pamela monitors and assesses in a variety of ways, depending on the type of activity. For example, she monitors students' understanding of the concepts in the daily review activities, and she adjusts her daily plan to include additional work on the concepts when needed. In the activities in which the students are using the social language needed for appropriate workplace communication, Pamela gives oral feedback directly, through recasts or explicit correction, while supporting the students' continued communication. She understands that it is important to match the type of feedback to the goals of the activity.

Principle 6. *Engage and Collaborate within a Community of Practice*

Pamela and Niu work closely throughout the course. They discuss the students' progress and identify which students need more support in the class and which may need more support during the practicum work experience. Both also work closely with each guest expert to make the new concepts comprehensible to the students and to scaffold the students' learning.

Pamela also participates in a community of practice on the subject of contextualized instruction, which is defined as "a process of providing language and literacy services contextualized to the skill demands of work or career and technical training [in which] instruction is offered in a supportive environment and uses authentic materials gathered from workplace and technical training" (Wrigley, 2015, p. 4). Talking with other teachers who are using and developing content-and-language-integrated teaching strategies helps Pamela with her own learning. In particular, the emphasis on authentic materials from the workplace has influenced Pamela to regularly reach out to workplaces in order to stay current on the skills they require and with the materials they use; she does this to assure that her course continues to be relevant to Canadian workplaces.

Preparing for Work in Australia

Paul McGowan teaches in the Skills for Education and Employment (SEE) program (www .education.gov.au/skills-education-and-employment) in a large city in Australia. The SEE program is funded by the Australian government for people who are unemployed, are looking for work, and have registered with the government for financial support. The program provides "language, literacy and numeracy training to eligible job seekers, with the expectation that such improvements will enable them to participate more effectively in training or in the labour force" (Skills for Education and Employment, 2018).

Students participate in up to 650 hours of free training, based on an individual plan. Participation in assigned courses is mandatory. Full-time students attend class at a center in the local community four days per week, for five hours each day.

The curriculum is quite broad, with many opportunities to customize for local community needs and students' needs. Each 10-week course is organized into five themes, each theme lasting for two weeks. For each level, two or three themes must relate to job seeking and employment skills. Each class includes 18–25 students. Throughout each term, students leave as they complete their required hours and new students enroll as seats become available.

The Australian Core Skills Framework guides the curriculum (Australian Government Department of Education and Training, 2015). The students in Paul's program are in low level 1, level 1, and level 2. Paul teaches the low level 1 (see table 5.5).

Table 5.5	Australian Core Skills Framework performance indicators for level 1 learners
Oral communication	Gives or elicits basic information in a short, simple spoken context
	Listens for basic information in short, simple oral texts
Reading	Identifies personally relevant information and ideas from texts on highly familiar topics
	Uses a limited range of strategies to locate specific information and construct meaning from explicit and highly familiar texts
Writing	Conveys a simple idea, opinion, factual information or message in writing
	Displays limited vocabulary, grammatical accuracy and understanding of conventions of written text
Learning	Demonstrates some awareness of self as a learner
	Takes first steps towards developing explicit learning strategies

(Australian Government Department of Education and Training, 2015)

Principle 1. *Know Your Learners*

Paul's students fall into one of four categories:

- Learners who have completed an English program for new immigrants but who may have started with less educational experience or no native-language literacy. Their English literacy is in early development. Their learning may have been influenced by negative forces such as trauma or illness.

- Learners who have been in Australia for three to four years but who had to go to work in non-English-speaking environments, such as fishing or farm work, immediately after immigration.

- Women (ages 30–45) with children in primary or secondary school. Their children are often doing well in school. Until now their focus has been on their children's education rather than their own. Their English skills are not sufficient for work but they now want or need to work. Many of these students are developing cottage industries, such as sewing clothing, cake decorating, or cooking, often sold online.

- Learners whose developing English skills are strong enough in some domains to proceed to the next level, but not strong enough in all of them. For example, they may place in listening and speaking at level 2 but reading and writing at level 1. Their language profile is said to have a spiky pattern.

Principle 2. *Create Conditions for Language Learning*

In the SEE program, participation in assigned classes is required, which means that learners are not necessarily highly interested in each class. To support learner motivation, one of the teacher's tasks is to create classes that are relevant but also fun and engaging.

Paul schedules class time in a way that supports student motivation. He starts with an easy warm up, moves to the more intensive and demanding tasks, and then ends with game-like activities. He also supports motivation for learning by talking about lifelong learning as a complement to students' many life accomplishments so far.

The program also supports student motivation by selecting themes for each 10-week term that are relevant and appealing to the students. In Paul's course this term, one of the themes is living in the community, specifically housing in the community, which is currently a key personal issue for his students.

Principle 3. *Design High-Quality Lessons for Language Development*

The goal for this day is to describe the types of housing that are available in the community. Paul selected this goal for several reasons. First, housing is a vital issue for his students and second, the topic fits well with one of the assessments, which is to write as much as possible to describe a selected image.

Today, the students are working on language to describe the housing in which they live. In the previous class, Paul and the students discussed the importance of being able to describe things in English, specifically things related to housing. Paul helped the students imagine being able to describe their housing to English speakers in their communities, in English. So far in this theme, students have learned a variety of nouns related to housing, such as *house*, *kitchen*, and *garden*. The following textbox shows a day in Paul's class during this unit.

A Day in a SEE Program Class

Paul breaks the five-hour class into three blocks of instructional time.

Block 1: Warm up and review (1.5 hours)
Paul's goal during block 1 is to have a light warm up and review while the students arrive and get settled. He designs an informal review of previously learned language by using the same language in a new format. For example, today he gives the students the choice of a word search, a crossword, or a word game that all use the vocabulary from the previous class. He invites students to help each other during this activity, and students who finish one game can move on to another. While the students are completing the activities, Paul tries to have at least one short impromptu conversation with each of his students. Impromptu conversation is an important skill, but his students have few opportunities to engage in such conversations in English.

Block 2: Main focus of the lesson (1.5–2 hours)
During the second block of time Paul designs activities that are more intensive and connect explicitly to a specific assessment task. The activities in the second block typically target features of a type of text. Today, the activities focus on the features of descriptions.

Paul is keenly aware that there are a variety of levels within his low level 1 class. When planning, he thinks of his students as three different groups and prepares class activities that will challenge all of the learners without overwhelming them.

(continued)

In the theme of housing, Paul prepares three differentiated activities. For the lowest level, he prepares a list of five adjectives. He guesses that the students know these words in their first languages, which serves as important prior knowledge. For their task, Paul asks the students to use their smartphones (all of the students know how to access the program's free wireless internet) to translate the words and write down definitions in any language.

For the middle group, Paul prepares a longer list of adjectives and several activities for them to interact with the meaning of the adjectives, including looking up definitions using their smartphones, an opposites-matching activity, and an activity that asks learners to pair an adjective with one of the nouns that they have been learning, in phrases such as *old house*, *modern kitchen*, and *beautiful garden*.

Paul gives the higher level group the same list of adjectives, but their task is more complex. Their task is to learn the adjectives and then form questions to ask their classmates. This group works cooperatively to generate their questions and create a kind of informal survey with questions such as *Do you live in an old house?*

In the last part of the second block, just before the lunch break, the students walk around and ask and answer questions in the informal survey. In this activity, all students have the opportunity to practice their listening and speaking skills. Finally, they compile their results to find out how many students live in each type of housing and make a graph. Paul has prepared results from another Australian city, and, in a whole class discussion, the students compare results from the two cities. The activities in block 2 are quite intensive for the students, and they are ready for a break when lunchtime arrives.

Block 3: Lighter activities, including pronunciation (1 hour)

After the lunch break, Paul schedules pronunciation and vocabulary practice guided by tutorial videos that are freely available on YouTube (e.g., those made by Mark Kulek: www.youtube.com /channel/UC9VWyvdF-91McG6kt27MeKA). These tutorials use animation and visuals to demonstrate vocabulary and pronunciation, which is a nice change of pace from the cognitively demanding listening and speaking activities from earlier in the class. Paul also conducts a whole-class digital quiz with Kahoot, an online quiz tool (www.kahoot.com). Both activities practice vocabulary related to the theme and engage students actively. Paul ends the class on a positive note by revisiting the day's goal of describing the place where students live. At this level, homework is not required, but Paul prepares some optional take-home tasks for each lesson.

Principle 4. *Adapt Lesson Delivery as Needed*

Not only does Paul provide feedback to students during the course of the class, but he also adapts his instruction based on what he learns. For example, when Paul sees that a student or small group of students is misinterpreting new vocabulary items during block 1, he works with them to demonstrate the meaning through pictures and drawings. When Paul notices that another group is struggling with writing questions for a class survey, he works with that group to show a model and to create with them several sentence frames that they can refer to.

Principle 5. *Monitor and Assess Student Language Development*

Paul regularly monitors student production through various assessment strategies and gives feedback. His feedback varies based on the type of activity. During the activities in block 1, Paul uses a feedback strategy in which he models the corrected language in his reply, but he keeps the focus on communication and does not interrupt the flow of conversation. He has found that students like direct correction of their pronunciation, and so, during the third block, Paul walks around the class and provides direct and explicit correction of pronunciation.

On written assignments, Paul is careful to provide feedback in the early drafts only on the language elements that are the current target of instruction. For example, he focuses on giving feedback on the present verb tense in a sentence describing an apartment, or an adjective that comes after a noun rather than preceding it. He wants to help the students improve in their ability to meet the demands of the assessment, but he understands that too much correction erodes student motivation and does not contribute to additional learning. In future drafts, Paul will provide feedback on other areas they have studied, such as the correct use of pronouns and auxiliary verbs.

Learning in Affordable Housing in the United States

Katie Hinton teaches ESL to adults in a midsize city in the Midwest United States. The ESL class takes place in a housing complex that is subsidized by the city to make rents affordable. Run by a community-based organization, the complex has a common area, which includes a room with a whiteboard, movable tables and chairs, wireless internet, and a cabinet with a set of tablets. Tutors use this room to work with children on their homework after school. The housing organization encourages partnerships with local organizations that provide opportunities for residents to build their skills in all areas of life, including employment skills. Because digital literacy is an important employment skill, course instructors are encouraged to include digital literacy in their instruction. The long-term goal is for the residents to be able to pay the full amount of rent without subsidy.

The only ESL class offered meets twice a week, from 9:30 a.m–11:00 a.m., a time selected because school-aged children are in school. Any resident can enroll in the class. The schedule of the ESL classes mirrors the public school calendar. The housing organization does not dictate a curriculum nor require reporting of outcomes; the teacher develops the curriculum based on the goals and interests of the students.

Principle 1. *Know Your Learners*

Sixteen students are in this class, from a variety of language and education backgrounds.

Four of the students have very early emerging levels of literacy in their first language and report that they didn't go to school. The rest of the students completed six or more years of education and have at least moderate literacy in their first language. The students range in age from 25–60. Most have smartphones that they use for telephone calls and for texting in their first language or with limited English phrases. All are beginning English learners.

To determine the curriculum for the course, Katie conducted a needs assessment during the first week of class. She selected pictures on the topics that beginning level ESL students most often request, including the following:

- children's education
- health/medical
- job skills and careers
- transportation
- money and banking

Katie represents each topic with an image that depicts people interacting. As a class, they discuss the images, using the multiple languages spoken by the students; in English, they point out the different tasks that the individuals in the image need to do. For example, using their various languages and Google Translate, students talk about reading notes and emails from their children's schools, reading the online school calendar, and talking with teachers at school conferences. The discussion gives Katie information about the students' oral English abilities and the non-English linguistic resources they bring to the classroom. It also helps the students begin to imagine themselves as users of English in the different settings. After a robust (and chaotic) discussion, each student votes on their preferred topic by putting two sticker dots next to the images that show the topics that they would like to study. Katie and the students then work together to tally the sticker dots, selecting the main topics for the course.

Principle 2. *Create Conditions for Language Learning*

There are additional benefits to having the students help select the curriculum in this kind of activity. Because many adult English learners do not have positive school experiences, they can be nervous in class. Having an activity in which students can use their linguistic resources, thereby demonstrating one of their strengths and giving them a voice in their own learning, reduces learner anxiety and creates a positive learning environment.

Beyond basic information, the students in this class are reluctant to talk about their own situations, especially regarding how long they have been in the United States, details about their educational experiences, and specifics about their family situations. Knowing that it is important to respect students' desire for privacy, Katie creates activities that feature fictional characters instead of having students talk about themselves. For example, in a unit on talking with the doctor, Katie creates a page with a fictional name, an image, and a set of symptoms. Katie is careful to use names that come from the cultures and languages of her students.

Principle 3. *Design High-Quality Lessons for Language Development*

Katie designs lessons that are embedded in contexts that are relevant to her students and align with their goals, and she provides multimodal input to increase comprehension and engagement. Every class follows the same pattern of activities; Katie knows that having a consistent routine helps students know what to expect, saves them effort in trying to understand instructions, and allows them to devote more attention to the new language.

Principle 4. *Adapt Lesson Delivery as Needed*

Katie utilizes work station activities. One of the benefits is that students can study at their preferred level. Katie prepares a set of activities at different complexity levels for each station. For example, one activity is a vocabulary card game in which students can practice body part vocabulary with the game of concentration, looking for matches of images and written words. Another activity teaches basic writing: learners can copy words from cards onto a handwriting sheet, or they can assemble target vocabulary terms with letter tiles. Another activity has pairs of students take turns giving each other spelling tests.

At another station, students work on activities with tablets, which is part of the daily routine (Harris, 2015). Katie has prepared a simple website for the class with three different tabs. Each tab contains images linking to activities aimed at different beginning levels. On the website, one of the tabs contains a link to an online book, *Amir Gets Sick*, which was used in a previous class and which students like to reread (globalaccess.bowvalleycollege.ca/esl-readers/amir-gets-sick). The other tabs contain spelling activities with the target vocabulary and typing practice. Katie provides some guidance to students about what activities might suit them best, but Katie also knows that selecting their own learning activities helps the students gain confidence in their ability to learn, promoting self-directed learning.

One of the stations is teacher facilitated. There, Katie works with small groups and revisits the language that students are struggling with. Katie can plan activities or decide what to focus on based on her observations of the class that day. Working with small groups also allows Katie to gather a single language group and leverage their linguistic resources so students can collaborate to solve a problem or work together on a concept in more depth.

The following textbox shows a day in Katie's class during the unit about the doctor's office.

A Day in the Housing Organization's ESL Class

The lesson for the day relates to answering questions about symptoms at a medical appointment. In the needs assessment, students had indicated they wanted to learn about health and medicine and to be able to talk with the doctor.

In the past several classes, the students have learned vocabulary about describing symptoms. To select authentic vocabulary, Katie had spoken to her own doctor about the questions doctors usually ask their patients about symptoms. As a result, the thematic vocabulary includes items such as *shortness of breath, chest pain, nausea, diarrhea,* and *chills.* The students completed multiple oral and written activities with the new vocabulary prior to this class. They also studied the question form *Do you have _____?* and practiced with oral activities.

> While talking with medical providers is a real-life language need, it is also important to be sure that students know how to ask for an interpreter in medical settings.

Katie starts by talking about the lesson objective for the day, which is "Learners will be able to answer questions about symptoms." She continues with activities that review the symptom vocabulary, first in oral form, then in written form, in a familiar pattern. First, she projects slides, each with an image and a word on the screen, and asks the students to say the word. If there are questions about meaning, Katie switches the computer to Google Translate and the class looks on while they translate the word into all of the students' languages. Then, students break into pairs and use flashcards to match the written English word with the image. The students quiz each other, showing the image and asking for their partner to say the word. The images help students comprehend the vocabulary, and the activity provides an opportunity to practice the new words.

The next activity asks the students to orally produce the language in a role-play. To prepare, Katie has created a set of fictional patient identity cards each with a name, birthdate, and four images that represent symptoms, using the same images as on the slides. She has also created strips of paper, each with a question that asks about a symptom, such as *Do you have chest pain?* Half of the students get a fictional patient identity and half are given a question. Students move around the room, with half asking and half answering *Yes, I do* or *No, I don't,* according to their fictional identity. This activity allows students to actively engage in skills and to practice without anxiety, scaffolded by images and text.

Katie invites student pair volunteers to perform the whole role-play. The student in the role of doctor gets a full set of question strips, puts on a lab coat, and asks the questions to the student in the role of patient, who answers the questions in character. A lot of laughter accompanies this activity, because students are dramatic in their roles as a fictional patient or stern doctor. By the end of the activity, all of the students have volunteered at least once, many more than once. A role-play activity is one way to make learning outcomes observable; both the teacher and the students can see that they have achieved the learning objective for the day.

After a break, the next activity uses the same language, but in the written modality. Katie has prepared a questionnaire that asks for the patient's name and date of birth, and asks the patient to review a list of symptoms and mark those that he or she is experiencing. Katie knows that it is important that the language used is exactly the same as they had practiced in the oral activities so that only the written modality is new. The class completes one questionnaire together, and then all of the students fill in a questionnaire using their fictional patient identity.

(continued)

The last activity is working at stations, tables where related activities are set up for students to complete on their own or in small groups. As part of the classroom routine, students rotate through a set of work stations to practice with the language of the day or to review language from previous classes. At one station is a set of tablet computers; at another, vocabulary activities; and at a third, writing and spelling activities. Katie sits at the fourth station to work with students in small groups. Having a variety of activities in the classroom allows students to choose their preferred activities at least some of the time.

At the tablet computer station, learners know how to turn on the devices and select an icon for the class home screen. The students are free to choose any of the activities there; most make good selections of activities at their level. The main activity for the day at the tablet station is to complete the online form, which is exactly the same as the paper form students completed in the earlier activity, repeating the task in a different modality.

In her design of the curriculum, Katie wanted to integrate into the class digital literacy activities. She decided that for each of the themes she would use online forms because students can practice literacy with online forms outside of the classroom. See table 5.6 for the forms that correspond to each theme. By having a single type of digital activity for all of the themes, over time the students become skilled at using electronic devices to complete online forms. In preparing these forms, Katie learned how quick and easy it is to create them.

Table 5.6   Forms that correspond to each theme

Theme	Paper and digital form
Children's education	Personal information form
Health/medical	Health information form
Job skills and careers	Job application form
Money and banking	Credit application form

Principle 5. *Monitor and Assess Student Language Development*

The role-play activity serves as a performance task that gives Katie information about each student's learning progress. Katie also uses the information in a formative way, and, for the next class, she adjusts the lesson plan and the station activities to target language that needs more practice.

Katie is very careful about providing oral feedback to learners during their oral interactions. This group of students lacks confidence in their English language abilities, and Katie has learned that they instantly stop talking when she provides corrective oral feedback. As a result, in oral interactions Katie focuses her feedback only on meaning, and not on form. She primarily uses clarification requests, such as *Do you mean shortness of breath?*, or requests for repetition, such as *Can you say that again?*

To provide the opportunity for feedback, Katie tries to create station activities that have built-in feedback mechanisms, such as games, self-checking on spelling tests, or letter-matching in which students compare their answer to a model.

Principle 6. *Engage and Collaborate within a Community of Practice*

As the sole English teacher at the site, Katie does not have direct access to other English teachers, but she wants to continue to learn how to best serve her students. She has joined an online discussion group for teachers of English language acquisition (community.lincs.ed.gov), where she enjoys reading what other teachers are doing, and she sometimes poses a question to get suggestions for what she is dealing with in her class.

An Adult Basic Education ESOL Program at a Community College

Evan Miller teaches in an ESOL Adult Basic Education program at a community college in a midsize city in the eastern United States. The ESOL program is for adults who are learning English for work, education, or training opportunities or for family and community purposes. It is not an intensive English for academic purposes program for those entering an academic track at the college. Classes are offered in the morning and evening on the main campus. Classes meet for two hours twice each week and run for 14 weeks on the schedule set for all of the community college courses.

Evan teaches a variety of ESOL classes for the community college and, among other classes, he is currently teaching level 4 Oral Communication. Students in this course gain listening, speaking, vocabulary, and grammar skills while developing oral English. Students are placed into levels based on their score on a test administered by the ESOL program.

All courses in the community college have an online course website in the college's learning management system (LMS), and teachers are encouraged but not required to use it. Evan thinks carefully about whether to use the LMS with his ESOL students. He knows that the LMS will be quite a challenge for some of his students, but it will help them develop their digital literacy skills, especially those students who want to continue with additional education. For this course, Evan has decided to use the LMS in a way that will introduce his students to it and give them regular practice accessing it. To make the introductory experience manageable, he has decided to make available just two sections: the announcements and calendar functionalities.

Evan's community college is in a U.S. state that has adopted the College and Career Readiness (CCR) Standards for Adult Education (U.S. Department of Education, Office of Vocational and Adult Education, 2013), and the curriculum of the ESOL program is aligned to these CCR Standards. Evan's level 4 Oral Communication class has several standards to attain, one of which is Speaking and Listening CCR Anchor 4, which is described in table 5.7.

The CCR Standards for Adult Education are supported by the English Language Proficiency (ELP) Standards for Adult Education, which detail the academic language that ESOL students need "to engage with and meet state-adopted content standards" (U.S. Department of Education, Office of Career, Technical and Adult Education, 2016, p. 1). Most of Evan's students fall into ELP Levels 2 and 3 as described by the ELP Standards that are related to Speaking and Listening CCR Anchor 4 and are shown in table 5.7.

The standards-based curriculum for Evan's class states that students will give several oral presentations; Evan has designed activities that prepare students to achieve this expectation.

Table 5.7	College and Career Readiness Standard, Speaking and Listening Anchor 4, with English Language Proficiency Standards for Adult Education Standard 3

Speaking and Listening, CCR Anchor 4

Present information, findings, and supporting evidence such that listeners can follow the line of reasoning and organization, development, and style appropriate to task, purpose, and audience.

English Language Proficiency Standards for Adult Education Standard 3

An [English language learner] can speak and write about level-appropriate complex literary and informational texts and topics.

Level 2	Level 3
By the end of English language proficiency level 2, an [English language learner] can . . . with support, • deliver short oral presentations • compose simple written narratives or informational texts about familiar texts, topics, experiences, or events.	By the end of English language proficiency level 3, an [English language learner] can . . . with support, • deliver short oral presentations • compose written informational texts • develop the topic with a few details about familiar texts, topics, or events.

(U.S. Department of Education, Office of Career, Technical and Adult Education, 2016, p. 23)

Principle 1. *Know Your Learners*

Many of the students in Evan's class are enrolled in several courses and move from one class to the next during the day. The group of students in this Oral Communication course will only be together for 14 weeks, so Evan is diligent during the first week of the term to make sure that he can get to know the learners and they get to know each other. Evan knows that having a sense of community supports language learning; students are more comfortable speaking with people that they know, at least a little. In the first week of class, Evan has each student fill out an information sheet with basic information about themselves that could be relevant to their experience in his course, including their language learning background, educational experience, and comfort with technology. The students in this course are from a variety of countries and speak different languages. All have had more than eight years of education in their countries of origin and have studied English in classes in the United States and elsewhere.

Principle 2. *Create Conditions for Language Learning*

Also during the first week of class, Evan has the students work in pairs to answer a few questions about themselves and their goals for learning English. Evan knows that developing trust is important, and he is careful to tell students to give only the information that they are comfortable sharing with the class. After their discussion, student pairs take turns introducing their partner to the whole group. In this way, Evan starts to build a base for making presentations throughout the term, thinking about purpose and audience as mentioned in CCR Anchor 4, while also helping the students learn each other's names and get to know one another. Evan knows that speaking in front of the class can produce anxiety for many students, so he creates many opportunities for rehearsal, including paired practice and having students digitally record their presentation for feedback from him. Because Evan is planning several group projects, it is especially important that the students in his class start to work in collaborative groups from the beginning of the term.

The curriculum for the course is based on topical units that include job search, job skills, housing, health, and education. Evan knows that adults learn best when they make choices that serve their learning goals, so in every course that he teaches, he asks the students to select one of the topical units that they will study. This group raised the issue of getting internet access: they wanted to know what options they had and how much it would cost. They voted to have internet access be their self-selected topic for a unit of study that will last for three weeks. Evan reminds the students to check the LMS daily because he will mark on the course calendar the dates of the various activities and tasks, and he will use the announcement page to post the target vocabulary for each unit and the links to resources that they will use.

Principle 3. *Design High-Quality Lessons for Language Development*

Evan is always looking for ways students can apply their English skills outside of the classroom to investigate a real-life topic, and the topic of internet access provides that opportunity. Evan decides that students will gather information for their presentations from an interview of students on campus. Evan plans a unit, which includes these activities:

- elicit what students already know while building vocabulary knowledge
- allow students to practice higher order thinking skills
- build informational literacy with authentic materials
- allow learners to interact using authentic language
- build student confidence to make an oral presentation

Elicit what students already know while building vocabulary knowledge

Evan introduces the unit by telling his own story with costly internet access: how he tried various free wireless networks and ran up his cell phone bill when his son depleted his data plan watching a video for homework. As he is talking, many students nod in agreement; several share their own similar experiences. Evan puts key words on the board as they occur in his story and in the experiences of others. These begin the vocabulary list for the unit.

Evan describes how the class will focus on the self-selected topic for the next unit, which will culminate in oral presentations. He reminds students of the importance of being able to make a good presentation for work, school, and sometimes community activities; he gives out the rubric that he will use to evaluate the presentations, which is already familiar to students from previous tasks in the course.

Evan designs the first activity to get the students thinking about what they already know about the topic. He divides the class into small groups to discuss how much time each person accesses the internet in various ways. The students fill out a grid like that shown in table 5.8.

Table 5.8	Information grid for initial small group discussion		
Where do you access the internet? In a week, how much time do you spend on each?			
Name	Cell phone data	Wireless at home	Wireless in a public place like our school, or the library
Example: Luis	7 hours	0	21 hours
Student #1:			
Student #2:			
Student #3:			
Student #4:			
Student #5:			

After this discussion, Evan asks the students to join a group based how they access the internet the most. He has created table signs for each type of internet access (cell phone data, wireless at home, wireless in a public place) and students select the appropriate group. Each group discusses the cost of their internet access. Evan knows that many students will not have a clear under-standing of the cost because their service may be provided, for example, by a parent, spouse, or landlord. For homework, Evan asks the students to investigate the information for themselves or for someone else if they would prefer not to talk about the costs of their own internet access.

In the next class, students get back into the same groups and share information about the cost of internet access. Evan has prepared information sheets for those who did not bring their own data.

Allow students to practice higher order thinking skills

Evan leads a whole class discussion about comparing the different types of internet access, building on the discussions from the previous class. He is deliberate about offering vocabulary he has identified that the students need, including *convenient, 24 hours a day, time limit, high cost, included*, and so on, defining them in the context of the discussion. As a model, he lists on the board several advantages and disadvantages of the different types of access.

Evan asks the students to discuss with their table group the advantages and disadvantages of the way they access the internet—starting with the cost—and to fill out a T-chart, like the one shown in table 5.9. The activity supports both critical thinking and active engagement with the language task.

Table 5.9	T-chart to analyze advantages and disadvantages	
Your internet access type		
Advantages		**Disadvantages**
Low cost: $_____/month		High cost: $_____/month

The groups take turns telling the rest of the class what they have discussed as advantages and disadvantages of their internet access mode, displaying their T-chart on the board. Evan has the student groups talk from their seats for this activity because he knows it is less anxiety-provoking than talking while standing in front of the class. The other groups listen carefully, mentally com-paring the information on their charts to those of the presenting group. As a follow up, Evan has designed a language activity for students to write about each advantage and disadvantage using sentence frames as a scaffold, such as: Cell phone data is _____ but it is _____. (Students might write in *convenient/expensive*.)

Build information literacy with authentic materials

After these two activities, the students are highly interested in the topic, their familiarity with the information is growing quickly, and they are eager to learn more. Evan selects two resources for the class to get more information. He puts the links to both resources on the announcements page of the LMS for students to access any time. The first resource is a short video about internet access and cost in the United States, which includes information about people whose primary access is through their cell phone, and the associated high cost and disadvantages. It is based on research from the Pew Research Center (www.pewinternet.org/fact-sheet/mobile). The second is a website called EveryoneOn (www.everyoneon.org), which informs about getting low-cost internet access. Evan develops a series of pre- and postactivities, and over the next two classes the students work with the texts, identifying the key details and central ideas, after which they do an activity to compare the new information with their previous information.

Allow learners to interact using authentic language

In the last part of the unit, the students create an internet access and cost questionnaire to conduct interviews around the campus. Evan is mindful that grouping students for collaborative work provides rich opportunities for language practice, so he has student groups write the questions, revise their drafts with his feedback, and then practice by asking the questions to each other, for fluency practice. Students break the questionnaire into sections and each group takes one section out on campus to interview five or six people. Two students ask the questions, and two other students record the answers in a grid format.

As a follow up, the students compile the answers that they have received. Each group creates a chart of the answers that they collected and puts them onto a series of slides for a presentation. Evan is careful to provide support as needed as the students are working in groups.

Build student confidence to make an oral presentation

Evan knows that presenting before the whole class can trigger anxiety and takes careful steps to build students' ease and confidence to make an oral presentation. Each student takes one question and prepares to present the questionnaire results for that question to the whole class. The students rehearse their part in small groups, using a rubric to give feedback to each other. The students each audio record their part on their phone and send the recording to Evan for feedback, which he also provides in a recorded audio format. In the last class of the unit, all students make presentations with their groups while standing in front of the class and showing their slide. Because the students have been working with the same topic for the whole unit, both the language and the information are familiar, which gives the students a lot of confidence. The rest of the class listens carefully because they are interested to find out what each group learned in their interviews.

Principle 4. *Adapt Lesson Delivery as Needed*

In the initial class discussion, there are many vocabulary items that cause confusion. Evan makes note of these items and starts a glossary on the LMS announcement page. After class, he adds the definitions of the vocabulary items that were discussed in class. This process is a regular part of Evan's class, and the students know to look to the LMS for vocabulary items. In addition, Evan creates digital flashcards based on those vocabulary items and assigns practice with these for homework. The students know to expect a vocabulary test at the end of each unit, including the unit on internet access. By this time in the term, the students have learned how to study vocabulary independently.

Throughout the unit, Evan listens to his students carefully; he knows that he will need to adapt the lesson based on the students' experiences. He can reteach vocabulary to small groups who need it, add multimedia to illustrate concepts, or allow additional time for activities that are difficult.

Principle 5. *Monitor and Assess Student Language Development*

Throughout the unit, Evan carefully monitors the learners' use of the new language to decide when the students are ready to move on. For example, in the first two activities of the unit, the students discuss information from their own experience, or they discuss information that is very familiar to them. Evan monitors the students' language use carefully through their discussions, their mini-presentation, and their sentences to gauge when they are ready for more new information. Even though it is on the same topic, adding new information will increase the difficulty of the activities.

Evan is aware that providing useful feedback at the appropriate time aids student language learning. In this unit, he gives feedback to students as they work on drafts of questions for their questionnaires and on recorded drafts of their presentation. Based on the pattern of errors that he sees and hears, he offers grammar mini-lessons when he judges that a group of students need it.

In their final presentations, Evan has the opportunity to assess the students' language performance through their slides and their oral presentations. Using the rubric, he provides written feedback to each person, pointing out their strengths and the areas where they still need work.

Principle 6. *Engage and Collaborate within a Community of Practice*
The ESOL program at Evan's community college has a culture of communication around teaching. For example, many of the instructors who teach intermediate level Oral Communication include a student-selected unit in their course. They meet regularly to help each other plan the units, exchange resources, discuss what worked well, and share ideas for how to improve. Evan finds a lot of support in these professional discussions. The same teachers work together to create a rubric for the presentation assignment and discuss its effectiveness in guiding students to create good presentations. Because of this positive experience with coplanning high-interest oral communication units, the group is considering proposing a presentation for their upcoming regional TESOL affiliate conference.

A Look Back and Final Observations
The 6 Principles provide a lens for viewing English language classes and seeing exemplary instruction that supports adult learners' success with language acquisition. As we have seen, exemplary teaching does not depend on any particular methodology, expensive resources, flashy technology, or even program type. Exemplary teaching has to fit both program contexts and the individual learners who participate. In chapter 5, we described how teachers who work within fundamentally different program contexts can implement The 6 Principles and how we can recognize the principles in what they do.

In looking at The 6 Principles in action in each of the classes, chapter 5 highlights the following takeaways:

- Effective instruction takes advantage of what students already know as competent adults who are experienced in the world.

- The students' other languages are an important resource for the classroom. Using learners' home languages in the classroom in intentional ways can support English language learning.

- The ways to create conditions for language learning depend in large part on the needs of the students. For example, students who have had negative formal learning experiences need safe spaces, and learners tired from work need an active pace.

- Learners are motivated when they have a voice in the instruction. For example, learners can help select the themes in the class or select the activities that best suit their learning.

- Learners are also motivated when the topics and language in their classes are related to their real-life needs outside of class. Using and adapting authentic materials from students' real-life needs helps to keep language activities relevant to them.

- Many English language classes include learners with a mix of language proficiency levels, and these learners face a mix of challenges. There are a variety of ways to design effective and appropriate instruction for these learners.
- High-quality instruction maximizes language comprehension and production by building on the language that students already know, by giving feedback in a variety of ways, and by scaffolding learner comprehension with multimodal input.
- Teachers can assess student learning by collecting evidence that indicates what students can do with language and what they are ready to learn next.
- Technology can create opportunities for differentiated instruction as well as for independent learning.

Exemplary English language instruction is not one-size-fits-all. We have seen how The 6 Principles work in different contexts as a framework for high-quality instruction. In every case, teachers begin their planning with the individual learners in mind. They are knowledgeable about stakeholders' desires for the program through careful needs assessment. They connect their instruction directly to learners' goals. They are aware of the standards for English language development that apply to their context and use the standards to guide instruction. These teachers use multiple strategies so that instruction is relevant to the learners, allows them to be actively engaged in using their new language, and empowers them to see themselves as legitimate users of English. These teachers provide feedback in ways that support learners' motivation and their learning. They encourage learners to apply learning strategies in and out of the classroom and to become lifelong learners.

Themselves lifelong learners, these teachers engage in communities of practice to continue to develop their knowledge and skills through collaboration with others in the field. English language teachers continue to learn because they know that high-quality instruction truly matters in the lives of the adult students served in adult education and workforce preparation programs.

Additional resources pertaining to this chapter are available at www.the6principles.org/adult-education.

APPENDIXES
GLOSSARY
AND REFERENCES

Appendix A

Instructional Techniques

This appendix provides descriptions of the techniques that have been discussed in this book.

Annotation: Adding notes, explanations, or translations to a text in order to aid reading comprehension and show the main ideas and key details to remember. Also known as *marginal notes*.

Anticipation chat: A learning task to activate prior knowledge and motivate new learning. Students complete a questionnaire about content they are going to learn and discuss with a partner or small group why they selected their responses. For more, see Zwiers (2014). Also known as *anticipation/reaction guide*.

Chart and share: Students work in a small group on a problem or investigation. Each group creates a poster on chart paper to organize, summarize, and illustrate their findings. Each group member practices presenting with the poster. Groups present their posters to each other. The activity allows multiple rehearsals and in-depth discussions of the content. Created by Isabel Ramirez and Lois Hardaway. (Vogt, Echevarría, & Washam, 2015)

Collaborative instructional formats: Learning strategies and activities that prompt learners to interact in an organized way, depending on each other for team success. For example, small learning teams or partner sharing. Also known as *cooperative structures* (Kagan & Kagan, 2009). Many of these formats are known by names that Spencer Kagan coined, such as Stir-the-Class, Numbered Heads Together, Quiz-Quiz-Trade, Talking Chips, StandUp-HandUp-PairUp, Inside-Outside Circle.

Critical incident scenario: A story that presents situations in which people from different cultural and language backgrounds interact and bring different perspectives to how they understand the situation. For examples of critical incidents, see DeCapua and Wintergerst (2016).

Formula 5-2-1: A learning structure in which teaching occurs in eight-minute blocks. For the first five minutes, the teacher presents using comprehensible input. For two minutes, students process the information while talking quietly with a partner. After this, in one minute, students provide the teacher with feedback on what they understood, using a response pad or mini dry-erase board. Created by Lindsay Young. (Vogt, Echevarría, & Washam, 2015)

Framed outlines: The teacher supplies an outline to the presentation/video/lecture with some of the key information missing. Students listen or search for the missing information. They discuss their guesses with each other. (Vogt & Echevarría, 2008)

Gallery walk: The teacher hangs poster paper on the wall around the classroom. The number of posters corresponds to the number of small groups who participate in the activity. The teacher writes a title or question in large letters on each poster. Each group is assigned to one of the posters. For a few minutes, group members discuss the poster topic or question. After the discussion, they write their notes on the poster using a marker color that identifies their group. Groups rotate from poster to poster, examining the contributions of previous groups, reacting and adding on their own ideas. When they have completed the round and arrive back at their first poster, they summarize all of the ideas and report them to the whole class, like tour guides in a museum. (Vogt & Echevarría, 2008)

Guess and replace: A reading comprehension and vocabulary strategy. The reader guesses the meaning of an unknown word and substitutes a known word that can complete the sentence. The students can cross out the word physically and write in the word they prefer to use.

Information gap task: A communication task in language learning where students work in pairs. Each partner has partial information, and they communicate to exchange information in order to build unified understanding of an image, a map, an event, a character, directions, or a task that they need to perform together.

Insert method: Students read a text with a partner and insert codes to mark their reactions: a check mark for what they already know, a question mark for what they don't yet understand, a plus sign for a new idea or new concept they noted in the text. (Vogt & Echevarría, 2008)

Jigsaw what you know: Each student receives an index card with one concept, one subtopic, or one important quality of the central topic of the lesson. Each student focuses on this one aspect and learns about it through reading and researching. After they have completed learning about their index card topic, students fit their information together to develop the central topic of the lesson. They create a poster, table, or graphic organizer to show how their subtopics connect to each other. (Vogt & Echevarría, 2008)

Journal jumpstart: The teacher provides an open-ended prompt to direct a journal entry and to get students to start writing quickly. Example: "The title of this article reminds me of . . ."

Key word method: A much-researched vocabulary technique to help learners remember new words. The learner thinks of a word in the home language that sounds similar, or contains similar sounds, to the new word in the target language (e.g., *book* in English—*bök* in Hungarian, which means *poke*). Then, the learner invents an image to associate the two words. (E.g., the image could be to be poking [*bök*] a ballerina with a *book*.) The more unusual the image, the easier it is to recall the associated words. (Nation & Webb, 2011)

KWL chart: This is a note-taking technique that helps students activate background knowledge, direct new learning, and review. Students create a chart with three columns. First, they write down the topic. In the first column of the chart, they list what they already know (K) about that topic. In the second column, they write what they want to learn (W) about the topic. At the end of the lesson, they complete the third column, where they record what they have learned (L) during the lesson. The technique is also useful to support reading comprehension with texts. Created by Donna Ogle.

Notecard method: Many variations exist of this research-supported method for studying vocabulary with packs of cards. The front of each card contains the target word, and the back contains the home language translation, an image, or a target language synonym. Learners practice with the cards frequently to retrieve either word form or meaning. They say the words to themselves, using packs of 20 cards at first, then gradually increasing to packs of 50. (Nation & Webb, 2011)

Quick-write: A short writing task. Students respond to a prompt in one to five minutes; they write without stopping, usually to activate their background knowledge and to get some ideas on paper quickly. Also known as *freewriting*.

Quiz-quiz-trade: This is a cooperative assessment technique. Each student prepares an index card individually by writing a quiz question on the front and the answer to the question on the back. When ready, students stand up and move around the room. They pair up and quiz a partner using their index card. After both partners answer a question (quiz-quiz), they trade cards, acknowledge each other with a high five, and move on to pair up with another student. The activity continues until students have answered most or all of the quiz questions on the index cards that are circulating. (Kagan & Kagan, 2009)

Sentence analysis: A technique where students analyze the relationships of ideas by examining compound and complex sentences that mark contrast, sequence, condition, or cause-effect. (Vogt, Echevarría, & Washam, 2015)

Simulation: A learning activity whose goal is to imitate or model in the classroom real-life processes and actions.

SQP2RS ("Squeepers"): This is a six-step instructional approach to teaching with a text. The six steps provide students with oral language support for the reading process. S stands for survey. In this first step, students activate their background knowledge by surveying the text. Q stands for *question*. In this second step, students formulate and orally share their questions about the text. P stands for *predict*, which is the third step. Students discuss and record their predictions about the text. The first R stands for *read*. Students read selections from the text with a partner or a small group. They interact with each other to identify sentences that are relevant to their questions. During the fifth step (the second R), students *respond*, that is, they answer their questions based on the text and evaluate their predictions. During the final step (S), they *summarize* the text by key points. Created by MaryEllen Vogt. (Vogt & Echevarría, 2008)

Status update: This activity is the classroom version of posting a personal update on a social media site. Students summarize their takeaways at the end of class using some of the key vocabulary featured during the lesson. They can post their "status update" to the class learning platform or social media group or on a sentence strip to pin on a bulletin board. Created by Catherine Hopkins. (Vogt, Echevarría, & Washam, 2015)

Student-created cloze sentences: Students write fill-in-the-blank sentences about a key concept or vocabulary item in the lesson. They quiz each other using their own cloze sentences. Created by Brooke Vecchio. (Vogt, Echevarría, & Washam, 2015)

Study buddy teaming: A teaching technique in which students initially work in pairs on problem solving or shared reading. They then compare and discuss with other teams to achieve consensus with each study pair. Created by Leslie M. Middleton. (Vogt, Echevarría, & Washam, 2015)

Word splash poster: The teacher writes a topic on a large sheet of paper. Students collectively write every word they can think of about the topic. This activity activates vocabulary and background knowledge about a lesson topic.

Appendix B

Resources for Teachers of Adult English Learners

General Resources

Meeting the Language Needs of Today's Adult English Language Learner: Issue Brief
Parrish, B. (2015). Washington, DC: U.S. Department of Education, Office of Career, Technical, and Adult Education.

This short issue brief explains the need for rigorous language instruction and literacy skills. It cites specific elements that research has shown to be critical for adult ESL learners to have full access to academic and work opportunities in sections such as "Context: A Changing Landscape in Adult English Language Instruction" and "Key Considerations: Making Instruction Rigorous Right from the Start," concluding with information helpful for administrators. Available at https://lincs.ed.gov/sites/default/files/ELL_Increasing_Rigor_508.pdf

Meeting the Language Needs of Today's English Language Learner:
Professional Development Module
Parrish, B. (2015). Washington, DC: U.S. Department of Education, Office of Career, Technical, and Adult Education.

Consisting of four related units, this self-paced online module addresses the increasingly complex language that adult ELs need to succeed in today's world. With a focus on increasing rigor, academic language, language strategies, and critical thinking, the overarching goal of this module is to give professionals who work with adult ELs the tools to provide rigorous instruction that will help all learners transition to new opportunities. Available at https://courses.lincs.ed.gov

Meeting the Language Needs of Today's Adult English Language Learner:
Companion Learning Resource
Vinogradov, P. E. (2016). Washington, DC: U.S. Department of Education, Office of Career, Technical, and Adult Education.

This 27-page practice-oriented digital magazine provides examples of specific instructional strategies. Including sections such as "Engaging Learners With Academic Language," "Accessing Complex Informational Texts," and "Employing Evidence in Speaking and Writing," the clickable online resource helps instructors effectively prepare their learners to meet the increased language and literacy demands of postsecondary education and the workplace. Available at https://lincs.ed.gov/sites/default/files/LINCS_CLR-3_508.pdf

Preparing English Learners for Work and Career Pathways: Companion Learning Resource
Adelson-Goldstein, J. (2015). Washington, DC: U.S. Department of Education, Office of Career, Technical, and Adult Education.

This 60-page practice-oriented clickable digital magazine describes ways to embed English skill development within themes such as career awareness, career exploration, and goal setting. Including sections on learning to learn, developing workplace and training vocabulary, demonstrating workplace soft skills, problem solving, and more, this resource provides concrete examples of how English language teachers can work to prepare their students for work or training. Available at https://lincs.ed.gov/sites/default/files/LINCS_CLR-1_508_0.pdf

Teaching ESL to Adults: Classroom Approaches in Action
New American Horizons Foundation. (2010–2011). Newtonville, MA.

This online resource uses video from eight adult English language teachers in their classrooms to demonstrate exemplary practices. Each of the twelve 30-minute segments focuses on one topic, such as "Growing Vocabulary with Beginning Learners," "Building Literacy with Adult Emergent Readers," and "Tasks to Promote Critical Thinking and Learning Skills" through video of students participating in classroom activities and the teacher explaining his or her rationale. Available at https://www.newamericanhorizons.org/training-videos

Language Support for Adult Refugees: A Council of Europe Toolkit
Council of Europe. (2018). Strasbourg, France.

Available in seven languages, this website contains 57 tools designed to assist organizations, programs, teachers, and volunteers in providing language support for adult refugees, which includes asylum seekers and refugees. Relevant for all beginning language learners in a new country, the tools can be downloaded and adapted to meet the needs of different contexts. The website housing the toolkit is organized into sections that include introduction, preparation and planning, activities, and resources. The preparation and planning section presents a robust set of tools to determine learners' needs, including "Tool 24: Identifying refugees' most urgent needs" and "Tool 25: Finding out what refugees can already do in the target language and what they need to be able to do." Available at https://www.coe.int/en/web/language-support-for-adult-refugees/home

Curriculum and Lesson Plans: ABE and Adult ESL Curriculum Units
Minnesota Literacy Council. (2012). St. Paul, MN.

The mission of the Minnesota Literacy Council is "to share the power of learning through education, community building and advocacy," and their curriculum units are available to serve all adult ELs. The Pre-beginning ESL Curriculum and Beginning ESL Curriculum each include downloadable lesson plans and materials, with English language learning infused with transition skills to build foundations for work and academic pathways. Available at https://mnliteracy.org/curriculum-lesson-plans

Teaching English
British Council & BBC. (n.d.). London, England.

This practical guide offers lesson plans, activities, and articles to help teachers of adults who are new to English. There are lesson plans on many topics of interest to adult learners, including getting to know the neighbors and money conversations (level A1/A2), changing ideas of beauty and shopping and sales tricks (level B1/B2), and left handers (level C1/C2). Available at https://www.teachingenglish.org.uk/teaching-adults

Language for Work: CLB Essential Skills for ESL Instructors (PDF-E-43) and Essential Skills Lesson Plans
Centre for Canadian Language Benchmarks. (2015). Ottawa, ON, Canada.

Section 3 of this free downloadable document describes how teachers can build on downloadable Essential Skills lesson plans to teach the skills needed for people to participate fully in the Canadian workplace and community. Available at https://www.language.ca/product/language-for-work-clb-essential-skills-for-esl-instructors-pdf-e and http://www.language.ca/resourcesexpertise/essential-skills

EAL/D Teacher Resources—Adult
Australian Council of TESOL Associations. (2018). Manuka, Australia.

This website contains links to curriculum, assessment, and professional development resources as well as archives from *Prospect*, an Australian journal of TESOL. Available at http://www.tesol.org.au/RESOURCES/EALD-Teacher-Resources-Adult

Teaching Adult English Language Learners: A Practical Introduction
Parrish, B. (2019) Cambridge, England: Cambridge University Press.

This comprehensive, teacher-friendly book describes the context for and teaching of adult ELs. The 10-chapter volume includes chapters on topics such as teaching language for meaningful purposes, planning for teaching and learning, and selecting instructional materials and resources.

Resources with a focus on learning English while also learning literacy for the first time

A Practical Guide to Teaching ESL Literacy
Bow Valley College. (2018). Calgary, Alberta, Canada: Bow Valley College.

This online book contains six chapters that describe the required skills and strategies for the development of literacy in the context of adult ESL literacy. Teachers will find descriptions of effective approaches to teaching adult ESL literacy learners, including creating a supportive learning environment, planning instruction, teaching oral language skills, teaching literacy skills, and finding materials and resources. Available at https://globalaccess.bowvalleycollege.ca/sites/default/files/ESL-Literacy-Book-August-24-2018-Digital_0.pdf

ESL Literacy Readers
Bow Valley College. (n.d.). Calgary, Alberta, Canada: Bow Valley College.

This site contains 40 theme-based readers designed for adults learning literacy at the same time that they are learning English. Organized into seven levels, the digital and printable books are on topics relevant to learners' lives with vivid images and audio files. An instructor guide provides directions for using the readers in an adult ESL class. Available at https://globalaccess.bowvalleycollege.ca/tools/esl-literacy-readers

Glossary

21st-century workplace skills: These are not traditional skills, but factors—a mix of knowledge, skills, and dispositions—that researchers have identified with statistical methods from survey items that were administered to employers from different fields. These factors represent clusters of priorities that employers seek in general, for employees in all occupations, usually including problem solving, technical skills, teamwork, communication, customer service, and flexibility/persistence/dependability.

Academic language: A register of the English language; the formal variety of language used for academic purposes (e.g., in academic conversations, lectures, and textbooks) and connected with literacy and academic achievement. Includes reading, writing, listening, and speaking skills used to acquire new knowledge and accomplish academic tasks. In the United States, sometimes known as *academic English*.

Accountable talk: A classroom practice in which students engage in frequent conversations and active listening to what every speaker has to say. Students build on each others' contributions, negotiate their ideas, and verbalize their thinking.

Anecdotal records: An assessment strategy in which the teacher or learner keeps informal records of incidents that show specific behaviors (e.g., evidence of learning, stories of small successes, a list of what the learner can do, errors, or problem behaviors).

Authentic language: Language that has not been modified or simplified. Typically refers to language that is written for a native-speaking or proficient audience and created by a native speaker to convey a message.

Benchmark assessment: A short assessment administered at regular intervals to give teachers feedback on how well students are meeting the academic standards that have been set; a tool to measure student growth and tailor curriculum or design an intervention to meet individual learning needs. Sometimes known as *formative assessment*.

Career training program: A vocational education program that prepares students for jobs. The training is usually short term, consisting of a combination of practical experience and coursework.

CASAS: A widely used assessment framework in the United States for measuring the English language proficiency of adult English learners. Formerly known as the Comprehensive Adult Student Assessment System (see www.casas.org).

Civics program: A course of study to prepare for the citizenship exam. In the United States, it includes preparation in the basics of U.S. history and the Constitution.

Collaborative inquiry: A group of educators study together to improve their practice. They identify a problem or critical question, research the topic, and decide what data they need to answer the question. They collect and analyze data, solve the problem/answer the critical question, and share their findings with colleagues. This process may be a cyclical form of teacher professional learning. Also known as *practitioner inquiry* or *action research*.

Collaborative learning: An approach to teaching in which students spend the majority of class time working in pairs and small groups. They work as team members, talking and discussing, dividing tasks, and taking turns with different roles. Also known as *cooperative learning*.

College and Career Readiness Standards: An adaptation of the Common Core State Standards for adult education. It sets benchmarks for five levels to achieve 12-grade equivalency in English language arts and mathematics. These standards are used by adult basic education programs in the United States to plan curriculum and to track learners' progress.

Comprehensible input: Oral or written input (e.g., new information) to the learner, structured or presented in such a way as to help him or her negotiate the meaning of the communication (e.g., through visuals, gestures, annotations). Over time, the input may increase in complexity of the language structures used or the amount of information shared.

Cultural broker: A person who serves to facilitate communication and to build connections between individuals and groups from different cultures. They facilitate mutual understandings and advocate on behalf of persons and groups from minority cultures.

Dynamic bilingualism: The ability to use more than one language flexibly and strategically, depending on the audience, conversational partners, or the situation.

English language proficiency (ELP) standards: Sets of concise statements identifying the knowledge and skills that English learners are expected to know and be capable of doing in English; statement-by-statement articulations of what students are expected to learn and what schools are expected to teach. May refer to national, state, or district standards. Each U.S. state is required by the federal government to have ELP standards and related assessments.

English-speaking countries: Countries where English is the primary language of the majority of the population, such as the United Kingdom, the United States, Ireland, Canada, Australia, and New Zealand. Because the use of English is widespread in other countries, some qualify these countries as inner circle English-speaking countries. Note that many smaller nations are also English-speaking countries (e.g., Jamaica, the Bahamas, Trinidad and Tobago, Barbados).

Family literacy: A program whose goal is to improve everyone's skills in the family with reading, writing, numeracy, and critical thinking.

Filler phrase: A meaningless or redundant expression that speakers use to fill in gaps in their speech (e.g., *I mean, like, you know, the thing is that, stuff like that*).

Funds of knowledge: Knowledge gained through nonacademic means, usually from family and community members in traditional societies. It may include knowledge of the natural world, farming, food preparation, crafts, customs, personal histories, legends, and stories.

Genre: A form of communication that has recognized conventions. For example, a work memo, a weather report, a formal invitation, an editorial, a stand-up comedy routine, an academic lecture.

High-frequency words: Words that occur most frequently across many different types of texts and transcripts of spoken language. Most are function words, such as articles (*a/an, the*), prepositions (*in, on, at, of*), auxiliaries (*do, be, have, can, may*), pronouns (*that, I, they, it, what, who*), conjunctions (*and, but, so*), conjunctive adverbs (*finally, however*), or quantifiers (*some, much*). They also include common verbs (*go, take, want, make*), nouns (*way, type, thing*), adjectives (*good, nice, great*), and adverbs (*here, now, sometimes, never, well*). These words are the most important to teach to beginners. For more, see The New General Service List (www.newgeneralservicelist.org).

Higher order thinking: Thinking that requires more than memorization, recall, and the comprehension of ideas from texts or teacher presentation. Higher order thinking involves using ideas actively: applying, analyzing, evaluating, synthesizing, and creating.

Input: Oral or written language provided to the learner.

Intake assessment: A systematic approach to document students' skills and knowledge before they begin a course of study. It usually involves the collection and analysis of different types of information: answers on forms and questionnaires, interviews, placement test, transcripts.

Integrative motivation: A person's strong desire to be included as a member in a community.

Just-in-time teaching: A student-centered strategy in which the teacher applies feedback from learners to determine what skills or information they need to make progress with a project or task and teaches that to them in small bursts. The advantage is that learners are motivated to obtain this knowledge and have immediate application for what they learn.

Just-right text: A text that is neither too easy nor too difficult for a developing reader; it suits the reader's independent reading level.

Language modalities: Ways to use language orally and in writing.

Late-onset language learner: A person who begins to learn a new language after the first decade of life.

Lesson objective: A statement of what students will be able to do by the end of the lesson. Its purpose is to focus students' attention on what is important in the lesson. The statement usually begins with "Students will be able to (SWBAT) . . ." or "I can. . . ." Teachers who have English learners may have separate content and language objectives for the same lesson. The content objective relates to the content standards or content curriculum, and the language objective states what language skill students need to focus on during the lesson.

Leveled reader: Series of books that are created or modified to match the skills of developing readers, based on their scores on a reading test. The number of levels varies for each series.

Literacy practices: The ways in which groups and individuals employ of reading, writing, and numeracy in their lives.

Low literacy: Experiencing major challenges with performing basic reading, writing, numeracy, and critical thinking tasks.

Multilingualism: The use of more than one language by an individual or a community of speakers or within a geographical area. A multilingual person speaks more than one language. A multilingual community consists of a group with speakers of more than one language, but some members of the community may speak only one language.

Native-like proficiency: The ability to perform with language skills similarly to people who speak the language as their primary or native language. Native-like proficiency does not preclude having an accent or making mistakes with grammar and word choice.

Needs assessment: An inquiry process that documents the current conditions and the desired conditions of stakeholders. The goal is to use the information to identify approaches that can bridge the gap between the current and the desired conditions. Educators use this process to evaluate learners' skills and to analyze the skills they need to succeed with specific tasks.

Output: Oral or written language generated by a person.

Practice: The collective name of activities whose goal is to improve the fluency and accuracy of language use with any subskill (e.g., active listening, speaking, reading, writing, grammar, or vocabulary).

Primary language: The language an individual uses the most, especially at home. Often, this is the first language learned. Also known as *home language, first language, L1, mother tongue,* or *native language.*

Register: A variety of language that is associated with specific social situations. For example, academic language, legal language, the language of mathematics, or the language of sportscasting.

Scaffolding: Classroom support given to assist students in learning new information and performing related tasks. Often provided by the teacher through demonstration, modeling, verbal prompts (e.g., questioning), feedback, adapted text, graphic organizers, and language frames, among other techniques. Provided to learners over a period of time but gradually modified and then removed in order to transfer more autonomy to the learner, leading to independence.

Settlement services: This term designates services to those who are newcomers to Canada. Service providers receive federal funding to deliver a range of services (e.g., housing, document translation, job training, obtaining employment and social services, and language classes).

Settlement worker: A staff member at an agency that provides settlement services.

Social capital: Resources, affordances, or various forms of support that a person can access through social connections.

Standards-based lesson: A planned lesson in which the learning goals are aligned with an applicable standards document. These lessons fit an overall plan of study, which is detailed in a specific standards document, usually skill-by-skill and grade-by-grade. Standards documents contain descriptors of skills and knowledge, which define what learners can do at each step of development on their way to proficiency or toward a suitable learning target.

Strength-based approach: An attitude in professional practice. Practitioners focus primarily on each individual's abilities, skills, knowledge, and potential contributions over any weaknesses and special needs they may have.

Target language: The language that the student is learning. Also known as *new language*, *additional language*, *second language*, and *foreign language*.

Text-to-voice protocol: Using a built-in or added-in feature within software applications that will read back the text.

Translanguaging: The strategic choice to mix two or more languages to serve a specific purpose in a communicative situation or accomplish a task.

Vocabulary size test: Tests that are designed to estimate vocabulary size. They test knowledge of words that represent a sample of different word-frequency bands. For more on measuring vocabulary size, see my.vocabularysize.com.

Workforce Innovation and Opportunity Act of 2014 (WIOA): Federal law in the United States that defines the types of career services and adult education programs that are eligible for funding through the federal government. The law emphasizes efficiency by requiring a unified statewide plan and a one-stop system for assisting job seekers.

Workplace education program: Classes that serve the employees of a company or members of a workers union, sometimes delivered in partnership with an educational institution, such as a community college.

References

PREFACE

Crystal, D. (2019). *The Cambridge encyclopedia of the English language* (3rd ed.). New York, NY: Cambridge University Press.

TESOL International Association. (2018). *The 6 principles for exemplary teaching of English learners: Grades K–12*. Alexandria, VA: Author.

CHAPTER 1

Australian Government Department of Education and Training. (2015). *Australian core skills framework*. Canberra, Australia: The Department of Industry, Innovation, Science, Research and Tertiary Education. Retrieved from http://docs .education.gov.au/node/37095

Batalova, J., & Fix, M. (2017). *New brain gain: Rising human capital among recent immigrants to the United States*. Washington, DC: Migration Policy Institute. Retrieved from https://www .migrationpolicy.org/research/new-brain-gain -rising-human-capital-among-recent-immigrants -united-states

Bergson-Shilcock, A. (2017). *Foundational skills in the service sector*. Washington, DC: National Skills Coalition. Retrieved from https://www .nationalskillscoalition.org/resources/publications /file/NSC-foundational-skills-FINAL.pdf

British Council. (2013). *The English effect: The impact of English, what it's worth to the UK and why it matters to the world*. London, England: Author. Retrieved from https://www.britishcouncil .org/sites/default/files/english-effect-report-v2.pdf

Centre for Canadian Language Benchmarks. (2012). *Canadian Language Benchmarks: English as a second language for adults*. Ottawa, ON: Author. Retrieved from https://www.canada.ca/content /dam/ircc/migration/ircc/english/pdf/pub/language -benchmarks.pdf

Crystal, D. (2019). *The Cambridge encyclopedia of the English language* (3rd ed.) New York, NY: Cambridge University Press.

Gambino, C. P., Acosta, Y. D., & Grieco, E. M. (2014). *English-speaking ability of the foreign-born population of the United States: 2012. American Community Survey reports*. Washington, DC: U.S. Census Bureau. Retrieved from https://www.census .gov/content/dam/Census/library/publications/2014 /acs/acs-26.pdf

Gryn, T., & Walker, L. (2018, April 25–28). *The foreign-born labor force in the United States, 2016*. Poster presented at the Annual Meeting of the Population Association of America, Denver, CO. Retrieved from https://www.census.gov/content /dam/Census/newsroom/press-kits/2018/paa/2018 -aa-poster-fb-labor-force.pdf

National Academies of Sciences, Engineering, and Medicine. (2015). *The integration of immigrants into American society*. Washington, DC: The National Academies Press. doi:10.17226/21746

Organisation for Economic Cooperation and Development. (2018). *International migration outlook 2018* (42nd ed.). Paris, France: OECD Publishing. doi:10.1787/migr_outlook-2018-en

Parrish, B. (2015). Meeting the language needs of today's adult English language learners: Issue brief. *LINCS ESL PRO*. Retrieved from https:// lincs.ed.gov/sites/default/files/ELL_Increasing _Rigor_508.pdf

Refugee Processing Center. (2018). *Refugee admissions report. September 30, 2018*. Retrieved from http://www.wrapsnet.org/s/Refugee -Admissions-Report-2018_09_30.xls

U.S. Department of Education, Office of Career, Technical, and Adult Education. (2016). *Adult English language proficiency standards for adult education*. Washington, DC: Author. Retrieved from https://lincs.ed.gov/publications/pdf/elp-standards -adult-ed.pdf

Wonderlic, Inc. (2016). *Hard facts about soft skills: An actionable review of employer perspectives, expectations and recommendations*. Vernon Hills, IL: Author. Retrieved from https://www .wonderlic.com/wp-content/uploads/2017/05 /HardFactsAboutSoftSkillsHandout.pdf

Workforce Innovation and Opportunity Act of 2014, Pub. L. No. 113-128 § 128 Stat. 1425 (2013–2014).

CHAPTER 2

Anderson, S. R., & Lightfoot, D. W. (2002). *The language organ: Linguistics as cognitive physiology*. New York, NY: Cambridge University Press.

Appleby, Y. (2010). Who are the learners? In N. Hughes & I. Schwab (Eds.), *Teaching adult literacy: Principles and practice* (pp. 29–47). Maidenhead, England: National Research and Development Centre and Open University Press.

REFERENCES FOR CHAPTER 2, *CONTINUED*

August, D., & Shanahan, T. (Eds.). (2006). *Developing literacy in second-language learners: Report of the national literacy panel on language-minority children and youth.* Mahwah, NJ: Lawrence Erlbaum.

Australian Government Department of Education and Training. (2015). *Australian core skills framework.* Canberra, Australia: The Department of Industry, Innovation, Science, Research and Tertiary Education. Retrieved from http://docs.education.gov.au/node/37095

Baker, C. (2014). *A parents' and teachers' guide to bilingualism* (4th ed.). Bristol, England: Multilingual Matters.

Baker, S., Lesaux, N., Jayanthi, M., Dimino, J., Proctor, C. P., Morris, J., Gersten, R., Haymond, K., Kieffer, M. J., Linan-Thompson, S., & Newman-Gonchar, R. (2014). *Teaching academic content and literacy to English learners in elementary and middle school* (NCEE 2014-4012). Washington, DC: National Center for Education Evaluation and Regional Assistance, Institute of Education Sciences; Washington, DC: U.S. Department of Education.

Birdsong, D. (2016). Age of second language acquisition: Critical periods and social concerns. In E. Nicoladis & S. Montari (Eds.), *Bilingualism across the lifespan: Factors moderating language proficiency* (pp. 163–182). Berlin, Germany: De Gruyter Mouton. doi:10.1037/14939-010

Borgwaldt, S. R., & Joyce, T. (2013). Typology of writing systems. In S. R. Borgwaldt & T. Joyce (Eds.), *Typology of writing systems* (pp. 1–11). Amsterdam, Netherlands: John Benjamins.

Brown, S., & Larson-Hall, J. (2012). *Second language acquisition myths.* Ann Arbor, MI: University of Michigan Press.

Calderón, M. E., & Slakk, S. (2018). *Teaching reading to English learners: Grades 6-12* (2nd ed.). Thousand Oaks, CA: Corwin.

Centre for Canadian Language Benchmarks. (2012). *Canadian Language Benchmarks: English as a second language for adults.* Ottawa, Ontario, Canada: Author. Retrieved from https://www.canada.ca/content/dam/ircc/migration/ircc/english/pdf/pub/language-benchmarks.pdf

Council of Europe. (2001). *Common European framework of reference for languages: Learning, teaching, assessment.* Cambridge, England: Cambridge University Press. Retrieved from https://rm.coe.int/1680459f97

De Angelis, G. (2007). *Third or additional language acquisition.* Clevedon, England: Multilingual Matters.

DeKeyser, R. M. (Ed.). (2007). *Practice in a second language: Perspectives from applied linguistics and cognitive psychology.* New York, NY: Cambridge University Press.

DeKeyser, R. M. (2010). Practice for second language learning: Don't throw out the baby with the bathwater. *International Journal of English Studies, 10,* 155–165.

DeKeyser, R. (2013). Age effects in second language learning: Stepping stones toward better understanding. *Language Learning, 63*(1), 52–67. doi:10.1111/j.1467-9922.2012.00737

DeKeyser, R. M. (2018). Age in learning and teaching grammar. In J. Liontas (Ed.), *The TESOL encyclopedia of English language teaching: Volume V. Teaching grammar. Teaching vocabulary* (pp. 1–6). Hoboken, NJ: Wiley-Blackwell. doi:10.1002/9781118784235.eelt0106

Delaney, M. (2016). *Special educational needs.* Oxford, England: Oxford University Press.

Dörnyei, Z., & Ushioda, E. (2011). *Teaching and researching motivation* (2nd ed.). New York: NY: Routledge.

Echevarría, J., Vogt, M., & Short, D. J. (2017). *Making content comprehensible for English learners: The SIOP model* (5th ed.). Boston, MA: Pearson.

Ellis, R. (2017). Oral corrective feedback in L2 classrooms. In H. Nassaji & E. Kartchava (Eds.), *Corrective feedback in second language teaching and learning: Research, theory, applications, implications.* New York, NY: Routledge.

Ellis, R., & Shintani, N. (2014). *Exploring language pedagogy through second language acquisition research.* New York, NY: Routledge.

Fairbairn, S., & Jones-Vo, S. (2010). *Differentiating instruction and assessment for English language learners: A guide for K-12 teachers.* Philadelphia, PA: Caslon.

García, O., Johnson, S. I., & Seltzer, K. (2017). *The translanguaging classroom: Leveraging student bilingualism for learning.* Philadelphia, PA: Caslon.

Gardner, R. C. (1985). *Social psychology and second language learning: The role of attitudes and motivation.* London, England: Edward Arnold.

Gibbons, P. (2015). *Scaffolding language, scaffolding learning: Teaching English learners in the mainstream classroom* (2nd ed.). Portsmouth, NH: Heinemann.

González, N., Moll, L., & Amanti, C. (Eds.). (2005). *Funds of knowledge: Theorizing practices in households, communities, and classrooms*. Mahwah, NJ: Lawrence Erlbaum.

Grabe, W. (2009). *Reading in a second language: Moving from theory to practice*. New York, NY: Cambridge University Press.

Hadaway, N. L., & Young, T. A. (2010). *Matching books and readers: Helping English learners in grades K-6*. New York, NY: Guilford Press.

Herrera, S. G., Perez, D. R., & Escamilla, K. (2014). *Teaching reading to English language learners: Differentiated literacies* (2nd ed.). Boston, MA: Allyn & Bacon.

Jeon, E-Y., & Day, R. R. (2016). The effectiveness of ER on reading proficiency: A meta-analysis. *Reading in a Foreign Language, 28*(2), 246–265.

Johnson, K. (1995). *Understanding communication in second language classrooms*. Cambridge, England: Cambridge University Press.

Knowles, M. S., Holton, E. F., III, & Swanson, R. A. (2015). *The adult learner* (8th ed.). New York, NY: Routledge.

Kohnert, K. (2013). *Language disorders in bilingual children and adults* (2nd ed.). San Diego, CA: Plural.

Krashen, S. (1985). *The input hypothesis: Issues and implications*. New York, NY: Longman.

Krekeler, C. (2006). Language for special academic purposes (LSAP) testing: The effect of background knowledge revisited. *Language Testing, 23*(1), 99–130. doi:10.1191/0265532206lt323oa

Lesaux, N., Koda, K., Siegel, L., & Shanahan, T. (2006). Development of literacy. In August, D., & Shanahan, T. (Eds.), *Developing literacy in second-language learners: Report of the national literacy panel on language-minority children and youth* (pp. 75–122). Mahwah, NJ: Lawrence Erlbaum.

Lightbown, P., & Spada, N. (2014). *How languages are learned* (4th ed.). New York, NY: Oxford University Press.

Lin, Z. (2002). Discovering EFL readers' perception of prior knowledge and its roles in reading comprehension. *Journal of Research in Reading, 25*(2), 172–190.

Lynch, E. W. (2011). Developing cross-cultural competence. In E. W. Lynch & M. J. Hanson (Eds.), *Developing cross-cultural competence: A guide for working with children and their families* (4th ed., pp. 41–78). Baltimore, MD: Brookes Publishing.

Lyster, R., & Saito, K. (2010). Oral feedback in classroom SLA. *Studies in Second Language Acquisition, 32*, 265–302. doi:10.1017/S0272263109990520

MacIntyre, P. D., & Doucette, J. (2010). Willingness to communicate and action control. *System, 38*, 161–171.

Mackey, A., Abbuhl, R., & Gass, S. M. (2012). Interactionist approach. In S. Gass & A. Mackey (Eds.), *The Routledge handbook of second language acquisition* (pp. 7–23). New York, NY: Routledge.

Merriam, S. B., & Bierema, L. L. (2014). *Adult learning: Linking theory and practice*. San Francisco, CA: Jossey-Bass.

Minnesota Literacy Council. (2017). *Journeys: An anthology of adult student writing, 2017*. Saint Paul, MN: Author. Retrieved from http://mnliteracy.org/journeys/past-journeys-related-resources

Muñoz, C. (2011). Input and long-term effects of starting age in foreign language learning. *International Review of Applied Linguistics in Language Teaching, 49*(2), 113–133.

Nagy, W. E., & Scott, J. A. (2000). Vocabulary processes. In M. Kamil, P. Mosenthal, P. D. Pearson, & R. Barr (Eds.), *Handbook of reading research, Volume III* (pp. 269–284). Mahwah, NJ: Lawrence Erlbaum.

Nakanishi, T. (2015). A meta-analysis of extensive reading research. *TESOL Quarterly, 49*, 6–37. doi:10.1002/tesq.157

Nassaji, H., & Kartchava, E. (Eds.). (2017). *Corrective feedback in second language teaching and learning: Research, theory, applications, implications*. New York, NY: Routledge.

Nation, I. S. P., & Webb, S. (2011). *Researching and analyzing vocabulary*. Boston, MA: Heinle.

National Academies of Sciences, Engineering, and Medicine. (2017). *Promoting the educational success of children and youth learning English: Promising futures*. Washington, DC: The National Academies Press. doi:10.17226/24677

National Academies of Sciences, Engineering, and Medicine. (2018). *How people learn: Learners, contexts, and cultures*. Washington, DC: The National Academies Press. doi:10.17226/246783

National Research Council. (2012). *Improving adult literacy instruction: Options for practice and research*. Washington, DC: The National Academies Press.

REFERENCES FOR CHAPTER 2, *CONTINUED*

Ó Laoire, M., & Singleton, D. (2009). The role of prior knowledge in L3 learning and use: Further evidence of psychotypological dimensions. In B. Hufeisen & L. Aronin (Eds.), *The exploration of multilingualism: Development of research on L3, multilingualism, and multiple language acquisition* (pp. 79–102). Amsterdam, Netherlands: John Benjamins.

Parrish, B., & Johnson, K. (2010). *Promoting learner transitions to postsecondary education and work: Developing academic readiness skills from the beginning.* Washington, DC: Center for Applied Linguistics. Retrieved from http://www.cal.org/caelanetwork/pdfs/TransitionsFinalWeb.pdf

Patterson, M. B. (2018). The forgotten 90%: Adult nonparticipation in education. *Adult Education Quarterly, 68*(1), 41–62. doi:10.1177/0741713617731810

Pavlenko, A., & Norton, B. (2007). Imagined communities, identity, and English language teaching. In J. Cummins & C. Davidson (Eds.), *International handbook of English language teaching* (pp. 669–680). New York, NY: Springer.

Reder, S. (2012). *The longitudinal study of adult learning: Challenging assumptions. Research Brief.* Montreal, Quebec, Canada: The Centre for Literacy.

Rex, L. A., & Green, J. L. (2008). Classroom discourse and interaction: Reading across the traditions. In B. Spolsky & F. M. Hult (Eds.), *The handbook of educational linguistics* (pp. 571–584). Malden, MA: Blackwell.

Rutgers, D., & Evans, M. (2015). Bilingual education and L3 learning: metalinguistic advantage or not? *International Journal of Bilingual Education and Bilingualism, 20*(7), 788–806. doi:10.1080/13670050.2015.1103698

Sato, M., & Ballinger, S. (2016). Understanding peer interaction: Research synthesis and directions. In M. Sato & S. Ballinger (Eds.), *Peer interaction and second language learning: Pedagogical potential and research agenda* (pp. 1–30). Amsterdam, Netherlands: John Benjamins. doi:10.1075/lllt.45.01int

Saunders, W. M., & O'Brien, G. (2006). Oral language. In F. Genesee, K. Lindholm-Leary, W. M. Saunders, & D. Christian (Eds.), *Educating English language learners* (pp. 14–63). New York, NY: Cambridge University Press.

Schmitt, N., Jiang, X., & Grabe, W. (2011). The percentage of words known in a text and reading comprehension. *Modern Language Journal, 95,* 26–43.

Short, D., & Echevarría, J. (2016). *Developing academic language with the SIOP Model.* Boston, MA: Pearson.

Swain, M., & Suzuki, W. (2008). Interaction, output, and communicative language learning. In B. Spolsky & F. M. Hult (Eds.), *The handbook of educational linguistics* (pp. 557–570). Malden, MA: Blackwell.

Turkan, S., Bicknell, J., & Croft, A. (2012). *Effective practices for developing the literacy skills of English language learners in the English language arts classroom* [Research Report ETS RR-12-03]. Princeton, NJ: Educational Testing Service. Retrieved from http://files.eric.ed.gov/fulltext/EJ1109828.pdf

U.S. Department of Education, Division of Adult Education and Literacy. (2017). *NRS technical assistance guide for performance accountability under the Workforce Innovation and Opportunity Act: Exhibit 2.2.* Retrieved from https://www.nrsweb.org/sites/default/files/NRS_TA_Guide_FINAL_4-20.pdf

U.S. Department of Education, Office of Career, Technical and Adult Education. (2016). *Adult English Language Proficiency Standards for Adult Education.* Washington, DC: Author. Retrieved from https://lincs.ed.gov/publications/pdf/elp-standards-adult-ed.pdf

Valdés, G., Kibler, A., & Walqui, A. (2014). *Changes in the expertise of ESL professionals: Knowledge and action in an era of new standards.* Alexandria, VA: TESOL International Association. Retrieved from http://www.tesol.org/docs/default-source/papers-and-briefs/professional-paper-26-march-2014.pdf

Van Patten, B., & Williams, J. (2014). *Theories in second language acquisition* (2nd ed.). New York, NY: Routledge.

Weingarten, R. (2013). Comparative graphematics. In S. R. Borgwaldt & T. Joyce (Eds.), *Typology of writing systems* (pp. 13–39). Amsterdam, Netherlands: John Benjamins.

Williams, M., Mercer, S., & Ryan, S. (2015). *Exploring psychology in language learning and teaching.* New York, NY: Oxford University Press.

Zacarian, D., Alvarez-Ortiz, L., & Haynes, J. (2017). *Teaching to strengths: Supporting students living with trauma, violence, and chronic stress*. Alexandria, VA: ASCD.

Zhou, M., & Kim, K. (2006). Community forces, social capital, and educational achievement: The case of supplementary education in the Chinese and Korean immigrant communities. *Harvard Educational Review, 76*(1), 1–29. doi:10.17763/haer.76.1.u08t548554882477

Zwiers, J. (2014). *Building academic language: Grades 5-12* (2nd ed.). San Francisco, CA: Jossey Bass.

CHAPTER 3

Adelson-Goldstein, J. (2015). *Preparing English learners for work and career pathways: Companion learning resource*. Retrieved from https://lincs.ed.gov/programs/eslpro

Andrade, M. S., & Evans, N. W. (2013). *Principles and practices for response in second language writing: Developing self-regulated learners*. New York, NY: Routledge.

Association of American Colleges and Universities. (2013). *It takes more than a major: Employer priorities for college learning and student success*. Washington, DC: Hart Research. Retrieved from https://www.aacu.org/sites/default/files/files/LEAP/2013_EmployerSurvey.pdf

August, D., & Shanahan, T. (Eds.). (2006). *Developing literacy in second-language learners: Report of the National Literacy Panel on Language Minority Children and Youth*. Mahwah, NJ: Lawrence Erlbaum.

Banas, J. A., Dunbar, N., Rodriguez, D., & Liu, S. (2011). A review of humor in educational settings: Four decades of research. *Communication Education, 60*(1), 115–144. doi:10.1080/03634523.2010.496867

Center for Applied Linguistics [COResourceCenter]. (2012, August 14). *Bhutanese refugees in the United States* [Video file]. Retrieved from https://youtu.be/N_o4GBpNj3Q

Roberts, C., & Cooke, M. (2007). *ESOL. Developing adult teaching and learning: Practitioner guides*. Leicester, England: NIACE.

Costa, A., & Kallick, B. (1993). Through the lens of a critical friend. *Educational Leadership, 51*(2), 49–51.

DeCapua, A., & Wintergerst, A. C. (2016). *Crossing cultures in the language classroom* (2nd ed.). Ann Arbor, MI: University of Michigan Press.

DeKeyser, R. M. (Ed.). (2007). *Practice in a second language: Perspectives from applied linguistics and cognitive psychology*. New York, NY: Cambridge University Press.

Delaney, M. (2016). *Special education needs*. Oxford, England: Oxford University Press.

Dewey, J. (1933). *How we think: A restatement of the relation of reflective thinking to the educative process*. Boston, MA: Heath.

Dörnyei, Z., & Ushioda, E. (2011). *Teaching and researching motivation* (2nd ed.). New York, NY: Routledge.

Echevarría J., Vogt. M., & Short, D. (2017). *Making content comprehensible for English learners: The SIOP model* (5th ed.). Boston, MA: Pearson.

Eddy, P. L., & Amey, M. J. (2011). Bridges across the P-16 continuum: The role of educational partnerships. *In Brief*. Retrieved from http://occrl.illinois.edu/files/InBrief/Brief-10-11.pdf

Ellis, R., & Shintani, N. (2014). *Exploring language pedagogy through second language acquisition research*. New York, NY: Routledge.

Finn Miller, S. (2010). Promoting learner engagement when working with adult English language learners. *CAELA Network Brief*. Washington, DC: Center for Applied Linguistics. Retrieved from www.cal.org/caelanetwork.

Fisher, D., Frey, N., & Rothenberg, C. (2008). *Content-area conversations: How to plan discussion-based lessons for diverse language learners*. Alexandria, VA: ASCD.

Flaitz, J. (2006). *Understanding your refugee and immigrant students: An educational, cultural, and linguistic guide*. Ann Arbor, MI: University of Michigan Press.

Freeman, Y. S., Freeman, D. E., & Mercuri, S. (2002). *Closing the achievement gap: How to reach limited-formal-schooling and long-term English learners*. Portsmouth, NH: Heinemann.

Gibbons, P. (2014). *Scaffolding language, scaffolding learning: Teaching English language learners in the mainstream classroom* (2nd ed.). Portsmouth, NH: Heinemann.

Goldstein, L. M. (2005). *Teacher written commentary in second language writing classrooms*. Ann Arbor, MI: University of Michigan Press.

REFERENCES FOR CHAPTER 3, *CONTINUED*

Harris, K. (2015). Integrating digital literacy into English language instruction: Issue brief. *LINCS ESL PRO*. Retrieved from https://lincs.ed.gov /publications/pdf/ELL_Digital_Literacy_508.pdf

Hellman, A. B. (2011). Vocabulary size and depth of word knowledge in adult-onset second language acquisition. *International Journal of Applied Linguistics, 21*(1), 162–182. doi:10.1111/j.1473-4192.2010.00265.x

Hellman, A. B. (2018a). Teaching/developing vocabulary at diverse age levels. In J. I. Liontas (Ed.), *The TESOL encyclopedia of English language teaching: Volume V. Teaching grammar. Teaching vocabulary*. Hoboken, NJ: Wiley-Blackwell. doi:10.1002/9781118784235.eelt0736

Hellman, A. B. (2018b). Teaching/developing vocabulary at diverse linguistic levels. In J. I. Liontas (Ed.), *The TESOL encyclopedia of English language teaching: Volume V. Teaching grammar. Teaching vocabulary*. Hoboken, NJ: Wiley-Blackwell. doi:10.1002/9781118784235.eelt0739

Honigsfeld, A., & Dove, M. G. (2010). *Collaboration and co-teaching for English learners: A leader's guide*. Thousand Oaks, CA: Corwin.

Kagan, S., & Kagan, M. (2009). *Kagan cooperative learning*. San Clemente, CA: Kagan.

Larrivee, B. (2000). Transforming teaching practice: Becoming the critical reflective teacher. *Reflective Practice, 1*(3), 293–307.

Levine, L. N., & McCloskey, M. (2013). *Teaching English language and content in mainstream classes: One class, many paths* (2nd ed.). Boston, MA: Pearson.

Long, M. H. (2005). Methodological issues in learner needs analysis. In M. H. Long (Ed.), *Second language needs analysis* (pp. 19–76). Cambridge, England: Cambridge University Press.

Lyster, R., & Saito, K. (2010). Oral feedback in classroom SLA: A meta-analysis. *Studies in Second Language Acquisition, 32*(2), 265–302. doi:10.1017/ S0272263109990520

Mayer, R. E. (1992). Cognition and instruction: Their historic meeting within educational psychology. *Journal of Educational Psychology, 84*, 405–412.

Merriam, S., B., & Bierema, L. L. (2014). *Adult learning: Linking theory and practice*. San Francisco, CA: Jossey-Bass.

Mesmer, H. A. E. (2008). *Tools for matching readers to texts*. New York, NY: Guilford.

Michaels, S., O'Connor, M. C., Williams Hall, M., & Resnick, L. B. (2013). *Accountable talk sourcebook: For classroom conversation that works*. Retrieved from http://iflpartner.pitt.edu /index.php/download/index/ats

Miller, D. (2009). *The book whisperer: Awakening the inner reader in every child*. San Francisco, CA: Jossey-Bass.

Minnesota Literacy Council. (2016). *Journeys: An anthology of adult student writing, 2016*. Saint Paul, MN: Author. Retrieved from http://mnliteracy.org /journeys/past-journeys-related-resources

Minnesota Literacy Council. (2017). *Journeys: An anthology of adult student writing, 2017*. Saint Paul, MN: Author. Retrieved from http://mnliteracy.org /journeys/past-journeys-related-resources.

Morgan, K., Waite, P., & Diecuch, M. (2017, March). *The case for investment in adult basic education*. Syracuse, NY: Proliteracy. Retrieved from https:// www.proliteracy.org/Portals/0/Reder%20Research .pdf?ver=2017-03-24-151533-647

Nassaji, H., & Kartchava, E. (Eds.). (2017). *Corrective feedback in second language teaching and learning: Research, theory, applications, implications*. New York, NY: Routledge.

Nation, I. S. P. (2006). How large a vocabulary is needed for reading and listening? *The Canadian Modern Language Review, 63*(1), 59–82. doi:10.3138/cmlr.63.1.59

Nation, I. S. P., & Webb, S. (2011). *Researching and analyzing vocabulary*. Boston, MA: Heinle Cengage Learning.

National Academies of Sciences, Engineering, and Medicine. (2017). *Building America's skilled technical workforce*. Washington, DC: The National Academies Press. doi:10.17226/23472

O'Malley, J. M., & Chamot A. U. (1990). *Learning strategies in second language acquisition*. New York, NY: Cambridge university Press.

O'Malley, J. M., & Valdez Pierce, L. (1996). *Authentic assessment for English language learners: Practical approaches for teacher*. Reading, MA: Addison Wesley Longman.

Organisation for Economic Cooperation and Development. (2018). *Education at a glance 2018: OECD indicators*. Paris, France: Author. doi:10.1787/eag-2018-en

Oxford, R. L. (2017). *Teaching and researching language learning strategies: Self-regulation in context* (2nd ed.). New York, NY: Routledge.

Pimentel, S. (2013). *College and career readiness standards for adult education*. Washington, DC: MPR. Retrieved from http://lincs.ed.gov /publications/pdf/CCRStandardsAdultEd.pdf

Pimentel, S., Copeland, M., Shaw, K., Lakin, J., & Whealdon, W. (2011). *The Common Core State Standards: Supporting districts and teachers with text complexity*. Retrieved from http://www.ccsso .org/Resources/Digital_Resources/The_Common _Core_State_Standards_Supporting_Districts_and _Teachers_with_Text_Complexity.html

Ritchhart, R., Church, M., & Morrison, K. (2011). *Making thinking visible: How to promote engagement, understanding, and independence for all learners*. San Francisco, CA: Jossey-Bass.

Rosen, D. J., Stewart, C. (2015). *Blended learning for the adult education classroom*. Retrieved from http://app.essentialed.com/resources/blended -learning-teachers-guide-web.pdf

Rothstein, D., & Santana, L. (2011). *Make just one change: Teach students to ask their own questions*. Cambridge, MA: Harvard Education Press.

Salva, C., & Matis, A. (2017). *Boosting achievement: Reaching students with interrupted or minimal education*. Irving, TX: Seidlitz Education.

Schön, D. A. (1990). *The reflective turn: Case studies in and on educational practice*. New York, NY: Teachers College Press.

Swain, M., & Lapkin, S. (1995). Problems in output and the cognitive processes they generate: A step towards second language learning. *Applied Linguistics, 16*(3), 371–391. doi:10.1093/ applin/16.3.371

Tomlinson, C. A. (2014). *The differentiated classroom: Responding to the needs of all learners* (2nd ed.). Alexandria, VA: ASCD.

U.S. Department of Education, Office of Career, Technical, and Adult Education. (2015). *Promoting teacher effectiveness: Adult education teacher competencies*. Washington, DC: Author. Retrieved from https://lincs.ed.gov/publications/te /competencies.pdf

U.S. Department of Education, Office of Career, Technical, and Adult Education. (2016). *Adult English language proficiency standards for adult education*. Washington, DC: Author. Retrieved from https://lincs.ed.gov/publications/pdf/elp-standards -adult-ed.pdf

Vogt, M., & Echevarría, J. (2008). *99 ideas and activities for teaching English learners with the SIOP model*. Boston, MA: Pearson.

Vogt, M., Echevarría, J., & Washam, M. A. (2015). *99 more ideas and activities for teaching English learners with the SIOP model*. Boston, MA: Pearson.

Walqui, A., & van Lier, L. (2010). *Scaffolding the academic success of adolescent English language learners: A pedagogy of promise*. San Francisco, CA: WestEd.

World Education. (2018). *Adult education facts 2018*. Boston, MA: Author. Retrieved from https://www .worlded.org/Managed/docs/AdultEdFacts.pdf

Zwiers, J. (2014). *Building academic language: Meeting Common Core standards across disciplines* (2nd ed.). San Francisco, CA: Jossey-Bass.

CHAPTER 4

Ager, A., & Strang, A. (2008). Understanding integration: A conceptual framework. *Journal of Refugee Studies, 21*(2), 166–191.

Asher, J. (1969). The total physical response approach to second language learning. *The Modern Language Journal, 50*(2), 79–84.

Bow Valley College. (2017). *Strategies for teaching adult refugees in the ELL classroom*. Calgary, Alberta, Canada: Author. Retrieved from https:// globalaccess.bowvalleycollege.ca/sites/default/files /Strategies-for-Teaching-Adult-Refugees-in-the -ELL-Classroom-6517.pdf

Bow Valley College. (2018). *A practical guide to teaching ESL literacy*. Calgary, Alberta, Canada: Author. Retrieved from https://globalaccess .bowvalleycollege.ca/sites/default/files/ESL -Literacy-Book-August-24-2018-Digital_0.pdf

Clayton, M. (2015). *The impact of PTSD on refugee language learners*. Retrieved from https://www .researchgate.net/publication/299467247_The _Impact_of_PTSD_on_Refugee_Language _Learners

DeCapua, A. (2016). Reaching students with limited or interrupted formal education through culturally responsive teaching. *Language & Linguistics Compass, 10*(5), 225–237. doi:10.1111/lnc3.12183

Delaney, M. (2016). *Special educational needs*. Oxford, England: Oxford University Press.

Fazel, M., Wheeler, J., & Danesh, J. (2005). Prevalence of serious mental disorder in 7000 refugees resettled in western countries: A systematic review. *The Lancet, 365*(9467), 1309–1314.

REFERENCES FOR CHAPTER 4, *CONTINUED*

Figley, C. R. (1995). Compassion fatigue as secondary traumatic stress disorder: An overview. In C. R. Figley (Ed.), *Compassion fatigue: Coping with secondary traumatic stress disorder in those who treat the traumatized* (pp 1–20). New York, NY: Brunner Routledge.

Frontier College. (2017). *Final report: National forum on literacy and poverty.* Retrieved from https://www.frontiercollege.ca/getattachment/dcf15253-e641-41b3-92b5-0a309b8f83cc/2017-Report-National-Forum-on-Literacy-and-Poverty.aspx

Gardner, S. (2017). Counting words: Successful sentences for beginning ESL adult learners using the product approach. *TESOL Journal, 8,* 367–384.

Holder, S. (1999, June). *The development of service and sectoral standards for the immigrant services sector.* Toronto, Ontario, Canada: Ontario Council of Agencies Serving Immigrants and COSTI. Retrieved from http://atwork.settlement.org/downloads/Development_Sectoral_Standards.pdf

Horsman, J. (2000). *Too scared to learn: Women, violence, and education.* Mahwah, NJ: Lawrence Erlbaum.

Ishiyama, F. I., & Westwood, M. J. (2011). *The sociocultural competencies training program: The facilitator's guide.* Vancouver, British Columbia, Canada: Aurora Pacific.

Isserlis, J. (2009). Trauma and learning—What do we know, what can we learn? In T. Wall & M. Leong (Eds.), *Low educated second language and literacy acquisition symposium: Proceedings of the 5th symposium* (pp. 42–51). Calgary, Alberta, Canada: Bow Valley College. Retrieved from https://drive.google.com/open?id=1RogfSbTUxRYxcZ_bKJKk1qMBM4mT2WdR

Jeffries, D., Rahemtulla, Z., & Wilbur, A. (2017). Supporting refugee women: Barriers and opportunities in language and settlement programs, policies and research. *Canadian Diversity, 14*(2), 23–26. Retrieved from http://www.ciim.ca/img/boutiquePDF/canadiandiversity-vol14-no2-2017-tc64w.pdf

Jeffries, D., & Wilbur, A. (2016) *Beyond trauma: Language learning strategies for new Canadians living with trauma.* Retrieved from https://cmascanada.ca//wp-content/uploads/2016/09/1467063427_01_beyond_trauma_complete_1.pdf

Long, M. (2014). *Second language acquisition and task-based language teaching.* Malden, MA: Wiley Blackwell.

Marshall, H. W., & DeCapua, A. (2013). *Making the transition to classroom success: Culturally responsive teaching for struggling second language learners.* Ann Arbor, MI: University of Michigan Press.

Nieto, S., & Bode, P. (2018). *Affirming diversity: The sociopolitical context of multicultural education* (7th ed.). Hoboken, NJ: Pearson.

Patterson, M. B. (2018a). *Critiquing adult participation in education, Report 2: Motivation around adult education.* Media, PA: VALUEUSA. Retrieved from https://static1.squarespace.com/static/560d5789e4b015789104a87e/t/5b252a26f950b7fedffb4b18/1529162279757/CAPE+Report+2+Motivation+around+adult+education.pdf

Patterson, M. B. (2018b). The forgotten 90%: Adult nonparticipation in education. *Adult Education Quarterly, 68*(1), 41–62. doi:10.1177/0741713617731810

Patterson, M. B., & Song, W. (2018). *Critiquing adult participation in education, Report 1: Deterrents and solutions.* Media, PA: VALUEUSA. Retrieved from http://valueusa.org/s/CAPE-Report-1-Deterrents-and-Solutions.pdf

Pentón Herrera, L. J. (2017). Undocumented ESL students from El Salvador, Guatemala, and Honduras in the era of Trump: A personal narrative. *Berkeley Review of Education.* Retrieved from http://www.berkeleyreviewofeducation.com/cfc2016-blog/january-20th-2017

Quigley, B. A. (2006). *Building professional pride in literacy.* Malabar, FL: Krieger.

Ray, B., & Seely, C. (2015). *Fluency through TPR storytelling: Achieving real language acquisition in school* (7th ed.). Berkeley, CA: Command Performance Language Institute.

Ripley, D. (2013). Implementing portfolio-based language assessment in LINC programs: Benefits and challenges. *TESL Canada Journal, 30*(1), 69. doi:10.18806/tesl.v30i1.1126

Root, C. (1994). A guide to learning disabilities for the ESL classroom practitioner. *TESL-EJ, 1*(1), 1–7.

Schwarz, R., & Terrill, L. (2000). *ESL instruction and adults with learning disabilities.* Retrieved from https://files.eric.ed.gov/fulltext/ED443298.pdf

United Nations High Commissioner for Refugees. (2018). *Global trends: Forced displacement in 2017.* Geneva, Switzerland: Author. Retrieved from http://www.unhcr.org/5b27be547.pdf

Vinogradov, P. (2010). Balancing top and bottom: Learner-generated texts for teaching phonics. In T. Wall & M. Leong (Eds.), *Low-educated second language and literacy acquisition: Proceedings of the 5th symposium* (pp. 3–14). Retrieved from https://drive.google.com/file/d/1RogfSbTUxRYxcZ_bKJKk1qMBM4mT2WdR/view

Vinogradov, P., & Bigelow, M. (2010). *Using oral language skills to build on the emerging literacy of adult English learners*. Washington, DC: Center for Applied Linguistics. Retrieved from www.cal.org/caelanetwork/resources/using-oral-language-skills.html

Wales, L. M. (1994). A language experience approach in adult immigrant literacy programs in Australia. *Journal of Reading, 38*(3), 200–208.

Waterhouse, M. (2017). Telling stories of violence in adult ESL classrooms: Disrupting safe spaces [Special issue 10]. *TESL Canada Journal, 33*, 20–41. doi:1018806/tesl.v33i0.1244

Wilbur, A. (2016). Creating inclusive EAL classrooms: How Language Instruction for Newcomers to Canada (LINC) instructors understand and mitigate barriers for students who have experienced trauma [Special Issue 10]. *TESL Canada Journal, 33*, 1–19. doi:1018806/tesl.v33i0.1242

CHAPTER 5

Adelson-Goldstein, J. (2015). *Preparing English learners for work and career pathways: Companion learning resource*. Washington, DC: U.S. Department of Education, Office of Career, Technical and Adult Education. Retrieved from https://lincs.ed.gov/sites/default/files/LINCS_CLR-1_508_0.pdf

Australian Government Department of Education and Training. (2015). *Australian core skills framework*. Canberra, Australia: Department of Industry, Innovation, Science, Research and Tertiary Education. Retrieved from http://docs.education.gov.au/node/37095

Bartel, J. (2018). Teaching soft skills for employability. *TESL Canada Journal, 35*(1), 78–92. https://doi.org/10.18806/tesl.v35i1.1285

Centre for Canadian Language Benchmarks. (2012). *Canadian Language Benchmarks: English as a second language for adults*. Ottawa, Ontario, Canada: Author. Retrieved from https://www.canada.ca/content/dam/ircc/migration/ircc/english/pdf/pub/language-benchmarks.pdf

Condelli, L., & Wrigley, H. S. (2006). Instruction, language and literacy: What works study for adult ESL literacy students. In I. van de Craats, J. Kurvers, & M. Young-Scholten (Eds.), *Low-educated second language and literacy acquisition: Proceedings of the inaugural symposium* (pp. 111–133). Utrecht, Netherlands: Tilburg University. Retrieved from https://drive.google.com/file/d/15XIYPEgCzBrUWeyfDUztodA7TGIWFmDp/view

Harris, K. (2015). *Integrating digital literacy into adult English language instruction: Professional development module*. Washington, DC: U.S. Department of Education, Office of Career, Technical and Adult Education. Retrieved from https://courses.lincs.ed.gov

Parrish, B. (2015). *Meeting the language needs of today's adult English language learner: Professional development module*. Washington, DC: U.S. Department of Education, Office of Career, Technical and Adult Education. Retrieved from https://courses.lincs.ed.gov

Skills for Education and Employment. (2018). *Skills for education and employment: Fact sheet*. Retrieved from https://docs.education.gov.au/system/files/doc/other/introduction_to_see_factsheet_0.pdf

U.S. Department of Education, Division of Adult Education and Literacy. (2017). *NRS technical assistance guide for performance accountability under the Workforce Innovation and Opportunity Act: Exhibit 2.2*. Washington, DC: Author. Retrieved from https://www.nrsweb.org/sites/default/files/NRS_TA_Guide.pdf

U.S. Department of Education, Office of Vocational and Adult Education. (2013). *College and Career Readiness Standards for Adult Education*. Washington, DC: Author. Retrieved from https://lincs.ed.gov/publications/pdf/CCRStandardsAdultEd.pdf

U.S. Department of Education, Office of Career, Technical and Adult Education. (2016). *Adult English Language Proficiency Standards for Adult Education*. Washington, DC: Author. Retrieved from https://lincs.ed.gov/publications/pdf/elp-standards-adult-ed.pdf

Wrigley, H. S. (2015). *Preparing English learners for work and career pathways: Issue brief*. Washington, DC: U.S. Department of Education, Office of Career, Technical and Adult Education. Retrieved from https://lincs.ed.gov/sites/default/files/ELL_Context_Instruction_508.pdf

REFERENCES FOR APPENDIX A

DeCapua, A., & Wintergerst, A. C. (2016). *Crossing cultures in the language classroom* (2nd ed.). Ann Arbor, MI: University of Michigan Press.

Kagan, S., & Kagan, M. (2009). *Kagan cooperative learning*. San Clemente, CA: Kagan.

Nation, I. S. P., & Webb, S. (2011). *Researching and analyzing vocabulary*. Boston, MA: Heinle Cengage Learning.

Vogt, M., & Echevarría, J. (2008). *99 ideas and activities for teaching English learners with the SIOP Model*. Boston, MA: Pearson.

Vogt, M., Echevarría, J., & Washam, M. A. (2015). *99 more ideas and activities for teaching English learners with the SIOP Model*. Boston, MA: Pearson.

Zwiers, J. (2014). *Building academic language: Meeting Common Core standards across disciplines* (2nd ed.). San Francisco, CA: Jossey-Bass.